SUBSTITUTION EFFECTS, SPECULATION AND EXCHANGE RATE STABILITY

STUDIES IN INTERNATIONAL ECONOMICS

Editors

JAGDISH N. BHAGWATI
JOHN S. CHIPMAN

Volume 3

NORTH-HOLLAND PUBLISHING COMPANY
AMSTERDAM · NEW YORK · OXFORD

SUBSTITUTION EFFECTS, SPECULATION AND EXCHANGE RATE STABILITY

PATRICK MINFORD

1978

NORTH-HOLLAND PUBLISHING COMPANY
AMSTERDAM · NEW YORK · OXFORD

ISBN North-Holland for this volume 0 444 85055 4

Publishers

NORTH-HOLLAND PUBLISHING COMPANY
AMSTERDAM · NEW YORK · OXFORD

Sole distributors for the U.S.A. and Canada
ELSEVIER NORTH-HOLLAND, INC.
52 VANDERBILT AVENUE
NEW YORK, N.Y. 10017

Library of Congress Cataloging in Publication Data

Minford, Patrick.
Substitution effects, speculation, and exchange rate stability.

(Studies in international economics; v. 3)
Bibliography: p. 211
Includes index.
1. Foreign exchange problem. 2. Foreign exchange problem—Great Britain. 3. Balance of payments. 4. Balance of payments—Great Britain. 5. Substitution (Economics) I. Title.
HG3826.M54 332.4'5 77-13650
ISBN 0-444-85055-4

PRINTED IN THE NETHERLANDS

INTRODUCTION TO THE SERIES

This series is intended to embrace all aspects of international economic analysis: theoretical, empirical and econometric. It will equally encompass contributions to pure and monetary theory.

The series will include the publication of collected essays, conference proceedings of exceptional professional quality and interest, and edited volumes addressed to specific phenomena of importance in the analysis of international economics. It will particularly encourage, however, the publication of hitherto unpublished studies which represent fresh and valuable contributions to the analysis of international economic problems.

The *Journal of International Economics* now provides an excellent outlet for original scientific work in international economics in article length form. For pamphlet length contributions, the different series published by the *International Finance Section* at Princeton have long been of exceptional value, even though they have not generally extended beyond international monetary issues. It is the hope of the editors that the launching of this series, *Studies in International Economics,* will now fill the lacuna in the systematic publication of monograph and volume length research output of international economists, and succeed in doing so consistently with the high quality that the promotion of scientific study of international economic issues requires.

THE EDITORS

To Rosie

PREFACE

This book is an expanded and revised version of my Ph. D. thesis (submitted to London University in July 1973). I am particularly grateful to Alan Walters who acted as my Ph. D. supervisor and who has helped massively in getting this book realised. I owe an enormous debt of gratitude also to Harry Johnson for unlimited encouragement, help and fruitful suggestions – his recent death came as a very sad blow to me as to so many whom he helped.

I have received many useful and stimulating comments in discussions at L.S.E., Manchester, Chicago and H.M. Treasury. I should mention in particular the valuable influence of John Hutton, whose cooperation I enjoyed on much of the work reported in Chapters 3 and 4, of Professor J.B. Ramsey, who read the original thesis (an earlier version of Chapters 1–4) as external examiner, and of my Treasury colleagues, Michael Beenstock and Arnold Lovell, from whom I have learnt a great deal in numerous discussions. Finally, I am much in the debt of Professor William Branson who read the completed manuscript and offered numerous helpful suggestions for its improvement. The usual disclaimers of course apply, with particular force in the case of a book of this lenght.

The work reported here has been assisted by financial and research support from a number of sources. The material for Chapter 2 was largely prepared when I was working at Courtaulds Ltd. in 1970–71. I am grateful to the *Australian Journal of Agricultural Economics* for permission to reproduce material from 'Textile Fibre Substitution and Relative Prices', *A.J.A.E.*, December 1975, a shortened version of Chapter 2. Much of that for Chapter 3–5 was the by-product of my work as economic adviser in H.M. Treasury Balance of Payments Division during 1971–73. I am grateful to H.M. Stationery Office for permission to reproduce the material in these three chapters, on which Crown copyright prevails; in particular, Chapter 3 is closely based on material used in Government Economic Service Occasional

Paper No. 11, 'A Model of UK Manufactured Exports and Export Prices' (John Hutton, co-author) published by *HMSO* in 1975. The rest, as well as the revision of these early chapters, was undertaken during 1974–75 when I held a Hallsworth Fellowship at the University of Manchester. I gratefully acknowledge this support, which of course in no way implies that the bodies concerned share any of the views I have expressed.

Especial thanks are due to the London School of Economics who, apart from supporting the original Ph.D. work, gave the most active assistance and backing in arranging for its publication; this help, surely that of an alma mater in the truest sense, is warmly acknowledged.

The manuscript has been ably typed and re-typed, in particular, by Mrs. Patricia Hall and Miss Irene Blackett of the Treasury, Mrs. M. Jones and Miss Edith Gillett of Manchester University, Mrs. Frances Robinson of the *NIESR* and Mrs. Jackie Fawcett of Liverpool University. I am grateful to them, and to others who have assisted, for this often trying work. David Chappell kindly cross-checked the algebra and arithmetic of Chapters 6–8; but is not liable for the errors which almost inevitably will have gone undetected by both of us. Mrs. Christine Moore and Miss Anne Bennett of Manchester Econometrics Department provided respectively essential programming and computational assistance, for the work in Chapters 5, 6, and 8. I am also indebted to Alan Hodgkiss and Mrs. Sandra Mather in the Drawing Office of the Liverpool Geography Department, to whose professional draughtmanship are due the Figures in this book.

My final and greatest debt of gratitude is to my wife Rosemary without whose support this book could simply not have been written.

November, 1977 Patrick Minford
University of Liverpool

CONTENTS

Chapter 1

INTRODUCTION, SUMMARY AND CONCLUSIONS

This book is concerned with the role of substitution in the balance of payments, and the implications that it has for the dynamic behaviour of the reserves and the exchange rate. The attempt has been made to build a general framework or model of the external sector within an economy linked into a world economy, and to explore its applicability in particular to the UK both in detailed studies of the UK trade and capital accounts and by incorporating relevant previous work. But while the main focus empirically is on the UK, it is not entirely so, and both here and in other places (e.g. Beenstock and Minford [1975]), empirical work is presented that indicates quite general applicability.

It is possible to identify two main traditions in the theory of the balance of payments (or, equivalently, the exchange rate). The oldest is the 'monetary' tradition, originating with David Hume [1752]. The more recent began as an offshoot of Keynes' *General Theory* [1936] and simultaneously of the theory of imperfect competition developed by Robinson [1933] and Chamberlin [1932]. Since the war, it has been perpetuated most notably by Meade [1951]; it might be called the 'structural' tradition.

The essence of the monetary approach (see, for example, Johnson [1973]) is that the exchange rate, if flexible, insulates each country's money supply, so fixing the domestic price level; arbitrage between traded goods ensures that in equilibrium the exchange rate has to compensate exactly for the resulting difference between national and international prices of traded goods. If the exchange rate is fixed, then there is no scope for these prices to diverge and money supplies have to adjust through payments imbalances and reserves changes. Dynamics are introduced according to taste through rate of adjustment parameters in the demand for money (for example, Dornbusch [1973]), the relation of traded with non-traded goods prices, of national and international traded goods prices, and in other functions (some of these possibilities are explored in Parkin [1974] and Jonson [1976]).

In the structural approach, the trade balance is determined by relative traded goods price levels, allowed to diverge by the assumption of product differentiation, and relative economic activity, and separately capital flows respond to interest differentials adjusted for exchange risk; the two components of the balance of payments may be solved either for the exchange rate in the flexible case or for reserve changes if the rate is fixed. These in turn feed into a model of each domestic economy, so that the loop is closed. The framework was discussed succinctly by Johnson [1961] and is exemplified in a number of large models of individual economies (especially for Canada, where the external sector has been most thoroughly treated; see Helliwell et al. [1971]).

It is the author's view that to stress the 'difference' of one's approach while natural can often be unhelpful in a wider perspective. It will be argued repeatedly in the later parts of this book that though there are different strands in these traditions, they essentially converge, or are very likely to once the dynamics are properly understood, on the same general area. Thus while we refer to the monetary and the structural approaches to the balance of payments, the work reported below belongs properly to both (or neither), in that the focus largely is on disequilibrium behaviour, an area where neither has staked out at all definite claims. It is true that formally the work proceeds within a structural framework, in that the trade and capital flow equations are estimated separately; the monetary aspects are considered as determining equilibrium behaviour, and are integrated as such. Yet it will be apparent that an approach formally in the monetary framework could easily in considering disequilibrium be drawn into the distinction between the trade and capital balances. (Jonson comes close to this.)

1.1. Part I: Price-responsiveness in trade and payments

Part I consists of three pieces of empirical work in the general field of international trade and payments, all of them concerned with substitution in response to relative price changes. The precise methods used in each differ considerably, and this is inevitable when the subject matter is so diverse.

Chapter 2 deals with substitution between six types of textile fibre (cotton, wool, and four man-made categories), using the framework of the *CES* production function and deriving the elasticity of substitution between pairs of fibres and fibre groups. This study is micro-economic and very disaggregated; textile end-uses within the US market, the only one for which such detailed data are available, are separately treated. Its finding of high substitution elasticities between differentiated products in an important international market gives strong, specific backing to one recurrent theme of this book, that there is no reason for 'elasticity pessimism' in international trade in differentiated products (i.e. the majority of the trade of the *OECD* area).

Chapter 3 investigates demand and supply relationships in the determination of UK exports of manufactures. This study finds support for the same theme within a macro-economic framework. It adds to a growing body of work reaching similar conclusions for other countries' exports and imports – Beenstock and Minford [1976] is one example but see Stern, Francis and Schumacher [1976] for an annotated bibliography.

Chapter 4 examines international capital flows to and from the UK within a portfolio selection model akin to the Tobin–Markowitz model for domestic portfolio holdings. This too is a macro-economic study which joins the literature on capital flows to and from other *OECD* countries (Branson and Hill [1971] and Branson [1968] for example). It, like much of this other work, supports the notion that capital flows are significantly responsive to interest rates adjusted for foreign exchange risk (the equivalent of the substitution elasticity response to price in goods markets). When combined with a model of the domestic monetary sector, this provides a major channel through which monetary policy will have international repercussions (Part II of this book is extensively concerned with spelling out the mechanisms involved).

The general proposition, which all these studies are designed to test and do in fact support, that consumers of internationally tradeable goods and securities are significantly responsive to their relative prices and yields, is not here intended to be confined to UK experience, though two thirds of the work relates to the UK. On the contrary, this work is to be seen as one more contribution to the empirical literature, covering a large span of cases, which as a whole provides general support.

More specifically, these studies suggest that in the areas investigated relative price changes have a powerful impact, contrary to the often-encountered view that prices cannot perform their allocative function, and that therefore governments must perform it for them. Rather it is implied here that there are considerable dangers in such government intervention; since prices do have an effect, intervention on the assumption that they do not will have unforeseen consequences, often far-reaching, and probably damaging.

We can see examples of this in each of the three particular areas looked at in Part I.

Some specific policy lessons of Part I

The fibre study illustrates the dangers of supply restraint by primary producers acting as a cartel. On the face of it, supply restraint is an attractive way of assuring higher incomes to less-developed primary producing countries; alternatively, it might be seen as a legitimate application of optimum tariff theory. Yet, when the high elasticities of substitution are allowed for, it becomes clear that supply restraint is the opposite of these. Volume sales and incomes are severely cut; employment is reduced while those left in the industry (usually licensed by government quota) develop a vested interest in the higher prices. For this reason, the policy may be difficult to reverse, so that the authorities look to sub-economic projects (such as capital-intensive 'import-substitution') to utilise the unemployed resources. Of course, there are commodities where short-run substitution elasticities are low; oil and tin are examples. In these cases, a strategy of supply restraint will have a payoff for a period. But, though not the subject of this book directly, the return to technological innovation will be increased and this should ensure that in time man-made substitutes are developed. It is possible to see the mechanism working in the development of rayon filament in the early 1900s as a response to high silk prices, of nylon during the war (because of the high price of strong fibres required for strategic needs), and of the other man-made fibres (partly in the wake of the Korean War shortage). What is at issue in these cases is the length of time needed for development. A high price strategy may be justified, provided that the longer term consequences are allowed for.

But even here it must be remembered that, because technology once available cannot be destroyed, these consequences are irreversible.

In the export chapter, to the extent that the export demand elasticity turns out to be significantly greater than unity, there is similar evidence against 'elasticity pessimism'. A further area of interest to the price theorist lies in the length of the lags reported. What these two things suggest is that the doubters of the price mechanism are likely to appear correct on any superficial reading of events, because there will be very limited price effects in the first year or two after a change of price or of exchange rate. Such an analysis may lead to the prescription of direct controls on trade and similar measures (as in Godley et al. [1975,6,7]). Yet the lagged effects of previous price movements will tend to make the controls either redundant or inoperable. If by chance the situations remain static, experience shows that these controls are unlikely to be maintained for long without widespread evasion, or if they are, then not without increasingly serious distortions, as computed by Batchelor and Minford [1977] for the UK.

An alternative strategy suggested by this line of analysis would rely on variations in domestic absorption to correct current account imbalances. In a world of national price flexibility, this strategy would succeed under fixed exchange rates in restoring external equilibrium, without sacrificing internal balance. But the evidence is that national price levels react slowly to excess domestic demand (for example Eckstein et al. [1974] and Ando [1974]); and the result of this strategy, if pursued without exchange rate flexibility, will be needless internal disequilibrium. In the export chapter, the role of absorption is stressed; the mechanism by which, above a certain level of resource utilisation, supply constraints operate on export deliveries, is investigated and confirmed as a significantly strong one. But this by no means implies that absorption policies alone can correct external imbalances; they are necessary but not sufficient. They have in fact to be combined both with flexibility in the exchange rate (in the absence of adequate national price flexibility) and with allowance for the time-path of reaction. For example, it is no good 'making room' at once for a current account improvement as a result of a fall in the exchange rate, when it is not likely to come through with any strength for a year and more. On the contrary, absorption policy has to be geared to gradual external adjustment and may, as a result, produce temporary imbalances in the composition of demand in the attempt to maintain reasonable internal equilibrium.

The scope for manouevre in absorption and exchange rate policy is however crucially dependent on the behaviour of capital flows, studied in Chapter 4. Here we find there is a school of thought which believes that 'hot money' flows between countries for irrational motives, and not from a reaction to price incentives.

Thus we have Sir Harold Wilson telling the Royal Statistical Society late in 1972,[1] 'The underlying reality (of 'being very close to a balance in our payments in the early months of 1966') counted for nothing in the face of the run on sterling in a few days in July, which were the markets' response to the July 2nd publication of the run on sterling caused by the same people in response to the seamen's strike, by that time over. They had slashed their own, and the nation's wrists, and then fainted at the sight of their own blood. ...You are dealing (here) with the irrational, the imponderable, the immeasurable.' Later he refers to 'the excesses of mala fide speculators, qua speculators, selling sterling they do not possess,' to 'more or less bona fide bankers,' and to 'the unstable and extended Euro-currency market.'

Yet chapter 4 shows that it is possible to explain capital flows for the UK during the 1960s in terms of a model within which expectations of exchange rate change are formed in the light of the trend in the balance, as proxied by the lag-weighted trade balance; this method of forming expectations is argued to be rational in the light of the knowledge at the time of the relationships involved. It is likely that it will be subject to a normal learning process as more research into the determinants of the balance of payments becomes available and assimilated. We can grant Sir Harold and others that, at times of crisis within a fixed rate system, the capital flows become self-aggravating; and this element is not built into the model as it stands because there was only one such crisis (in 1967) during the period studied. However, it can quite easily be provided. As capital flows (in response to underlying expectations of exchange rate change) cumulate above some threshold, expectations of a change are progressively reinforced by the implications for the reserves and domestic liquidity of the flows themselves[2]. This is often described as a 'one-way option' for the foreign exchange market, in that not only are the expected gains from moving funds considerably greater than the expected gains of keeping them where they are, but also

[1] Presidential address to the *RSS*, Journal of *RSS*, Vol. 136, Part I, 1973.

[2] This process is simulated in Chapter 5 where it is shown that a 'fixed-but-adjustable' exchange rate will be highly unstable in conditions such as prevailed in the late 1960s.

the profit variance attached to moving funds to a non-suspect currency is less than that of keeping them in a suspect one, under the fixed-but-adjustable parity system.

This diagnosis suggests that it is fruitless to prop up 'fixed' rates by exchange controls or 'international monetary reform', simply because as long as they are in practice adjustable these crises are bound to recur. Exchange controls cannot deal with the many channels through which capital flows at the present time (Euro-currency markets and multi-national company accounts being particularly evasive). Any international reform short of unlimited financing combined with the general belief that it would be *used* to defend a particular pattern of rates would be ineffective; and both elements in this combination have yet to materialise[3].

This leaves some form of floating system, whether 'managed', 'smoothed', or quite free of intervention, as apparently the only viable alternative, in a world in which exchange rates must adjust because it is not a common currency area. Here the 'hot money' school argue that speculative irrationality would produce instability in the rate, just as it is supposed to produce large capital flows under the fixed rate system. Such arguments have exercised economists for decades (the voluminous literature is reviewed by Sohmen [1969]) and require a careful examination; this we attempt in Part II.

1.2. Part II: Developing a model of the floating exchange rate

In Part II we consider the possibilities of instability, or non-convergence, after allowing for feedback from the exchange rate into the current balance through prices and movements in the real economy. To do this it is necessary to link the capital account model onto a macroeconomic model with an appropriate foreign trade sector. Thus in this Part we develop a model of the floating exchange rate, which, as with the empirical work of Part I, is intended to be generic and to answer the general question: can floating rates be unstable and if so under what circumstances? However, it is natural that we should illustrate the model from the UK experience, given the predominant bias both of the work reported in Part I and of the other empirical work,

[3] For some penetrating, as well as amusing, observations on recent international monetary developments see Johnson's Stamp Memorial Lecture [1973a].

institutions etc. familiar to the author. Part II will therefore make liberal use of parameter estimates for the UK and focus at some length on the particular properties of the UK model.

We argue that speculators base their expectations on a model of the foreign exchange market but that this need not be the 'true' model (ie. the model as seen within the research set out in this book), at least initially. It is suggested that speculators learn gradually, as data and research becomes available, about the nature of the model (a 'model-learning' process), until ultimately they base their expectations on the true model itself. The initial state of affairs we call 'semi-rational expectations', the ultimate we call 'fully rational expectations' (in the sense defined by Muth [1961] in his original and perceptive work on this question). This 'ultimate' state may in fact never completely be attained, especially if there is continuous change in the structural parameters of the model. However, it is necessary for us to frame our hypothesis in a precise form in order to explore and test its implications, and we assume as an approximation (to the actual asymptotic process) that fully rational expectations are actually attained within some period following a violent structural change (specifically here the shift from fixed to floating exchange rates).

Within this framework, 'adaptive' or other expectations functions comprising lag distributions of the forecast variable imply particular restrictions on the nature of the model and are thus seen as special cases. Alternatively and more realistically, they can be seen as cost-effective forecasting devices where information about the model is costly to obtain. There is additionally a wide spectrum of compromise expectations functions, which in the spirit of rational expectations distinguish between the equilibrium value and a lag-weighted average of past deviations from equilibrium, but then go on to substitute estimates of the equilibrium and the lag-weights based on non-model sources (usually general statistical schemes). When the matter is put in this light, we are in effect arguing here that the cost of obtaining the relevant model information is worth incurring for the speculator whose livelihood depends primarily on the accuracy of his forecasting[4].

In Chapter 5 we consider the behaviour of a floating rate with semi-rational

[4] By contrast in the example of inflation, it might be argued that the cost was not worth incurring for the ordinary man, but was for the institutional investor; such an approach might yield insight into differential behaviour, eg. of financial and labour markets in the context of inflation. See Walters [1971] for a discussion of rational expectations in this context.

expectations about the exchange rate, specifically based on the lag-weighted current balance, the critical failing of which is that it assumes no lags (or J-curve) in the current balance response to the exchange rate. A number of simulations under somewhat different assumptions reveal a presumption of instability in the exchange rate, as well as clear cyclicality, in the initial 'teething-period' of the floating rate system.

However, as speculators learn, we move away from this behaviour towards full rationality. In Chapter 6, we derive the stability properties for the same model with fully rational expectations. At this point we run into the paradox that the model solution yields at least one unstable root in spite of full rationality; but it is shown that, if the solution is bounded (by some plausible ceiling and floor to the exchange rate) any unstable roots are ruled out. The solution then, for fairly wide variations in parameter assumptions, implies fairly slow convergence (over at least two years and probably more) and almost certainly cyclicality (also with a period of at least two years and probably longer); the higher the trade elasticities, as one would expect, the faster the rate of convergence but the solution is relatively insensitive to variations in the size of the speculative response (the elasticity of forward cover) and the relative importance of forward markets of different maturities.

There remains the issue of the extent to which we can use for the floating regime our estimate of the speculative response obtained for the pegged rate regime. The issue arises because the nature of uncertainty clearly changes significantly between regimes, since under the peg the rate changes discontinuously and usually by a large amount while a floating rate changes continuously by small amounts. In Chapter 7 we set out an analysis of the shift in a way intended to provide a numerical estimate of the relevant 'correction factor' to be applied to the speculative response.

Not surprisingly, the size of the correction depends on the one hand on the size of underlying payments shocks and on the other on the frequency and size of peg change in response to these shocks. Using the evidence to hand for the UK, we estimate in Chapter 8 that with a floating rate and semi-rational expectations, the speculative response is considerably larger (by a factor of 4.5) than under the pegged rate of the 1960s for which the UK estimate was derived, and that the response under a floating rate with fully rational expectations is very much more elastic again than with semi-rational expectations. This elasticity is so great that it effectively validates an 'efficient market' approach to the floating exchange rate, according to which the deviation of the exchange rate from purchasing power parity will be solely a function of the interest differential (net of the differential in expected inflation if applicable). A macroeconomic model embodying this approach has been proposed by Dornbusch [1976], and quite clearly has fertile implications for macroeconomic analysis, which we reluctantly defer to later investigation.

The final step in the analysis, to re-examine the stability properties of the exchange rate allowing for this correction, is also carried out in Chapter 8. We find that the original conclusions of chapters 5 and 6 require little modification. The presumption of instability in the floating rate remains for semi-rational expectations during the initial teething period. Cyclicality and slow convergence may remain in the fully rational case, but this of course now has less significance because the high speculative elasticity strongly dampens any shock from the start. We conclude finally therefore on the major question of exchange rate stability that Part II of this book has attempted to tackle:

(1) The foreign exchange market will not, as some critics of floating rates once suggested, fail to function after the transition into floating. There will always be a (non-absurd) market-clearing rate.

(2) But there may well be an initial tendency to long run divergence from equilibrium, as well as cyclicality, as the floating rate settles down (i.e. speculators learn about the nature of the system). We have no analysis here of how long this period of settling down might be, though since the information involved is subject to no restrictions there is no reason to believe it would be more than a few years. This would suggest that it would be prudent to allow for central bank market intervention on a contingency basis, until it became clear that it was over; such intervention would be undertaken in the spirit of improved stabilisation and the mistakes of market management made in the peg system would not be repeated.

(3) The floating rate will become stable once speculators have learnt the essential features of the market. In this situation, the authorities ex hypothesei will know no more than speculators and the previous rationale for intervention disappears. It is true that the authorities could still in principle stabilise the rate (i.e. more closely around its equilibrium movement) by adding to the elasticity of forward cover. However, this elasticity is seen to be so high that the volume of intervention would need

to be massive to have a significant effect and any intervention at all by the same argument is effectively redundant. Also, if we take a normative viewpoint, the decision to intervene would need to be justified to taxpayers on the grounds that the social net benefit of greater stability outweighed the private cost (as reflected in speculators' portfolio decisions) of taking the portfolio risks involved. In sum, the likelihood of serious intervention – other than some 'smoothing' operations of no consequence – is small in these circumstances. The main task of the monetary authorities remains that of controlling the domestic monetary aggregates, and through them the equilibrium exchange rate.

PART I

EMPIRICAL WORK

Chapter 2

TEXTILE FIBRE SUBSTITUTION AND RELATIVE PRICES: A STUDY IN RAW MATERIAL SUBSTITUTION[1]

In this chapter we investigate the relationships, in the US during the years 1949 to 1968, of relative fibre prices and the market shares of different fibres in the textile industry. This is a study of pure substitution effects at the most disaggregated level for an important traded goods category. The other chapters in this book largely deal with macroeconomic relationships in which substitution is either postulated or found to be a powerful force. This chapter is to be regarded as a case-study which helps to establish the credibility of this postulate at the micro-economic level. Competition between different types of fibre, each of which have different properties (e.g. strength, durability, washability), is typical of competition between differentiated manufactured products. We will find that competition between textile fibres exhibits neither 'infinite' nor 'negligible' elasticities of substitution, contrary to two popular extreme views about substitution between differentiated manufactures; rather the elasticities lie in the range 1–3, which is reasonably consistent with the findings of macroeconomic trade studies (see Stern et al. [1976]), as with Chapter 3 of this book on UK exports.

[1] I am grateful for helpful comments to J.P. Bradley, C. Blackorby, H.G. Johnson, J. Johnston, M.H. Miller, J.J. Thomas, H. Townsend, K.F. Wallis and particularly to A.A. Walters my Ph.D. supervisor. I am also grateful to Courtaulds Limited, and in particular to A.W. Knight (Chairman) and N.H. Smith (Deputy Chairman), for sponsoring this research and providing much of the data, also to D. Jaques and P. Thompson of the Economics Department for help in its interpretation. I am indebted for computational assistance to Miss A. Bennett in the Manchester Econometric Department.

2.1. Previous work

A similar study was attempted on the same data (for an early sub-period) by Powell, Polasek, and Burley [1963].[2] They followed Griliches [1957] in his pioneering paper on hybrid corn, and fitted simple logistic curves to the consumption of synthetic staple in the traditional markets of wool. They then allowed for the effects of price changes on the rate of substitution and the final 'ceiling' but found that the simple logistic trends gave the better fit. They concluded that price had no significant role in competition between new and traditional fibres, but rather that the growth in consumption of the new fibres was 'technically determined'.

Griliches had used the logistic to describe the development of hybrid corn penetration in a large number of US districts. He regressed the parameters of the logistic for each district, in a cross-section analysis, on the economic return to the planting of hybrid corn. He stated that 'the growth curves serve merely as a summary device, perhaps somewhat more sophisticated than a simple average, but which should be treated in the same spirit'.

The approach in this paper is different from these studies. The use of the logistic or any other time-trend is eschewed, on the ground that the data is sufficiently disaggregated by end-use to ignore technological learning curves beyond the first few years of 'teething'. Instead, it is assumed that the progress of a fibre within an end-use once it has made the quantum jump of penetrating the end-use, depends primarily and directly on price movements.[3] In what follows this assumption is explored and tested.

2.2. The model

There is assumed to be a perfectly competitive US textile industry, who are the users of fibre. All firms in the industry have a *CES* production function,[4]

[2] See also Polasek and Powell [1964 (1) and (2)], and Polasek [1965].

[3] If it were felt that technological change in quality etc. is an important factor requiring a separate explanatory variable, then a time trend (logistic or otherwise) would be too broad to qualify, since it includes the effect of price changes on the trend in fibre use. A variable based on known technological facts *for each end-use* would need to be constructed; this was not possible here and hence any such variable is omitted (i.e. implicitly included in the error term).

[4] The well-known function developed by Arrow, Chenery, Minhas and Solow [1961], also reviewed by Walters [1963].

identical in each case apart from a multiplicative 'efficiency parameter'. The production function consists of a fibre part and labour–capital part. The two parts substitute with one another (probably with a very low elasticity of substitution), and together may be subject to non-constant returns to scale over certain ranges of production. Within the labour–capital part there is substitutability between labour and capital. Within the fibre part, where several fibres are distinguished, there is substitutability between 'groups' of fibres, each 'group' consisting of fibres which share an elasticity of substitution equal to or greater than that between the group and other fibres.[5] Thus, for example, if only three fibres are competing, the production function for the ith firm would be expressed (where the F_j are fibres, K is capital and L is labour):

$$q_i = A_i[k_0(\{k_1F_1^{-r} + [(k_2F_2^{-s} + F_3^{-s})^{-\frac{1}{s}}]^{-r}\}^{-\frac{1}{r}})^{-w} + \\ + (\{k_3K^{-t} + L^{-t}\}^{-\frac{1}{t}})^{-w}]^{\frac{-v(q_i)}{w}}$$

where it is assumed that $s \leqslant r \leqslant w \geqslant t$.

The number of firms who are potentially 'in' the industry is assumed to be fixed; but they will produce zero output if by producing they would make losses, hence the number actually producing can vary. Each firm maximizes profits and is assumed to be in constant long run equilibrium, subject to 'commercial' error terms in the marginal productivity conditions.

It can be shown (see Appendix 2.A) that, because this production function has the property of homothetic separability, each 'group' of fibres has a price and quantity index, P_f and F respectively, such that the marginal productivity conditions can be rewritten in terms of these indices. For example, if we just look at the fibre part of the function,

$$\{k_1F_1^{-r} + [(k_2F_2^{-s} + F_3^{-s})^{-\frac{1}{s}}]^{-r}\}^{-\frac{1}{r}},$$

we find that instead of writing out the marginal productivity (MP) ratios as

$$\frac{P_1}{P_2} = \frac{MPF_1}{MPF_2} \qquad (2.1)$$

[5] This 'nested' *CES* production function was first propounded by Sato [1967].

and

$$\frac{P_2}{P_3} = \frac{MPF_2}{MPF_3}, \tag{2.2}$$

the first of which is a highly involved algebraic expression, we can rewrite them as

$$\frac{P_1}{P_f} = \frac{MPF_1}{MPF} \tag{2.3}$$

and

$$\frac{P_2}{P_3} = \frac{MPF_2}{MPF_3}, \tag{2.2}$$

where P_f and F are the price and quantity indices of F_2 and F_3 taken as a group. This has the important implication that the ratio of the two fibres inside the group (in this case F_2 and F_3) is fixed quite independently of the ratio of the group to the other fibre.

It follows, by similar reasoning, that the ratio of capital to labour is fixed independently of fibre ratios and that the ratio of the capital–labour part to the fibre part of the production function is fixed independently of all these subsidiary ratios. In each case, the higher-level ratio is solely dependent on the ratio of the corresponding price indices.

The final logic of this hierarchy is that, all these ratios being fixed, the output level of the firm is determined by the ratio of an index of factor prices to the price of final output. Hence factor ratios are independent of both the output level of the firm, and by implication that of the industry. Thus we can write fibre ratios, in particular, as functions solely of fibre price ratios; and in general we can say that the marginal productivity conditions are recursive (see Appendix 2.B).

This way of treating factor inputs is of course directly parallel to the 'utility tree' approach suggested for consumer spending by Strotz [1958]. The basic idea of both is that decisions by the economic unit, whether producer and consumer, can be taken in descending order of complexity;

first, the decision to produce or consume at all, then the breakdown into main categories, then the further breakdown of these, and so on. At each stage, the same vector of prices is manipulated to produce the appropriate price indices; and the quantity decision is taken in terms of the appropriate quantity indices which at the end of the process imply a unique quantity vector.

The textile industry is distinguished into seventy-four sub-industries, each of which produces for a separate 'end-use' (examples are men's suits, women's and children's sweaters, and curtains). Each sub-industry is assumed to have the characteristics described in connection with the industry as a whole.

Some of the implications of this model may be controversial. In particular, it is implied:

(i) That once introduced into an end-use in significant quantities, fibres do not change in 'quality' in that end-use.
(ii) That there are no lags in the 'acceptance' of a new fibre or in the adjustment of fibre ratios.
(iii) Since there is no lag in adjustment, there is no role for expectations of future fibre prices (on the grounds that, if prices change in the future, adjustment of fibre ratios can be immediate).

However, there are good reasons for adopting these assumptions, even if they inevitably represent something of an oversimplification.

The data in the first place consists of annual observations, hence the model is concerned with average annual rates. The saying goes in the industry that 'a year is a very long time in textiles'; this is the result of having to keep pace with fashion, and it is a fact that textile firms, more than most, have to keep up with new developments.

The second point about the data is that, if consumption of a fibre is less than 50,000 pounds in an end-use, it is counted as zero. This means that a fibre is not considered to be in significant use until it has passed this threshold, which at the time of introduction of the new synthetic fibres, the mid-1950s, represented just under 0.1% of total fibre consumption in an average end-use. This threshold has implications for the model which are considered below.

Turning to lags in adjustment, we find that textile machinery is fairly rapidly converted to the handling of any fibre or fibre blend once the technical problems have been overcome; the costs of adjustment are low.

For example, a machine for tufting carpets can be easily reset to tuft a different fibre combination; a change in fibre (for example from rayon to acrylic) will require readjustment of tensions, cams, angles of cutting blades, and so on, all of which can be completed in a few hours (or at most a few days, depending on the exact changes). Of course, there are fibres which cannot be handled on machinery designed for a certain end-use. But this simply means that such a fibre will never be introduced in significant quantities in that end-use so that lags in adjusting to it do not arise.

As for lags in the acceptance of new fibres, these belong, if anywhere, to prewar days when the idea of 'artificial' fibres was quite new. There was indeed a long acceptance lag in the case of rayon filament in the first three decades of this century. But by 1949, when the period examined opens, viscose filament had been in existence for fifty years, viscose staple for fifteen, acetate filament for twenty-seven, acetate staple for ten and nylon filament for eight. The textile industry had by then grown familiar with artificiality and come to expect new developments.

Furthermore, a new fibre in the post-war era has a long 'pre-launching' phase in any end-use to which it is to be introduced. By the time it appears in significant quantities in that end-use (as defined earlier), it has been reasonably well-known to fibre buyers, and has been tested in small quantities, for several years. There follows, in the first few years of significant usage, the period of teething when fibre technicians will spend a lot of time solving minor headaches. But its essential quality is fixed once it is used in significant quantities and its acceptance in that end-use has usually occurred by then, though some scepticism will remain until the end of the teething period.

There is one final assumption to be added to complete the model: that each fibre price ratio is exogenous (that is, independent of random changes in the ratio of fibre demand in any individual end-use). This can reasonably be defended. Most end-uses contribute only a small proportion of the US demand for a particular fibre. There are some exceptions. In 1968, women's dresses absorbed 16% of total US rayon filament demand and 11% of US rayon staple demand. Women's coats and jackets contributed 16% of US demand for wool. Tufted-carpet yarns took 11% of wool. Apparel lining took 10% of rayon filament; tyres 19% of rayon filament, 22% of synthetic filament. But all other sixty-eight end-uses contributed under 10% of total US demand for any one fibre.

Furthermore, each of the man-made fibres is produced in the US under conditions of oligopoly.[6] US man-made fibre producers tend to aim for price stability, this being probably the result of the need to maintain pricing discipline (see Scherer [1970]). Hence current changes in demand are unlikely to affect the prices charged; instead capacity utilisation, stocks, and possibly queues are likely to be varied.

Wool, unlike man-made fibres, is imported by the US in large quantities; just over 75% of its wool requirements were met by imports in 1968. Changes in the US domestic wool price will therefore be closely related to changes in the world price. The largest of the US end-uses for wool, namely women's coats and jackets, only contributed 2.2% of world wool consumption in 1968. Changes in wool demand from this end-use therefore could have had at most an insignificant effect on the world price of wool and hence also on the US price.

The price of cotton in the US was pegged to the user by a Government support price and export subsidy system, until 1966, when the Government replaced this with a direct production subsidy so that since then the US domestic price has been closely related to the world price. Thus, from 1949 to 1966, the cotton price was exogenous because of Government regulation, and from 1966 onwards, individual end-uses for cotton, none of them as we have seen constituting more than 10% of US cotton demand, were competing in a world market for cotton six and a half times as large as the US market.

The model therefore can be written down in its reduced form, as a set of marginal productivity conditions, recast as in equations (2.2) and (2.3) above, but with prices as the independent variable. In full mathematical detail and including the error terms, u_{1F} and u_{23}, we can write them, for the same three-fibres case, as:[7]

$$\frac{F_1}{F} = k_1^{\sigma}\left(\frac{P_1}{P_F}\right)^{-\sigma} u_{1F}, \tag{2.4}$$

$$\frac{F_2}{F_3} = k_2^{\eta}\left(\frac{P_2}{P_3}\right)^{-\eta} u_{23}, \tag{2.5}$$

where $\sigma = 1/(r + 1)$ and $\eta = 1/(s + 1)$.

[6] The point made in this paragraph should not of course be confused with the assumption made above that fibre *users* are perfectly competitive.

[7] See Appendix 2.A for the full derivation.

2.3. Data

The data on US fibre quantities (in pounds weight) are taken from the *Textile Organon*, a monthly magazine published by the US Textile Economics Bureau. Each year the *Textile Organon* carries out a survey of fibre consumption by end-use; the survey is regarded by the US textile industry as their prime source of statistics on inter-fibre competition. The survey results are available for a continuous span of years from 1949, and it is these that have been used here.

The usual problems of revisions in the series apply in this case. For the years 1949 to 1959 the figures were collected on a rather different basis than those from 1960 to 1968 and were not revised, though admitted to contain errors, particularly in the classification of the new synthetics that emerged in the late 1950s. Within each period, however, the data are on a broadly consistent basis; and fortunately data are available for 1960 on both bases. It was assumed that in general the error in the earlier period was as a percentage equal to the percentage error in 1960. But in a few cases, where this caused early relationships to 'blow-up' implausibly, the error was assumed to be additive.

Six types of fibre are distinguished: the traditional fibres (cotton and wool), the cellulosics (filament and staple), and the synthetics (filament and staple). Historically, the cellulosics or rayon[8] (produced by either the viscose or the acetate process) emerged in the first quarter of this century, initially only in filament form, but later also as a staple. The synthetics, which consist of nylon, polyester, acrylic and polypropylene fibres, emerged in that order, nylon filament in the 1940s, polyester filament in the early 1950s, polyester, nylon and acrylic staple in the late 1950s, and polypropylene (filament and staple) most recently of all in the mid 1960s.

This classification isolates the most important differences (from the demand side, with which we are concerned) among the man-made fibres. Cellulosics, obtained by processing woodpulp, have significantly different properties from synthetics, which are made by synthesising petro-chemicals. For example synthetics are stronger, more resilient, can be heat set, and, because strong, are easy to use in textile processes; but they are less moisture-absorbent (important, for example, in underwear), suffer from pilling (fluffiness when

[8] Strictly only viscose is 'rayon'; but I have loosely used the term to cover all cellulosics.

the fabric is used) and static, and are more difficult to dye. The distinction between filament (man-made fibre produced in a continuous thread) and staple (filament cut into short lengths similar to cotton or wool staples), is also fundamental, since in filament form a man-made fibre has maximum strength, while in staple form it can compete in the end-uses which require the properties of spun fibre (its rougher texture, its bulkiness, its 'breathing' quality, and so on).

Any classification of fibres must do some violence to real distinctions that have to be ignored. In this case, the distinctions between the two rayon processes, viscose and acetate, and between the four synthetic types, nylon, polyester, acrylic and polypropylene, have been ignored. We have unweighted quantities for each of the six fibre types.

For the prices of cotton, wool, rayon filament and rayon staple, the *Textile Organon* have published monthly price series that are on a broadly consistent basis over the whole period; unweighted twelve-month averages of these series were taken as the average price of each fibre.

There has been a minor change in basis for the cotton price (to domestic users), which was an average of ten domestic markets up to and including 1954, and since then has been an average of fifteen (sometimes fourteen) domestic markets; this change had no perceptible effect on the monthly series, which is what one would expect from a mere broadening of the basis.

Of the two main rayon processes, viscose and acetate, by far the most widely used has been viscose. Hence viscose was chosen as the representative rayon price (price changes in the two series have been similar).

For prices of synthetic fibres, not reported by the *Textile Organon*, the Economics Department of Courtaulds Limited have kept a record, based on a reading of the textile trade journals. From this record were extracted the prices of a typical nylon filament (70/23 normal tenacity), polyester filament (70/54), acrylic staple (Orlon, 3 denier regular), and polyester staple ($1\frac{1}{2}$ denier, 54); again an unweighted monthly average of each was used as the annual average price. The prices of nylon and polyester filament were then combined in an unweighted average to give a price for synthetic filament, those of acrylic and polyester staple combined in the same way to give a price for synthetic staple.

The price data is affected by the existence of quantity, and other, discounts given by the US man-made fibre producers against the list prices which have been used here. There is no problem if the discounts are a constant percentage of listed prices; the percentage discount can then be treated as a logarithmic constant, and, since we know roughly that this factor is around 10% in a normal year, we can allow for the bias in the constant term of the regression. The problem arises if the percentage discount varies, or more precisely, if different fibre discounts vary by different proportions. It is in fact well-known that discounts on man-made fibres do vary according to the level of capacity utilisation;[9] but the response of the discount to the level of sales may well differ between fibres and capacity utilisation rates may not be synchronised, so that for any given pair of man-made fibres, the relative discount may well also vary. Since there are no discounts on natural fibres, the relationships between any man-made fibre and cotton or wool will also be affected. However, the connection between discounts and capacity utilisation suggests that the error term would follow the business cycle, specifically the cycle in the textile activity, and would be autocorrelated. We can rewrite, for example, model equation (2.5) as:

$$\frac{F_2}{F_3} = k_3^\eta \left(cv \frac{P_2}{P_3} \right)^{-\eta} u_{23}$$

$$= k_3^\eta \left(c \frac{P_2}{P_3} \right)^{-\eta} v^{-\eta} u_{23}, \tag{2.6}$$

where c is the constant part of the fractional discount (the 'normal' discount), v is the variable part. However, when we tested for this connection, there was little evidence of it (see Appendix 2.C) and on the face of it, therefore, to neglect discounts is not an unduly serious omission.

2.4. Estimation techniques

The marginal productivity conditions are the equations from which the parameters of the fibre section of the production function are estimated. The basic method is that made familiar by Arrow, Chenery, Minhas, Solow [1961] and subsequently others in their work on *CES* production functions. A marginal productivity equation of the form

[9] See, for example, Markham [1952, especially pp. 79–80].

$$\frac{F_i}{F_j} = k^{\sigma}\left(\frac{P_i}{P_j}\right)^{-\sigma} u_{ij} \tag{2.7}$$

can be written in the loglinear form:

$$\log \frac{F_i}{F_j} = \sigma \log k - \sigma \log\left(\frac{P_i}{P_j}\right) + \log u_{ij}, \tag{2.8}$$

which is the form of all the equations estimated here. (Natural logarithms were used throughout.)

The first stage was to estimate the elasticity of substitution between individual fibres. Those fibres which shared a high and significant elasticity were then classed as a group. There might be several potential sets of groups.

The next stage was to estimate the elasticities of substitution between the groups in each potential set. This was done by using indices as described earlier.[10] A typical equation was:

$$\frac{F_1}{F} = k_2^{\sigma}\left(\frac{P_1}{P_f}\right)^{-\sigma} u_{1F} \tag{2.9}$$

where $\sigma = \frac{1}{(r+1)}$, P_f and F are the indices of price and quantity for F_2 and F_3 together, and u_{1F} is assumed to be independent of u_{23}. Formally

$$F = (k_2 F_2^{-s} + F_3^{-s})^{-\frac{1}{s}} \tag{2.10}$$

and

$$P_f = P_3\left(\frac{F_3}{F}\right)^{s+1} \tag{2.11}$$

However, we do not know the true values of k_2 and s, so we substitute the estimated values into the expression for F and P_f.

$$\hat{P}_f = P_3\left(\frac{F_3}{\hat{F}}\right)^{\hat{s}+1} \tag{2.12}$$

[10] The sensitivity of the results to different methods of indexing is discussed in Appendix 2.D.

is independent of u_{1F}, by virtue of the recursiveness of the system and the independence of u_{1F} and u_{23}; in other words F_3/F is exogenous in this equation, because it is a function solely of P_2/P_3 and u_{23}, both of which are independent of u_{1F} by assumption. The equation is fitted in loglinear form.

All fibres that at no point in the period absorbed a significant proportion of consumption in a particular end-use were excluded from the analysis of that end-use; clearly, the substitution represented by their variation is of no importance either to their own consumption or to the consumption of other fibres. This restriction reduced the number of potential sets to a manageable size.

Where a choice had to be made between potential groupings, three criteria were borne in mind:

(1) A condition imposed by the model is that the elasticity of substitution of any group of fibres be not significantly less than the elasticity between that group and other fibres. This condition follows from our definition of a group, defined as a number of fibres which substitute at least as, or more, closely with each other than with fibres outside the group. For example, if coffee is found to substitute more closely with tea than different types of tea do among themselves, then it is wrong to consider coffee and tea as groups; we might look instead at the substitution between coffee, grade A, and tea, grade A. Or we might find that Indian tea is a close substitute for coffee, with China tea as a general substitute for both.

(2) The comprehensiveness of the grouping was considered. For example, if there were four fibres involved, then a grouping which succeeding in relating all four would in general be preferred to one that only related three.

(3) The relative statistical significance of the elasticities as measured (albeit imperfectly, as discussed below) by their t-statistics was taken into account.

In most cases, the most satisfactory grouping was reasonably clear. However, in some end-uses, particularly those with five or six competing fibres, an element of subjective judgment inevitably entered.[11] The regression results,

[11] Formal methods of cluster anlaysis (see for example Hartigan [1975]) were not used for this problem; 'eyeball' clustering based on the application of these criteria appeared adequate. However formally one proceeds, it is impossible to avoid an element of arbitrariness in the choice or weighting of criteria.

for the grouping which emerged in this manner, are presented end-use by end-use in Table 2.1.

The statistical significance of the results presented in Table 2.1 require careful interpretation for two reasons. First, the data was relied upon not only to estimate the elasticity of substitution between fibre pairs but also to select the correct groupings of the fibres. The process of selection involved to some extent passing over fibre pairs with lower or wrongly-signed or 'insignificant' elasticities. The benefit of this is that more information is extracted from the data; the loss, as discussed by Theil [1971, Ch. 12, pp. 603–6], 'is that the standard significance tests no longer strictly apply to the "final" group's elasticities, because the probability of obtaining "significant" results is raised by the selection process'. A similar loss occurs in many econometric studies when the resercher follows the 'regression strategy' of improving his equations' specification in response to trial regressions. The usual convention (a not entirely satisfactory one – but followed here) is to report only final results and not to attempt to quantify the loss of significance.[12]

The likelihood of autocorrelated residuals was noted earlier; in many cases there was in fact evidence of autocorrelation. Since no lagged endogenous variables are used in the regressions, parameter estimates will be unbiased in spite of autocorrelation. Its effect will, however, be to remove their minimum variance property and to lead to understimates of their standard errors.[13]

The hypothesis was suggested, in discussion of the data, that the residuals were correlated with the cycle in textile activity. The residuals of the successful equations were examined but only in a very few cases (shown in Appendix 2.C) was the null hypothesis rejected with the strictly limited data available on the textile cycle; better data may increase the number. But a general explanation of the serial correlation must be the subject of further research, and could be pursued in conjunction with the investigation of non-price factors generally.

[12] Theil [1971] suggests that in these circumstances one should 'apply ... significance limits liberally', after noting that the true significance limits cannot, in the present state of the arts, be determined precisely, since they depend on the true (and unknown) values of the coefficients and error variance.

[13] Autocorrelation will introduce inconsistency if relative prices themselves respond to lagged movements in relative fibre quantities (i.e. are predetermined rather than exogenous). However, because the end-uses considered are small in relation to total use of each fibre, such feedbacks can reasonably be neglected.

Table 2.1
Regression results (see end of table for notes).

End-use	Regression pair	s (t)	$\bar{R}^2$	d	T	Regression pair	s (t)	$\bar{R}^2$	d	T	Regression pair	s (t)	$\bar{R}^2$	d	T
A. Men's & boys' wear															
1. Reg, mid & light-weight suits	Ss/Wo	2.26 (2.38)	0.22	0.60	51–68	(Ss–Wo) /Rs	1.20 (2.34)	0.21	0.72	51–68	(Ss–Wo) –Rs/Co	0			
2. Tailored civilian uniforms	Rs/Ss	4.85 (4.47)†	0.56	0.91	53–68	(Rs–Ss) /Wo	5.60 (4.26)†	0.53	1.06	53–68					
3. Separate coats, tailored	Ss/Wo	4.79 (4.92)†	0.56	0.88	50–68	Rs/Co	0				(Ss–Wo)/ (Rs–Co)	0			
4. Separate slacks	Ss/Co	2.81 (3.46)*	0.37	0.74	49–68	(Ss–Co) /Rs	2.10 (1.95)	0.13	0.09	49–68	(Ss–Co) –Rs/Wo	2.28 (14.33)†	0.91	1.82	49–68
5. Overcoats, top coats & rainwear	Ss/Co	4.12 (3.15)	0.37	0.70	53–68	(Ss–Co) /Wo	2.87 (5.67)†	0.68	0.41	53–68	(Ss–Co) –Wo/Rs	1,99 (4.62)*	0.58	0.86	53–68
6. Outdoor jackets & athletic uniforms	Ss/Co	2.75 (5.95)†	0.64	0.78	49–68	(Ss–Co) /Wo	1.37 (1.92)	0.12	0.19	49–68	(Ss–Co) –Wo/(Ry–Rs)	0.40 (2.82)*	0.27	0.88	49–68
	Ry/Rs	1.22 (2.02)	0.14	0.58	49–68	(Ss–Co) –Wo–(Ry–Rs) /Sy	0.92 (2.70)*	0.25	0.51	49–68					
7. Sweaters	Ss/Co	6.18 (7.14)†	0.72	0.83	49–68	(Ss–Co) /Wo	1.91 (1.81)	0.11	0.30	49–68	(Ss–Co) –Wo/Sy	0			56–68
8. Swimwear	Ry/Sy	0.70 (2.17)	0.16	1.10	49–68	(Ry–Sy) /(Ss–Co)	0			53–68	Ss/Co	3.38 (2.80)	0.31	0.46	53–68
9. Robes & neckties	Rs/Sy	3.38 (2.96)	0.49	0.93	60–68	(Rs–Sy) /Ry	2.20 (5.50)	0.78	1.60	60–68	(Rs–Sy) –Ry/(Ss–Co)	0.71 (3.67)	0.61	1.30	60–68
	(Ss–Co)	4.52 (3.05)	0.41	0.81	66–68	(Rs–Sy) –Ry–(Ss–Co) /Wo	0			60–68					
10. Utility clothing	Ss/Co	6.96	0.70	0.67	49–68										

shirts		(3.90)†				/Wo	(1.85)				Wo/Co	[illegible]			
12. Business & dress shirts	Sy/Ss	6.13 (6.64)†	0.69	0.68	49–68	(Sy–Ss) /Co	5.59 (2.75)*	0.26	0.58	49–68					
13. Sports shirts, woven	Rs/Ss	4.03 (6.85)†	0.71	0.75	49–68	(Rs–Ss) /(Ry–Co)	0			49–68	Ry/Co	3.93 (5.48)†	0.60	0.31	49–68
	(Rs–Ss) –(Ry–Co) /Wo	0			49–68										
14. Sports shirts, knit	Ry/Rs	10.01 (4.01)	0.65	1.63	60–68	(Ry–Rs) /(Ss–Co)	0.79 (2.74)	0.45	1.97	60–68	Ss/Co	8.36 (5.47)†	0.66	0.93	53–68
	(Ry–Rs) –(Ss–Co)/Sy	0			60–68										
15. Underwear, woven	Ry/Ss	4.17 (4.48)†	0.61	1.58	56–68	Ss/Co	4.39 (1.95)	0.19	0.50	56–68	Ry/Co	2.16 (5.11)†	0.58	1.81	50–68
16. Underwear, knit	Ss/Co	1.50 (3.22)*	0.36	1.14	51–68	(Ss–Co) /Ry	0			51–68					
17. Nightwear, woven & knit	Ry/Sy	4.52 (5.67)†	0.65	0.90	51–68	(Ry–Sy) /(Ss–Co)	1.85 (2.23)	0.33	1.13	60–68	Ss/Co	5.55 (1.62)	0.17	0.53	60–68
18. Hosiery, all types	Ry/Rs	5.64 (6.69)†	0.70	1.23	49–68	Rs/Ss	4.97 (6.16)†	0.66	0.72	49–68	Ry/Ss	5.63 (8.72)†	0.80	0.50	49–68
	(Ry–Rs–Ss) /Wo	2.28 (4.13)*	0.46	0.88	49–68	(Ry–Rs–Ss) –Wo/Co	1.37 (3.93)*	0.43	0.60	49–68	(Ry–Rs–Ss) –Wo–Co/Sy	0			49–68
B. Women's, girls', children's and infants' wear															
19. Suits & skirts	Ry/Sy	7.02 (6.49)†	0.68	0.84	49–68	(Ry–Sy) /Ss	2.57 (10.55)†	0.85	0.93	49–68	(Ry–Sy) –Ss/Rs	2.19 (2.02)	0.14	0.20	49–68
	(Ry–Sy) –Ss–Rs/Co	1.37 (2.15)	0.16	0.28	49–68	(Ry–Sy) –Ss–Rs–Co/Wo	0.47 (2.10)	0.15	0.39	49–68					
20. Slacks	Rs/Wo	3.68 (2.04)	0.28	0.45	60–68	(Rs–Wo)/ Ss	3.18 (5.33)	0.77	1.20	60–68	(Rs–Wo) –Ss/Sy	4.29 (1.74)	0.20	0.97	60–68
	(Rs–Wo)–Ss– Sy/Ry	0			60–68	(Rs–Wo)–Ss –Sy–Ry/Co	0			60–68					
21. Dresses	Ry/Sy	4.56 (7.55)†	0.75	0.67	49–68	(Ry–Sy) /(Ss–Co)	1.07 (3.76)*	0.41	0.27	49–68	Ss/Co	6.91 (8.27)†	0.78	0.99	49–68
	(Ry–Sy)–(Ss– Co)/(Rs–Wo)	0.61 (3.77)*	0.41	0.71	49–68	Rs/Wo	1.47 (2.56)*	0.23	1.14	49–68					

End-use	Regression pair	s (t)	$\overline{R}^2$	d	T	Regression pair	s (t)	$\overline{R}^2$	d	T	Regression pair	s (t)	$\overline{R}^2$	d	T
22. Coats & jackets	Ss/Co	4.08 (4.56)†	0.78	0.99	51–68	(Ss–Co)/Rs	4.46 (5.83)†	0.66	0.37	51–68	(Ss–Co)–Rs /Wo	3.03 (4.27)†	0.50	1.09	51–68
	(Ss–Co)–Rs–Wo/Ry	1.21 (4.30)*	0.51	0.51	51–68	(Ss–Co)–Rs –Wo–Ry/Sy	0			51–68					
23. Rainwear	Ry/Sy	1.84 (2.84)*	0.31	1.97	52–68	(Ry–Sy)/Ss	0			56–68	Ss/Co	1.65 (1.41)	0.08	0.56	56–68
	(Ry–Sy)–Ss–Co/Rs	0													
24. Playsuits, Sun-suits & shorts	Ss/Co	4.15 (6.66)†	0.73	1.30	52–68	(Ss–Co)/Rs	0			52–68					
25. Sweaters	Ss/Wo	2.23 (2.26)	0.18	0.26	49–68	(Ss–Wo)/Sy	0			55–68					
26. Swimsuits	Sy/Ss	1.09 (2.06)	0.18	1.10	53–68	(Sy–Ss)/Co	1.41 (2.09)	0.21	0.32	55–68	(Sy–Ss)–Co /Ry	0.57 (3.15)	0.41	0.39	55–68
27. Loungewear	Rs/Wo	2.08 (2.54)*	0.22	0.60	49–68	(Rs–Wo)/(Ss–Co)	0			60–68	Ss/Co	1.29 (1.46)	0.12	0.54	60–68
	(Rs–Wo)–(Ss–Co) /(Ry–Sy)	0			60–68						Ry–Sy	0.62 (1.41)	0.05	0.51	49–68
28. Washable service apparel	Sy/Ss	3.47 (2.47)	0.28	0.55	55–68	(Sy–Ss)/Co	0			55–68					
29. Work clothing	Ss/Co	4.38 (2.43)	0.29	0.45	56–68										
30. Blouses	Ry/Rs	2.72 (7.75)†	0.76	0.74	49–68	(Ry–Rs)/Sy	3.15 (3.01)*	0.30	0.23	49–68	(Ry–Rs)–Sy /(Ss–Co)	1.14 (2.77)	0.28	0.27	51–68
	Ss/Co	5.66 (5.03)†	0.59	0.95	51–68										
31. Brassieres & foundations	Ry/Sy	3.87 (9.52)†	0.82	0.56	49–68	(Ry–Sy)/Co	0			49–68					
32. Underwear, woven	Ry/Ss	6.49 (10.18)†	0.89	1.12	55–68	Ss/Co	6.04 (3.13)	0.40	0.59	55–68	Ry–Co	5.85 (7.21)†	0.73	0.36	49–68
	(Ry–Ss–Co)/Sy	2.06 (3.85)*	0.51	0.83	55–68										
33. Underwear, knit	Ry/Sy	2.38	0.54	0.45	49–68	(Ry–Sy)/Co	0								

[illegible]	[illegible]	(7.46)†					(8.18)†					(1.74)			
35. Nightwear, knit	Ry/Sy	4.32 (6.35)†	0.67	0.46	49–68	(Ry–Sy)/Ss	4.76 (1.77)	0.35	1.10	64–68	(Ry–Sy)–Ss /Co	0			64–68
36. Full-length hosiery	Ry/Sy	3.85 (6.26)†	0.67	0.42	49–68	(Ry–Sy)/Co	0			49–68					
37. Anklets & socks	Ss/Co	3.24 (4.27)†	0.51	0.82	49–68	(Ss–Co)/Sy	0			51–68					
38. Gloves	Ss/Co	3.72 (3.07)*	0.39	0.91	55–68	(Ss–Co)/Sy	0			55–68					
39. Apparel, lace	Ry/Sy	3.34 (4.76)†	0.53	0.70	49–68	Sy/Ss	1.72 (1.81)	0.16	0.98	56–68	Ry/Ss	2.73 (5.27)†	0.69	1.26	56–68
	(Ry–Sy–Ss)/Co	0			56–68										
C. Home furnishings															
40. Bedspreads & quilts	Ry/Rs	2.55 (6.26)†	0.67	0.92	49–68	(Ry–Rs)/ (Ss–Co)	1.39 (2.37)	0.54	1.61	64–68	Ss/Co	5.46 (2.15)	0.47	1.13	64–68
	(Ry–Rs)–(Ss–Co) /Sy	0.92 (2.22)	0.48	1.14	64–68										
41. Blankets & blanketings	Rs/Ss	3.64 (7.31)†	0.77	0.96	52–68	(Rs–Ss)/Co	4.31 (1.76)	0.12	0.34	52–68	(Rs–Ss)–Co /Wo	1.39 (1.73)	0.11	0.56	52–68
42. Sheets & other bedding	Ss/Co	9.21 (1.98)	0.42	0.97	64–68	(Ss–Co)/Rs	0			64–68					
43. Towels & towelling	Rs/Co	0			55–68										
44. Woven & lace napery	Rs/Ss	2.58 (4.20)	0.77	1.92	63–68	(Rs–Ss)/Co	0			63–68					
45. (i) Carpets, tufted, face yarns	Rs/Ss	4.71 (5.41)†	0.67	0.43	54–68	(Rs–Ss)/Wo	3.39 (5.49)†	0.68	0.07	54–68	(Rs–Ss)–Wo /Sy	0			57–68
	(Rs–Ss)–Wo–Sy/Co	0			57–68										
(ii) Carpets, woven, knit & needle punch, face yarns	Rs/Ss	9.15 (5.08)†	0.63	0.44	53–68	(Rs–Ss)/Wo	5.07 (4.53)†	0.56	0.82	53–68					
46. Curtains	Ry/Co	1.32 (3.76)*	0.41	0.66	49–68	(Ry–Co)/Sy	1.73 (2.19)	0.17	0.26	49–68					
47. Drapery	Ry/Sy	6.90 (4.73)†	0.53	0.31	49–68	(Ry–Sy)/(Ss–Co)	0			49–68	Ss/Co	4.13 (6.65)†	0.69	1.13	49–68
	(Ry–Sy)–(Ss–Co)/Rs	0			49–68										

End-use	Regression pair	s (t)	$\bar{R}^2$	d	T	Regression pair	s (t)	$\bar{R}^2$	d	T	Regression pair	s (t)	$\bar{R}^2$	d	T
D. Other consumer-type products															
49. Apparel linings	Ry/Rs	2.24 (3.38)*	0.35	0.53	49–68	(Ry–Rs)/(Ss–Co)	0.38 (4.18)*	0.51	0.82	52–68	Ss–Co	6.36 (8.64)†	0.82	1.46	52–68
	(Ry–Rs)–(Ss–Co)/Sy	1.32 (1.78)	0.13	0.44	53–68										
50. Retail piece goods	Ss/Co	4.81 (4.56)†	0.55	0.65	52–68	(Ss–Co)/Wo	0.98 (3.35)*	0.39	0.66	52–68	(Ss–Co)–Wo/(Ry–Sy)	0			52–68
	Ry/Sy	5.30 (6.91)†	0.74	0.57	52–68	(Ss–Co)–Wo–(Ry–Sy)/Rs	0			52–68					
51. Narrow fabrics	Ry/Sy	5.65 (7.67)†	0.78	0.60	49–68	(Ry–Sy)/Co	0			49–68					
52. Handwork yarns	Rs/Ss	3.58 (5.96)†	0.65	1.00	49–68	(Rs–Ss)/Co	3.85 (3.52)†	0.37	0.85	49–68	(Rs–Ss)–Co/Wo	0.35 (1.45)	0.05	0.56	49–68
53. Shoes & slippers	Ry/Sy	1.34 (1.69)	0.10	0.67	52–68	(Ry–Sy)/Co	0			52–68					
54. Luggage, handbags, etc.	Ry/Sy	1.42 (4.42)	0.70	1.31	60–68	(Ry–Sy)/Co	0			60–68					
57. Miscellaneous consumer type products	Rs/Ss	3.17 (10.70)	0.93	1.13	60–68	(Rs–Ss)/Ry	0			60–68					
E. Industrial uses															
58. Transport upholstery	Ry/Rs	2.28 (3.13)*	0.37	1.20	53–68	(Ry–Rs)/Co	2.19 (3.38)*	0.41	0.61	53–68	(Ry–Rs)–Co/(Ss–Wo)–Sy	0			53–65
	Ss/Wo	5.48 (2.77)*	0.29	1.08	49–65	(Ss–Wo)/Sy	0			49–65					
59. Automobile seat slip covers	Ry/Sy	2.31 (2.58)	0.23	0.33	49–68	Sy/Co	2.29 (1.62)	0.08	0.23	49–68	Ry/Co	3.29 (3.07)	0.31	0.27	49–68
60. Tyres	Ry/Sy	9.51	0.78	0.49	49–68	(Ry–Sy)/Co	0			49–68					

which consist of a considerable number of unbiased estimates of elasticities of substitution between fibres.

The salient features of the story behind these results are illustrated by Figures 2.1 and 2.2. Overall market shares of synthetic yarn and staple grew during the period at the expense of cotton, wool and rayon yarn in that order, with rayon staple broadly holding its share; there was a large drop in synthetic staple prices, a smaller slide in the prices of wool, rayon staple and synthetic yarn, with cotton prices falling less than these until the end of the period and wool briefly soaring during the Korean War, while rayon yarn prices grew steadily throughout. The role of price in the market growth of synthetic staple is evidenced by high elasticities with the dominant fibres in most end-uses; for example, in men's suits with wool, in sheets with cotton, in tufted carpets with rayon staple, in woven carpets again with wool. Rayon staple, while losing share to synthetic staple, gained mainly from cotton, significantly on price grounds. Price competiveness is generally high between synthetic yarn and rayon yarn, which the former displaced in a variety of end-uses requiring fibre strength (e.g. tyre cord, women's stockings). Yet the displacement of cotton and wool by synthetic yarn in several knitwear

Figure 2.1
Market shares of fibres in total US consumption, 1949–68 (per cent).

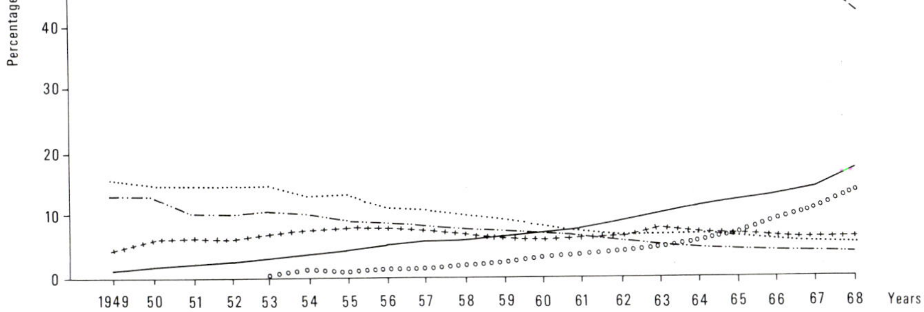

Figure 2.2
US fibre prices, 1949–68 (indices, 1949 = 100).

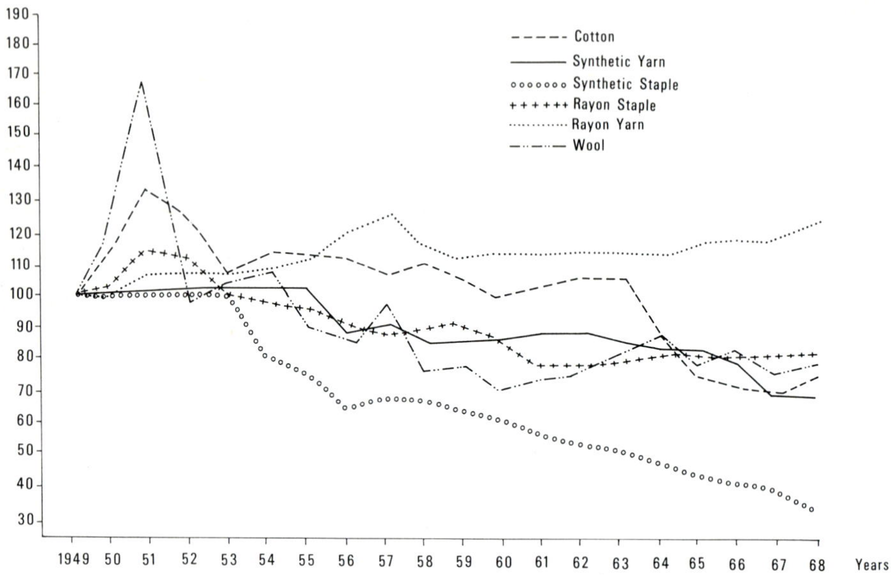

end-uses appeared not to be due to price but to the progress of machine-knitting technology with which it is complementary; and cotton gave way to made-made filaments as a group in many consumer-type and industrial uses primarily on non-price grounds. In further research, these technological changes could usefully be captured in additional variables; it may be that allowance for them would reveal more price competiveness than is at present apparent. Nevertheless, the extent of substitutability uncovered here carries conviction, at least as a minimum.

Economic theory suggests that fibres known to be 'competitive' with one another (in the jargon of the trade) should display substitution elasticities higher than unity, how much higher depending on the degree of 'competitiveness'. The range here mostly lies between 1 and 5 (see Table 2.2), which is consistent with the prediction of the theory. The mean elasticity for the whole sample is 2.5. For the sample of positive elasticities (i.e. for those fibre pairs which are apparently substitutes) it is 3.6. Thus these estimates, even when they are not significant, may be considered as reasonably plausible for the most part.

Table 2.2
Size distribution of elasticities estimated (disaggregated end-uses).[a]

Range of elasticity	Percentage of elasticities falling within range
$s = 0$	30.2
$0 < s \leqslant 1$	7.0
$1 < s \leqslant 2$	13.9
$2 < s \leqslant 3$	13.0
$3 < s \leqslant 4$	9.8
$4 < s \leqslant 5$	11.2
$5 < s \leqslant 6$	6.5
$6 < s$	8.4

[a] *Source:* Table 2.1. The total number of elasticities estimated is 215.

2.5. Testing the null hypothesis for textile fibres generally

We would like to draw some conclusions about fibre substitution in general from the individual results discussed above. Since these results represent unbiased elasticity estimates we may test the null hypothesis for fibre substitution generally as follows.

We suppose that our elasticity estimates for the i end-uses, s_i, are because unbiased distributed with a random error, v_i, of mean zero around σ_i the true elasticity; thus $s_i = \sigma_i + v_i$. We also suppose that the σ_i are distributed around the population mean σ with another random error w_i, also of mean zero (and unknown variance); thus $\sigma_i = \sigma + w_i$. We therefore have $s_i = \sigma + w_i + v_i$, and we may use the mean and standard deviation of the s_i to derive confidence limits for σ, and test the null hypothesis that $\sigma = 0$.

From Table 2.1 we find the mean of the s_i, $\bar{s}_i$, as 2.50 and the standard deviation of the s_i as 2.88. Thus by the central limit theorem $\bar{s}_i$ is distributed around σ approximately normally (since N is very large), with standard error, 0.196. Hence we may set 5% confidence limits for σ as 2.12 and 2.88, and reject the null hypothesis that $\sigma = 0$ with virtually total confidence; the null hypothesis that $\sigma \leqslant 1.70$ may be rejected with equal confidence.

It may be objected that, as a result of the procedure adopted (especially in the search for the correct grouping) elasticity estimates most favourable to rejection of the null hypothesis have been selected, and that a proper test would include all estimated elasticities (whatever their sign) either for all possible groupings or for a grouping selected on grounds independent of this data. There may be an element of truth in such an objection, though its seriousness may reasonably be doubted in view of the overwhelming rejection of the null hypothesis noted above.

Unfortunately, we are unable to carry out the test suggested for the disaggregated data; 'all possible groupings' is an impracticably large set, and we do not have sufficient information that is independent of the sample data to select a single grouping for each end-use *before* carrying out our regressions.

However, a further test can be devised based on more aggregated results. We assume that at a suitable level of aggregation, nesting disappears from the fibre production function and there is a single average elasticity of substitution between all or at least the main fibres; this implies an unambiguous one level grouping and within the aggregated end-use allows us to regress each individual fibre ratio against the corresponding fibre price ratio. Table 2.3 presents results on this basis for five groupings aggregated over the 74 subcategories previously considered.

These results, though based on a much cruder approach, are interestingly similar to the disaggregated results. Out of 75 estimates, 35 are significantly greater than zero and of these 30 are significantly greater than unity; both of these proportions were in fact somewhat larger than for the disaggregated. The size distribution of elasticities, shown in Table 2.4, is slightly more weighted towards zero, in spite of this greater proportional significance. The mean of all elasticities (counting those with the wrong sign as zero) is also somewhat lower at 1.8 (as against 2.5 for the disaggregated); for the non-zero elasticities only, it is 3.4, again rather lower than the 3.6 found for the disaggregated.

Nevertheless, our main interest in these aggregate results is to use them to test various hypotheses about the average elasticity of substitution for fibres generally. We assume as before that $s_i = \sigma + w_i + v_i$ where the interpretation is as above.

We perform two tests, first including all fibres, second excluding from each end-use those fibres with less than 10% of the end-use consumption both at the beginning and end of the period (see Table 2.5).

For all fibres the mean s_i (including wrongly signed values) was 1.37. The standard deviation of the s_i was 2.86, and with $N = 75$, the standard deviation of the mean, $\bar{s}_i$, was therefore 0.33. Hence we may reject the null hypothesis that $\sigma = 0$ with total confidence, while the 95% confidence interval for σ is 0.71 to 2.03.

Table 2.3
Regression results for 5 aggregated end-uses, 1949–68.[a]

	I. Male clothing (end-uses 1–18)			*II. Female clothing* (end-uses 19–39)			*III. Home furnishings* (end-uses 40–48)			*IV. Other consumer products* (end-uses 49–57)			*V. Industrial uses* (end-uses 58–74)		
Fibre pair	s (t)	$\bar{R}^2$	d	s (t)	$\bar{R}^2$	d	s (t)	$\bar{R}^2$	d	s (t)	$\bar{R}^2$	d	s (t)	$\bar{R}^2$	d
Ry/Rs	1.95 (10.86)†	0.86	1.10	1.63 (5.87)†	0.64	1.07	2.36 (9.83)†	0.83	1.19	4.79 (5.53)	0.61	0.43	3.30 (6.20)†	0.66	0.57
Ry/Sy	4.73 (6.32)†	0.67	0.48	2.97 (4.77)†	0.53	1.47	5.99 (7.62)†	0.75	0.43	1.89 (6.66)†	0.70	0.60	5.89 (9.22)†	0.82	0.59
Ry/Ss	−4.31 (15.00)	0.92	0.80	2.95 (5.95)†	0.65	1.87	5.42 (10.36)†	0.85	0.39	3.51 (9.11)†	0.81	0.84	1.93 (8.65)†	0.80	0.56
Ry/Co	1.44 (3.48)*	0.37	0.18	0.24 (0.50)	−.04	1.06	−.58 (4.37)	0.49	0.97	−.78 (5.48)	0.60	0.57	0.34 (1.33)	0.04	0.71
Ry/Wo	1.27 (8.55)*	0.79	1.20	0.67 (2.71)*	0.25	1.36	−.98 (3.01)	0.30	0.70	−.69 (3.35)	0.35	0.69	−1.74 (5.79)	0.63	0.96
Rs/Sy	1.39 (0.83)	−.02	0.12	−.31 (0.28)	−.05	1.05	−.31 (0.14)	−.05	0.08	−1.48 (0.78)	−.02	0.11	−.10 (0.07)	−.06	0.16
Rs/Ss	5.24 (8.55)†	0.79	0.73	−3.21 (4.01)	0.44	1.77	6.62 (6.65)†	0.69	0.42	4.16 (5.91)†	0.64	0.87	0.68 (3.35)*	0.35	1.38
Rs/Co	−.87 (2.70)	0.25	0.74	−1.34 (2.13)	0.16	1.09	0.23 (0.22)	−.05	0.11	−.09 (0.10)	−.05	0.08	−.02 (0.02)	−.06	0.12
Rs/Wo	0.51 (1.50)	0.06	0.34	0.49 (0.97)	−.003	0.65	−1.46 (1.09)	0.009	0.30	−1.63 (1.74)	0.10	0.45	−2.73 (1.68)	0.09	0.39
Sy/Ss	3.15 (9.55)†	0.83	1.25	2.54 (6.02)†	0.65	2.16	3.92 (4.78)†	0.54	0.39	1.86 (4.57)†	0.51	2.42	−1.60 (4.59)	0.51	0.66
Sy/Co	−1.11 (0.81)	−.02	0.19	−1.54 (1.42)	0.05	0.30	−3.14 (1.06)	0.006	0.09	−1.59 (0.61)	−.03	0.07	−1.49 (0.60)	−.03	0.08
Sy/Wo	1.13 (1.12)	0.01	0.29	−.07 (0.09)	−.05	0.36	−2.47 (1.13)	0.01	0.17	−3.28 (1.98)	0.13	0.32	−3.85 (1.89)	0.12	0.29
Ss/Co	5.35 (8.20)†	0.78	1.01	4.10 (5.41)†	0.60	1.42	9.81 (8.82)†	0.80	1.12	6.36 (7.59)†	0.75	1.36	2.84 (6.72)†	0.70	1.12
Ss/Wo	4.55 (4.58)†	0.51	0.71	3.60 (4.21)†	0.47	1.54	7.00 (3.37)†	0.35	0.47	4.32 (3.07)*	0.31	0.56	3.42 (4.07)†	0.45	0.69
Co/Wo	−.03 (0.13)	−.05	0.41	−.22 (1.41)	0.05	1.45	0.31 (0.84)	−.02	0.36	−.27 (1.31)	0.04	0.47	−.88 (1.55)	0.07	0.26

[a] Notes: As in Table 2.1. All regressions were estimated for the full period, 1949–68.

† significantly > 1 } (5% level, one-sided test) with corrected standard error – see Appendix
* significantly > 0 } 2.E.

Table 2.4
Size distribution of elasticities estimated (aggregated end-uses).[a]

Range of elasticity	Percentage of elasticities falling within range
$s = 0$	44.0
$0 < s \leqslant 1$	10.7
$1 < s \leqslant 2$	10.7
$2 < s \leqslant 3$	8.0
$3 < s \leqslant 4$	8.0
$4 < s \leqslant 5$	8.0
$5 < s \leqslant 6$	5.3
$6 < s$	5.3

[a] *Source:* Table 2.3. The total number of elasticities estimated over aggregate end-uses is 75.

Table 2.5
Consumption of fibres by main end-uses in 1949 and 1968 (million lbs.).[a]

		Ry	Rs	Sy	Ss	Co	Wo	Total
I. Male clothing	1949	39.0	64.7	4.3	2.9	835.3	168.1	1114.3
	1968	17.8	86.2	77.7	493.5	1068.7	170.3	1914.2
II. Female clothing	1949	204.5	75.1	39.6	4.5	321.2	152.5	797.5
	1968	258.6	210.0	340.1	358.6	561.0	175.2	1903.5
III. Home furnishings	1949	40.8	33.4	4.5	0.1	758.5	190.3	1027.6
	1968	99.0	399.3	485.8	585.7	1260.6	97.7	2928.1
IV. Other consumer products	1949	125.1	18.5	1.1	0.9	399.6	42.6	587.7
	1968	220.7	135.4	71.4	145.0	506.5	26.8	1105.8
V. Industrial uses	1949	262.0	7.2	28.7	2.1	893.3	47.5	1240.8
	1968	210.8	53.8	906.8	39.3	592.5	8.6	1811.8

[a] *Source: Textile Organon.*

Excluding minor fibres, the mean s_i (again including wrongly signed values) is 1.78, the standard deviation of the s_i is 3.06 and of the mean, $\bar{s}_i$, (with $N = 37$) consequently 0.5. Again, $\sigma = 0$ can be rejected with total confidence while the 95% confidence interval for σ is 0.78 to 2.78.

Whereas the test on the disaggregated results may have favoured rejection of the null hypothesis, it is clear that both of these latter tests on aggregated data are biased against rejection. By aggregating, we lose much of the information that enabled us to pinpoint σ rather precisely. Of the two tests, the first may be the worse; the inclusion of minor fibres, whose substitutability within the end-use is likely to be small, may give s_i a downward bias, since these minor fibres should probably be nested separately with a lower than average elasticity.

Therefore the truth appears to be somewhere between the results of the disaggregated and the aggregated tests (especially that excluding minor fibres). We might summarise the overall results, on this basis, by saying that: σ, the average elasticity of substitution between fibres, is almost certainly positive; very probably (80–90% confidence) greater than unity (elastic); is most likely to lie between $1\frac{1}{2}$ and $2\frac{1}{2}$; is very probably (95% confidence) less than $2\frac{3}{4}$; but is almost certainly less than $3\frac{3}{4}$.

2.6. Conclusions

Three questions that must be the subject of further research are discussed in a preliminary way in Appendices 2.B–D; these concern the recursiveness of the model, the serial correlation of the residuals, and the indexing procedure. There is also the question of how the fibre substitution not explained by fibre prices can be explained, and whether fibre prices play a subsidiary part in such an explanation; this question is closely linked with the serial correlation problem.

Nevertheless, it was shown that textile fibres are on the average definitely price-sensitive with an elasticity of subsitution significantly greater than unity and most probably in the region of 2. At the disaggregated level, it was found that about 40% of the individual elasticities examined were significantly positive and, of these, two-thirds were significantly greater than unity; the remaining non-significant (but unbiased) estimates were generally of a plausible magnitude. One general conclusion of this study is therefore that, in the area of textile fibres, the price mechanism works in the manner predicted by marginal productivity analysis.

In the context of this book the important conclusion is that the elasticity of substitution in the demand for differentiated products has been shown in a particular case at the detailed microeconomic level to be of a magnitude that is also found frequently in macroeconomic trade studies. This finding is sufficiently unusual, given the general absence of such good disaggregated data, to be a source of considerable reassurance for the macroeconomic work that we now go on to report below.

Appendix 2.A: Equivalence of marginal productivity conditions[15] (using indices and without using indices), in the case of a simplified CES production function with three fibres only.

Let the production function be

$$Q = K\{k_1 F_1^{-r} + ([k_2 F_2^{-s} + F_3^{-s}]^{-\frac{1}{s}})^{-r}\}^{-\frac{v}{r}}.$$

The problem is to maximize profits, $\Pi = PQ - P_1 F_1 - P_2 F_2 - P_3 F_3$, subject to this production function. Let $F = [k_2 F_2^{-s} + F_3^{-s}]^{-\frac{1}{s}}$.

(a) Without using indices: we can write the marginal productivity conditions as:

$$P_1 = vPK^{-\frac{r}{v}} Q^{\frac{r}{v}+1} k_1 F_1^{-r-1}, \tag{2.A.1}$$

$$P_2 = vPK^{-\frac{r}{v}} Q^{\frac{r}{v}+1} F^{s+1-r-1} k_2 F_2^{-s-1}, \tag{2.A.2}$$

$$P_3 = vPK^{-\frac{r}{v}} Q^{\frac{r}{v}+1} F^{s+1-r-1} F_3^{-s-1}. \tag{2.A.3}$$

This is equivalent to:

$$\frac{P_2}{P_3} = k_2 \left(\frac{F_3}{F_2}\right)^{s+1}, \tag{2.A.4}$$

$$\frac{P_3}{P_1} = \frac{1}{k_1} F^{s+1-r-1} F_3^{-s-1} F_1^{r+1}, \tag{2.A.5}$$

$$\frac{P_1}{P} = vK^{-\frac{r}{v}} Q^{\frac{r}{v}+1} k_1 F_1^{-r-1}. \tag{2.A.6}$$

(b) Using indices: we write the conditions as:

$$\frac{P_2}{P_3} = k_2 \left(\frac{F_3}{F_2}\right)^{s+1}, \tag{2.A.7}$$

[15] See also, for a general proof, Blackorby et al. [1970] and, for more discussion of the *CES* case, Armington [1969].

$$\frac{P_f}{P_1} = \frac{1}{k_1}\left(\frac{F_1}{F}\right)^{r+1}, \tag{2.A.8}$$

$$P = P_c \bigg/ \frac{\partial Q}{\partial C}, \tag{2.A.9}$$

where P_f, the price index of F, $= P_3(F_3/F)^{s+1}$, and P_c, the price index of C, $= P_1/(\partial C/\partial F_1)$ and

$$C = \{k_1 F_1^{-r} + ([k_2 F_2^{-s} + F_3^{-s}]^{-\frac{1}{s}})^{-r}\}^{-\frac{1}{r}}.$$

Proof of the equivalence of (2.A.4–6) and (2.A.7–9), (2.A.4) = (2.A.7). To show (2.A.5) = (2.A.8) expand (2.A.8),

$$\frac{P_f}{P_1} = \frac{1}{k_1}\left(\frac{F_1}{F}\right)^{r+1},$$

$$\therefore \frac{P_3\left(\dfrac{F_3}{F}\right)^{s+1}}{P_1} = \frac{1}{k_1} F^{-r-1} F_1^{r+1},$$

$$\therefore \frac{P_3}{P_1} = \frac{1}{k_1} F^{s+1-r-1} F_3^{-s-1} F_1^{r+1},$$

which is (2.A.5). To show (2.A.6) = (2.A.9) expand (2.A.9),

$$P = P_c \div \frac{\partial Q}{\partial C} = \left(P_1 \div \frac{\partial C}{\partial F_1}\right) \div \frac{\partial Q}{\partial C} = \frac{P_1}{\dfrac{\partial C}{\partial F_1} \cdot \dfrac{\partial Q}{\partial C}} = \frac{P_1}{\dfrac{\partial Q}{\partial F_1}},$$

$$\therefore P_1 = P \cdot \frac{\partial Q}{\partial F_1} = vPK^{-\frac{r}{v}} Q^{\frac{r}{v}+1} F_1^{-r-1},$$

which is (2.A.6). It follows that, using the indices set out above, it is possible to restate marginal productivity conditions (2.A.4–6) as conditions (2.A.7–9). To obtain the form of eqs. (2.4) and (2.5) we manipulate (2.A.7) and (2.A.8) and change notation so that

$$\sigma = \frac{1}{r+1}, \qquad \eta = \frac{1}{s+1},$$

and we add the error terms u_{23} and u_{lF} respectively, representing commercial misjudgement at each decision level. (These errors would therefore enter into the original marginal productivity conditions (2.A.2) and (2.A.3), respectively as $u_{23} \cdot u_{lF}$ and u_{lF}, so that the errors in those equations would not be independent.)

Appendix 2.B: Recursiveness of equations

For (2.4) and (2.5) to constitute a recursive system it is necessary and sufficient that:

(i) the equations can be ordered in such a way that the solution to any equation is not dependent on the solution to the equations following it;
(ii) the error, u_{ij}, in each equation is independent of the errors in the other equations.

(i) Ordering. If we write $F_{ij} = F_i/F_j$, $P_{ij} = P_i/P_j$, and u_{ij} as defined in Appendix 2.A, write (2.5) as:

$$F_{23} = k_2^{\frac{1}{s+1}}(P_{23})^{-\frac{1}{s+1}}u_{23}, \tag{2.B.1}$$

where P_{23} is exogenous. This equation gives a unique solution for F_{23}. We can write (2.4) as:

$$F_{1F} = k_1^{\frac{1}{r+1}}(P_{1F})^{-\frac{1}{r+1}}u_{1F} \tag{2.B.2}$$

where $P_{1F} = P_{13}(F/F_3)^{s+1} = P_{13}(\phi[F_{23}])^{s+1}$. This equation gives a unique solution for F_{1F}, in terms of P_{13}, F_{23} and u_{1F}.

(ii) Independence of error terms. The residuals from the successful equations were examined for inter-correlations. Only the results that did not confirm the hypothesis of independence are reported. The correlation matrix between the residuals is given for these cases, and the coefficients which are significant at the 95% level are starred, these being the 'offending' instances. Coefficients are bracketed if the residuals are in the same recursive block (e.g. Ry–Rs and Ss–Co in end–use 6).

The assumption of recursiveness can therefore be questioned in several end-uses. Investigation of this must be the subject of further research. Simple indexing (by shares in fibre expenditure) would have the advantage of making each equation independent (the recursiveness properties thereby becoming irrelevant), and is discussed in Appendix 2.D. Alternatively, it may be possible, by specifying other exogenous variables, to improve the fit and modify the residuals.

Table 2.B.1
Correlations between residuals.

End-use	Residuals from		Correlation matrix of residuals (2)	(3)	(4)	(5)	No. of observ-ations
2	Rs–Ss	(1)	–0.72*				16
5	Ss–Co	(1)	0.15	–0.15			16
	(Ss–Co)–Wo	(2)		0.61*			
	[(Ss–Co)–Wo]–Rs	(3)					
6	Ss–Co	(1)	(–0.03)	–0.44	–0.50*	–0.55*	20
	Ry–Rs	(2)		0.14	–0.21	–0.16	
	(Ss–Co)–Wo	(3)			–0.35	–0.79	
	[(Ss–Co)–Wo]–(Ry–Rs)	(4)				0.30	
	[(Ss–Co)–Wo]–(Ry–Rs)–Sy	(5)					
7	Ss–Co	(1)	0.60*				20
	(Ss–Co)–Wo	(2)					
9	Rs–Sy	(1)	(0.02)	–0.72*	0.68*		9
	Ss–Co	(2)		–.28	0.32		
	(Rs–Sy)–Ry	(3)			–0.60		
	[(Rs–Sy)–Ry]–(Ss–Co)	(4)					
11	Rs–Ss	(1)	–0.67*	0.28			12
	(Rs–Ss)–Wo	(2)		0.23			
	[(Rs–Ss)–Wo]–Co	(3)					
17	Ry–Sy	(1)	(0.57)	–0.90*			9
	Ss–Co	(2)		–0.31			
	(Ry–Sy)–(Ss–Co)	(3)					
18	Ry–Rs	(1)	(0.10)	(0.64*)	–0.33	–0.05	20
	Rs–Ss	(2)		(0.82)	–0.73*	0.09	
	Ry–Ss	(3)			–0.70*	0.11	

End-use	Residuals from		Correlation matrix of residuals (2)	(3)	(4)	(5)	No. of observ-ations
	(Ry–Rs–Ss)–Wo	(4)				0.18	
	[(Ry–Rs–Ss)–Wo]–Co	(5)					
19	Ry–Sy	(1)	–0.09	–0.43	0.35	–0.19	20
	(Ry–Sy)–Ss	(2)		–0.17	0.51*	–0.44	
	[(Ry–Sy)–Ss]–Rs	(3)			–0.02	0.63*	
	[[(Ry–Sy)–Ss]–Rs]–Co	(4)				–0.19	
	([[(Ry–Sy)–Ss]–Rs]–Co)–Wo	(5)					
21	Rs–Wo	(1)	(0.35)	(0.07)	0.59*	0.34	20
	Ry–Sy	(2)		(0.10)	0.47*	0.24	
	Ss–Co	(3)			0.34	–0.24	
	(Ry–Sy)–(Ss–Co)	(4)				0.01	
	[(Ry–Sy)–(Ss–Co)]–(Rs–Wo)	(5)					
22	Ss–Co	(1)	0.20	0.52*	–0.22		18
	(Ss–Co)–Rs	(2)		0.49*	0.64*		
	[(Ss–Co)–Rs]–Wo	(3)			0.02		
	[[(Ss–Co)–Rs]–Wo]–Ry	(4)					
30	Ry–Rs	(1)	(–0.37)	–0.54*	–0.48*		18
	Ss–Co	(2)		–0.27	0.06		
	(Ry–Rs)–Sy	(3)			0.73*		
	[(Ry–Rs)–Sy]–(Ss–Co)	(4)					
34	Ry–Sy	(1)	–0.30	–0.32			9
	(Ry–Sy)–Co	(2)		–0.72*			
	[(Ry–Sy)–Co]–Ss	(3)					
40	Ry–Rs	(1)	(–0.27)	–0.54	0.04		5
	Ss–Co	(2)		–0.26	–0.93		
	[(Ry–Rs)–(Ss–Co)]	(3)			0.51		
	[(Ry–Rs)–(Ss–Co)]–Sy	(4)					
41	Rs–Ss	(1)	–0.60*	–0.49			17
	(Rs–Ss)–Co	(2)		0.53*			
	[(Rs–Ss)–Co]–Wo	(3)					
45(i)	Rs–Ss	(1)	0.62*				15
	(Rs–Ss)–Wo	(2)					
49	Ry–Rs	(1)	(–0.13)	–0.14	0.04		16
	Ss–Co	(2)		0.60*	–0.38		
	[(Ry–Rs)–(Ss–Co)]	(3)			–0.07		
	[(Ry–Rs)–(Ss–Co)]–Sy	(4)					
50	Ss–Co	(1)	(–0.52*)	0.07			17
	Ry–Sy	(2)		0.13			
	[(Ss–Co)–Wo]	(3)					

Appendix 2.C: Serial correlation and the textile cycle

In the following few cases, the hypothesis, that the textile cycle was responsible for serial correlation in the errors, was confirmed. The textile cycle was taken to be the logarithmic deviations, from a third degree polynomial trend, of the mill consumption of textile fibres (all man-made fibres, cotton, wool and silk). The residuals from each equation were regressed on this variable. The coefficient which thus related the residuals to the textile cycle, its t-statistic and the Durbin–Watson statistic of the regression are given. The Durbin–Watson of the original equation is also given.

Table 2.C.1
Regressions of residuals on 'textile cycle'.[a]

End-use	Original equation	Coefficient relating residuals to textile cycle	t-statistic	Durbin-Watson statistic	Durbin–Watson statistic of original equation	No. of observ-tions
1	Ss–Wo	–7.40	1.65	0.69	0.60	18
6	Ry–Rs	–3.36	1.53	0.46	0.58	20
16	Ss–Co	–4.20	2.66	1.28	1.14	18
20	(Rs–Wo)–Ss	–4.54	1.94	1.68	1.20	9
27	Rs–Wo	3.70	1.98	0.71	0.60	20
31	Ry–Sy	–2.14	1.85	0.69	0.56	20
32	(Ry–Ss–Co)–Sy	–3.00	1.85	1.14	0.83	14
39	Ry–Ss	–6.56	3.13	1.15	1.26	15
40	(Ry–Rs)–(Ss–Co)	–1.72	1.82	1.62	1.61	5
50	Ry–Sy	–4.90	1.90	0.97	0.57	17
52	Rs–Ss	4.19	1.82	0.89	1.00	20
54	Ry–Sy	–1.60	1.59	2.24	1.31	9
57	Rs–Ss	–2.89	2.60	2.49	1.13	9
58	(Ry–Rs)–Co	–4.05	2.13	1.13	0.61	16
62	Ry–Sy	–7.36	1.84	0.65	0.49	17
68	(Ry–Sy)–Rs	9.44	2.32	1.36	1.16	9

[a] Mill consumption of these fibres between 1949 and 1968 was (in million lbs.): 5445, 6846, 6838, 6440, 6481, 6028, 6710, 6543, 6230, 5967, 6839, 6530, 6630, 7116, 7321, 7855, 8561, 9055, 9029, 9825. The following trend was fitted to the natural logarithms of these numbers: $8.705 + 0.023793T + 0.003346T^2 + 0.000174T^3$, ($\bar{R}^2 = 0.85$, $d = 1.79$) where T is time. The logarithmic deviations from this trend were:– –0.123, 0.091, 0.079, 0.012, 0.014, –0.061, 0.044, 0.016, –0.038, –0.088, 0.037, –0.025, –0.032, 0.011, 0.003, 0.028, 0.058, 0.048, –0.033, –0.041. These deviations were treated as the 'textile cycle' in these regressions.

It is clear that the hypothesis of varying discounts can only make a limited contribution to the explanation of the residuals.

Appendix 2.D: The problem of indexing

The general method of indexing described in the text offers as many alternatives for the price index of a fibre group as there are fibres in the group. This is simply because the 'price' of the fibre group is the marginal cost of producing it and this marginal cost can be equivalently measured in terms of each of the fibres. Theory offers no guide as to which is the right measure (or whether indeed we should take an average of them); and in the work that has been done, the quite arbitrary decision was made to use the fibre whose distribution parameter was normalised at unity. Thus, for example, where

$$F = (k_2 F_2^{-s} + F_3^{-s})^{-\frac{1}{s}},$$

as in Appendix 2.A, then P_f was measured, in terms of F_3, as

$$P_3 \div \frac{\partial Q}{\partial F_3} = P_3 \left(\frac{F_3}{F}\right)^{s+1}.$$

The alternative measure in this case is

$$\frac{P_2}{k_2}\left(\frac{F_2}{F}\right)^{s+1}.$$

The two measures are related by the marginal productivity equation,

$$\frac{P_2}{P_3} = k_2 \left(\frac{F_3}{F_2}\right)^{s+1} u_{23}.$$

Hence $P_3(F_3/F)^{s+1} = (P_2/k_2)(F_2/F)^{s+1} u_{23}^{-1}$.

The measures would thus only be the same if: (i) there were no error term in the marginal productivity equations; and (ii) the production function parameters were correctly estimated.

There is the further alternative of abandoning the general method of indexing completely in favour of the familiar method based on shares of expenditure. While simple indices of this kind do not satisfy the marginal productivity conditions mathematically, they do have the advantage that recursiveness is not required. Just as the other method poses an index number problem in the choice of price index, so the traditional problem arises with the familiar method in the choice of weights. In neither case is there a correct answer.

There is no solution to this generalised index number problem. All that we can say is that the estimates put forward in this chapter employ indices which (a) are derived from the model (i.e. satisfy the marginal productivity equations), (b) have the statistical properties discussed elsewhere in the paper. Indices, which included the alternative price index but were otherwise the same, would have the same properties; given the resources, we could therefore generate a whole alternative set of estimates, which were equally valid. We could then pool these estimates in some way, as if they were evidence from separate samples. Indices based on the familiar expenditure weighting method would not strictly fulfil (a) but would perhaps do better on (b) because recursiveness would not be needed; the fact however that they do not satisfy the model strictly, makes these simple indices something of a last resort.

How sensitive are the estimates to the different indexing methods? To attempt a preliminary answer to this question, one end-use (No. 19) was chosen and the same regressions as were reported in Table 2.1 above were carried out using the other methods, both measuring marginal cost in terms of the other price (there is one alternative price, in this end-use, at all levels of grouping), and using simple expenditure weights (1965 was chosen as the typical year). The results are compared in Table 2.D.1.

It is not possible to draw conclusions about sensitivity from this single trial. At level 2 the estimates differ little; here the A estimates were very robust with an $\bar{R}^2$ of 0.85. At the higher levels, the estimates differ considerably; but then the A estimates were not really significant. Very probably different indexing would have resulted in a different grouping in this case. Further exploration of this question is necessary.

Table 2.D.1
Comparison of different indexing methods for end-use no. 19.

Level of fibre grouping			s	t	$\bar{R}^2$	d	T
(2)	(Ry–Sy)–Ss	*A*	2.57	10.55	0.85	0.93	1949–68
		B	2.74	8.29	0.78	0.66	1949–68
		C	3.33	8.62	0.72	0.65	1949–68
(3)	[(Ry–Sy)–Ss]–Rs	*A*	2.19	2.02	0.14	0.20	1949–68
		B	0.95	0.43	0.27	0.65	1949–68
		C	3.41	6.77	0.70	1.12	1949–68
(4)	[[(Ry–Sy)–Ss]–Rs]–Co	*A*	1.37	2.15	0.16	0.28	1949–68
		B	–*	–	–	–	1949–68
		C	–*	–	–	–	1949–68
(5)	([[(Ry–Sy)–Ss]–Rs]–Co)–Wo	*A*	0.47	2.10	0.15	0.39	1949–68
		B†	0.39	2.34	0.19	0.42	1949–68
		C	2.18	4.19	0.47	1.14	1949–68

* The sign was wrong.
† The weights were taken from the *A* regression for Level 4, but the *B* regression for all other cases.
A = reported results.
B = results using price index based on price of other fibre (or group).
C = results using 1965 expenditure weights.

Appendix 2.E: Correcting coefficient standard errors for serial correlation

In the presence of serially correlated residuals, the variance of the estimated coefficient is not that calculated by the usual method. Instead, using Aitken's notation (see Christ [1966, pp. 309–5]; see also Johnston [1972, pp. 246–9], who sets out the derivation below in another notation), the variance/co-variance matrix is given by:

$$\text{cov}\,(\beta'\beta) = (ZZ')^{-1}\, Z\, E\, v'\, v\, Z'\, (ZZ')^{-1}. \tag{2.E.1}$$

Where Z consists of a single exogenous variable, p (relative fibre prices), measured in deviations from its mean, and β of the single slope coefficient (the constant term being dealt with separately and not considered here), this can be written as:

$$\text{var}\,\beta = \frac{1}{(\sum p^2)^2}\, pEv'vp'. \tag{2.E.2}$$

We assume that $v_t = \rho v_{t-1} + u_t$; then if ω^2 is the variance of u, $\mathrm{var}(v) = (\omega^2/1 - \rho^2)$, $\mathrm{cov}(v_t, v_{t-1}) = \omega^2\rho^2/(1 - \rho^2)$ and so on. Thus:

$$\mathrm{var}\,\beta = \frac{\omega^2}{(1-\rho^2)(\sum p^2)^2}\, p\Omega p', \tag{2.E.3}$$

where

$$\Omega = \begin{bmatrix} 1 & \rho & \rho^2 & \rho^3 & \cdots & \rho^{n-1} \\ \rho & \ddots & & & & \vdots \\ \rho^2 & & \ddots & & & \rho^3 \\ \rho^3 & & & \ddots & & \rho^2 \\ \vdots & & & & \ddots & \rho \\ \rho^{n-1} & \cdots & \rho^3 & \rho^2 & \rho & 1 \end{bmatrix}$$

and so collecting terms,

$$\begin{aligned} p\Omega p' = \{\textstyle\sum p^2 + 2[\rho(p_1p_2 + p_2p_3 + \ldots + p_{n-1}p_n) \\ + \rho^2(p_1p_3 + p_2p_4 + \ldots + p_{n-2}p_n) \\ \vdots \\ + \rho^{n-1}(p_1p_n)]\} \\ = \textstyle\sum p^2 + 2P, \end{aligned} \tag{2.E.4}$$

(P being the expression in square brackets). Therefore we may write:

$$\mathrm{var}\,\beta = \frac{\omega^2[\sum p^2 + 2P]}{(1-\rho^2)(\sum p^2)^2}. \tag{2.E.5}$$

We now derive an unbiased estimate of ω^2 in the presence of serially correlated residuals. We note that, adapting Christ [p. 369, eq. (3.39)]:

$$E\hat{v}\hat{v}' = E\sum \hat{v}_t^2 = \frac{\omega^2}{1-\rho^2}\left(n - 2 - \frac{2\sum_t \sum_s v_s v_t \cdot p_s p_t}{\sum p^2}\right). \tag{2.E.6}$$

It is readily apparent that the double summation term is $2P/\sum p^2$ and so:

$$E\hat{v}\hat{v}' = \frac{\omega^2}{1-\rho^2}\left[n - 2 - \frac{2P}{\sum p^2}\right], \tag{2.E.7}$$

and it is clear that the unbiased estimate of ω^2 is now:

$$w^2 = \frac{\hat{v}\hat{v}'(1-\rho^2)}{(n-2) - (2P/\sum p^2)}. \tag{2.E.8}$$

Substituting this for ω^2 in (2.E.5), we obtain:

$$\text{true } \widehat{\text{var}}\ \beta = \frac{\hat{v}\hat{v}'(\sum p^2 + 2P)}{[(n-2)\sum p^2 - 2P]\sum p^2}. \tag{2.E.9}$$

We compare this with the usual estimate of var β:

$$\text{usual } \widehat{\text{var}}\ \beta = \hat{v}\hat{v}'/\sum p^2(n-2). \tag{2.E.10}$$

We then easily obtain the correction factor for the coefficient standard error as usually reported:

$$\text{Correction factor} = \sqrt{\left(\frac{\text{true } \widehat{\text{var}}\ \beta}{\text{usual } \widehat{\text{var}}\ \beta}\right)} = \sqrt{\left(\frac{\sum p^2 + 2P}{\sum p^2 - \left(\frac{2P}{n-2}\right)}\right)} \tag{2.E.11}$$

In Table 2.E.1 that follows we show the correction factors that would result on this basis for regressions involving all fifteen possible fibre pairs, and on four different assumed values of ρ. (It should be noted that an estimate of ρ is provided by the Durbin–Watson statistic, d, since $\rho = (1 - 0.5d)$.)

The meaning of the correction factor for a given fibre pair is that for any end-use the *t*-statistic[16] for the estimated elasticity of substitution between these fibres is over-stated by the factor shown. It was unfortunately not possible to calculate the appropriate correction factor for all index-combinations of fibres; but clearly, this will lie somewhere in the range given by each fibre combination taken separately (e.g. the factor for a regression of (Ry–Sy) on Ss will be within the range given by Ry–Ss and Sy–Ss). These factors are applied to the *t*-statistics[17] of *s* in the main text tables.

Table 2.E.1
Correction factors for calculated standard errors of estimated elasticity of substitution.[a]

Fibre Pair	$\rho = 0.3$	$\rho = 0.5$	$\rho = 0.7$	$\rho = 0.9$
Ry–Rs	1.304	1.578	1.926	1.977
Ry–Sy	1.263	1.484	1.755	1.807
Ry–Ss	1.299	1.573	1.932	2.034
Ry–Co	1.293	1.537	1.824	1.852
Ry–Wo	1.268	1.503	1.777	1.749
Rs–Sy	1.172	1.252	1.238	0.893
Rs–Ss	1.269	1.512	1.827	1.910
Rs–Co	1.230	1.371	1.435	1.101
Rs–Wo	1.066	1.112	1.124	0.906
Sy–Ss	1.304	1.587	1.961	2.057
Sy–Co	1.147	1.212	1.212	0.933
Sy–Wo	1.146	1.260	1.347	1.103
Ss–Co	1.244	1.473	1.783	1.850
Ss–Wo	1.196	1.380	1.606	1.582
Co–Wo	1.211	1.379	1.492	1.153

[a] *Notes:* The *t*-statistics given in the main text tables should be divided by these correction factors (or the standard errors multiplied by them). The factors are calculated on the assumption that the estimation period is the full one ($N = 20$) from 1949 to 1968; some experimentation suggests that they are not sensitive to quite large reductions in the estimation period, however for regressions with 10 periods or less the factors have not been applied and no assessment made of significance levels.

[16] Strictly speaking, this does not have the *t*-distribution in the presence of serially correlated residuals; however, Johnston on p. 249 suggests that this is relatively not a serious problem.

[17] For ρ values lying between those shown in Table 5.1, the correction factors were interpolated. For higher-level fibre pairs, an average of the correction factors was taken; e.g. for (Ss–Wo)/Rs, the average of the factors for Rs–Ss and Rs–Wo was used. Similarly for the more complex (Ss–Co)–Wo/(Ry–Rs), an average of those for Ry–Ss, Ry–Co, Ry–Wo, Rs–Ss, Rs–Co, Rs–Wo was taken.

Chapter 3

A MODEL OF UK MANUFACTURED EXPORTS AND EXPORT PRICES[1]

3.1. Introduction

We now turn to the estimation of a macroeconomic relationship which is central to any model of the UK economy, that between UK exports of manufactures on the one hand and expenditures, foreign and domestic, relative prices, and domestic supply on the other hand. The underlying model for the demand for export goods is essentially the same as that of Chapter 2 for fibre demand. However, it is necessarily more aggregated; and, because of this, we cannot assume, as we did there at the micro level, that supply is always forthcoming at the prices set (for natural fibres) by the world market or (for man-made) by the fibre-producing industry. We, therefore, add the supply side to the demand problems of Chapter 2. As part of the full supply/demand model, we also investigate the determinants of export prices.

A more accidental difference is that the data are quarterly a opposed to annual and they cover a shorter period, 1958–71. Another is that the work is an attempt to explain the variations in exports as fully and in as much

[1] This chapter reports work substantially completed when I was in H.M. Treasury Balance of Payments Division, work on which I enjoyed the cooperation of John Hutton, University of York; it is a revised version of Hutton and Minford [1975], which appeared as Government Economic Service Paper No. 11, HMSO. I am grateful for valuable comments from colleagues in the Treasury and in the Department of Trade and Industry, as well as elsewhere in Whitehall; in particular to Michael Doig, Arnold Lovell, Donald MacDougall and Peter Sedgwick. I am also grateful to the DTI for providing much of the data and to Mrs Honor Stamler for writing most of the computer programmes used.

structural detail as possible because it was originally prompted by the needs of H.M. Treasury for forecasting and policy simulation; Chapter 2 was essentially concerned with testing a hypothesis about the elasticity of substitution and not with the full explanation of relative fibre use. This chapter, in fact, will contribute the first explicit 'building block' in a macroeconomic framework for predicting trade, payments and the exchange rate, with specific reference to the UK.

3.2. The Theoretical Framework of Existing Empirical Work

A convenient starting point for the argument is Ball's [1967] short theoretical analysis of the effects of demand pressure on exports. Viewing the problem in terms of Joan Robinson's [1933] analysis of the discriminating monopolist, Ball divided his analysis to distinguish two cases: price flexibility and price rigidity in the short run. He considered the rigid price model appropriate to the UK case, and developed some implications for excess demand and supply conditions, but concentrated his attention on the excess supply case which he considered characteristic of the UK economy during the 1950s. An important implication of Ball's position for empirical work is that under conditions of excess supply, exports must be demand-determined, so that the world demand for UK exports could be considered identified; in other words, the short run elasticity of supply is assumed to be infinite.

A recent example of a pure demand model justifiable only on these grounds is due to Houthakker and Magee [1969], where UK exports are a function of world trade (as a proxy for the income effect on demand for exportables) and the ratio of UK to competitors' prices. The usual form of model, however, does incorporate supply effects, by incorporating in the demand equation various measures of the pressure of domestic demand. These equations, as is argued later, are not the appropriate way to allow for supply factors because of the very special assumptions implicit in them; yet they have been used widely, apparently without much consideration of their precise theoretical justification or the precise interpretation of the coefficients obtained. Thus, Ball, Eaton and Steuer [1966], Brechling and Wolfe [1965], Smyth [1968], Artus [1970] and Renton and Duffy [1970] have all estimated estimated essentially similar models for UK exports. Smyth and Renton and Duffy, using somewhat different criteria from each other, claimed to have found an asymmetrical response of exports to the pressure of demand: Smyth differentiated between the effects of rising and falling pressure on the rate of growth of exports, while Renton [1970] and Renton and Duffy differentiated between high and low pressure on the level of exports. Renton and Renton and Duffy analysed total manufactured exports to each country of destination, as well as the aggregate. A number of writers (e.g. Cooper, Hartley and Harvey [1970] and Artus) have disaggregated by commodity rather than destination; others (e.g. Adams, Eguchi and Meyer-zu-Schlochtern [1969]) have confined themselves to the aggregate. All these writers have adopted the straightforward course of adding pressure of demand variables to the demand equation. There appears, however, to be no study at the aggregate level which can show satisfactory estimates of pressure of demand effects, together with the sort of relative price effects we expect from more disaggregated studies (see for example MacDougall's [1951], where he finds high 'long run' substitution elasticities across commodities; also Magee's findings, quoted in Branson [1972]).

The failure of aggregative studies to produce results consistent with the predictions of microeconomic theory has been attributed both to the inadequacy of price data and to the well-known problems of aggregation. Artus, Renton and Duffy, and Ball, Eaton and Steuer all use these arguments, as does Henry [1970]. In this study, he analyses pressure of demand effects at the industry level, but re-emphasises the essential features of Ball's [1967] article which postulated that excess demand *or* supply conditions characterised the market for exportables. Thus, instead of introducing a pressure variable into the demand equation (with or without asymmetrical effects), Henry showed that pressure effects had more radical consequences. His approach is closest to the one proposed here for dealing with supply factors.

However, he too fails to discover plausible price effects. Yet apparently no researcher has paid more than cursory attention to the lag structures of the price term with the exception of Junz and Rhomberg [1965 and 1973], who distinguish successfully between long and short run elasticities; others assume either no lag or at best a short fixed lag, the justification normally being that, treated in this way, the variable picks up the trend impact of prices. This justification seems inadequate, particularly when (as in the UK experience) an exchange rate change has given the relative price series an important discontinuity. In this paper we discuss the appropriate lag structure at some length.

3.3. Specification of the model

We now consider the specification of demand and supply schedules, and the behaviour of deliveries under conditions of disequilibrium between demand and supply.

3.3.1. Demand

The demand schedule presents least difficulties in specification, since our approach is quite conventional. Thus the general form we use is

$XD = XD(M, R{\cdot}PX, PW, WBC)$: we treat this as being loglinear.

The demand for manufactured exportables depends on the level of world imports of manufactures from the main manufacturing countries including the UK (M), the unit value index of UK manufactured exports (PX) converted to dollar terms by R the sterling/dollar parity, an index of competitors' unit values (in dollars) weighted both by the competitors' shares in UK markets and by each market's share in UK exports of manufactures (PW), and a world business cycle index from indices of capacity utilisation in *OECD* countries weighted by UK market shares (WBC). Variable definitions, sources and data are shown in the Appendix.

The only major restriction on the demand function is that $R.PX$ and PW have equal and opposite elasticities; this is a normal restriction where the trade expansion and income effects of price changes are captured as here by a world trade term. It implies that the estimated elasticity can be interpreted as the elasticity of substitution times one minus the UK share in world exports of manufactures, as shown by Armington [1969]. The elasticity of substitution between UK manufactures and its competitors' is, at an aggregate level, analogous to that between fibres in Chapter 2. In each manufactured end-use we assume that UK products are differentiated from products of other countries; there will also be competition between UK products in that end-use, just as there is between different brands of each fibre group in Chapter 2, but as there we ignore this and treat volume and price as indices for the group as a whole. The difference here is that we proceed to aggregate the end-uses into total manufactures.

We do not restrict the elasticity of *M* to unity, as is sometimes done (e.g. by Ball et al. [1966]). Our reason was that this 'elasticity' captures the effects of various non-price factors (such as new product penetration) whose influence varies with world trade, and also that, in the aggregate, market and product distribution different from the average could result in a changing UK share (i.e. non-unit elasticity). In this connection, it is worth noting that we attempted to include proxies for other non-price factors such as a time trend and export profitability (with varying lags, as a measure of sales effort); but these attempts met with no success.

The *WBC* term is included in order to pick up any cyclical income effects that are not associated with the movements of *M*. We would not be surprised to find that the relationship between the trend components of *XD* and *M* is different from that between the cyclical components, and this would make *WBC* significant. The difference could arise because of peculiarities of the market and commodity distribution of UK exports. Primary producers take a larger share of UK exports than of world manufactured exports, and their incomes are (because of ex-colonial links) more dependent on the state of the world business cycle than those of industrial economies. Similarly, intermediate and capital goods are a larger proportion of UK exports than of world trade in manufactures, and these too exhibit unusually strong cycles. In principle we could allow for these effects by a fine weighting of world imports by destination and commodity group; but the enormous computation involved makes it far less cost–effective than the simple inclusion of *WBC*.

We are also interested in the distributed lag effects of all the variables specified. Lags on *M* and *WBC* come about because 1) these are proxies for demands in different parts of the world and in different commodity groups, whose movements are not sunchronised; 2) not only their level but also their rates of growth determine export demand for goods (such as capital goods) where a stock-adjustment model is appropriate. We expect these lags to extend no further than a few quarters, because the principal demand proxy, world trade itself, consists of actual deliveries and so already includes, so to speak, the order-delivery lag.

Lags in international price responsiveness are likely to arise under four headings:

1. The gap between order and delivery.
2. Information search costs.
3. Costs of adjustment.

4. Formation of expectations.

The effect of the order-delivery lag will depend on 1) how far contracts are fixed-price and are adhered to; 2) how far changes in relative prices come about through exchange rate changes. If there were no exchange rate changes, then fixed-price contracts would in the absence of renegotiation imply that recorded deliveries and prices (unit values) would both correspond to the contracted quantities and prices at the time of order; so there would be no order-delivery lag in price response, the prices also being lagged. On the other hand, exchange rate changes would have an immediate effect on relative recorded prices because by convention the conversion to a common exchange rate is done at current exchange rates; an exchange rate could therefore only produce a change in recorded deliveries after the order-delivery lag. However, while evidence is hard to come by, it seems at least possible – particularly on the goods with longer order-delivery lags – that in the inflationary conditions of the 1950s and 1960s prices could have been revised upwards after the order was placed; it may also be that in these conditions there will be a difference between the price list at the time of the decision to order and the price list when the contract is drawn up, especially on capital projects where the equipment has to be made to specification and the decision in principle to use a certain supplier has to be made very far in advance of delivery. Such considerations suggest that the order–delivery gap, loosely defined as the gap between the time of delivery and the time when the decision to order is made, could contribute a lag to the price response.

The order–delivery lag will clearly be longer the more durable the commodity, since order books act as a buffer between flow demand and production while flow demand is more volatile as the ratio of replacement flow to existing stock decreases. It is clear from Table 3.1 that the proportion of UK manufactured exports represented by longer-lived goods is a high one; if we include capital goods, metals and metal manufactures, motor vehicle parts, and consumer durables, it comes to around 60%. This suggests a significant order–delivery lag; Zarnowitz [1962] finds a lag of around 2 months on typical light manufactures and of around $3\frac{1}{2}$ months on typical heavy manufactures. On this basis, we might expect the average order–delivery lag to be about 3 months. But it seems likely that for some extreme categories such as aircraft, hydro-electric equipment, it would be a matter of years (the RB211 example springs to mind where orders were were placed in 1968 and deliveries began in 1972).

The general nature of information and adjustment costs needs no elaboration here; see for example Stigler [1969] and Nerlove [1958]. However, adjustment costs will assume increasing importance 1) the longer the life of the commodity, 2) the greater its complementarity, 3) the greater are communications costs; while of course information costs principally depend on 3). In international trade communications costs will be higher than in the normal domestic context, while for the UK the high share on the one hand of capital goods (plus consumer durables), and on the other of intermediate inputs (see Table 3.1), emphasise the importance respectively of 1) and 2).

The role of expectations is complicated by the existence of forward markets.

Table 3.1
Exports of manufactures by commodity, 1971.

	SITC group	Value 1971 (£ million)	% of total manufactures
Capital goods			
Non-electrical machinery	71	1945	24.9
Electrical machinery (excl. domestic)	72 excl. 725	598	7.6
Commercial vehicles	732.2–5 & 7	241	3.1
Ships and aircraft	734 & 735	220	2.8
Total Capital goods		3004	38.4
Intermediate goods			
Chemicals	5	884	11.3
Textiles	65	426	5.4
Metals & metal manufactures	67–69	1005	12.9
Other manufactures classified by material	Rest of 6	802	10.3
Parts and accessories and miscellaneous for road motor vehicles	732.8–9	376	4.8
Miscellaneous for other transport equipment	731, 733	63	0.8
Total intermediate goods		3556	45.5
Consumer goods			
Cars	732.1,732.6	373	4.8
Domestic electrical equipment	725	50	0.6
Miscellaneous manufactures (clothing, footwear, etc.)	8	837	10.7
Total consumer goods		1260	16.1
Total Manufactures		7820	100.0

The trader can avoid exchange risk by covering forward and so avoid the need to form an expectation about the future exchange rate by obtaining a sure quote in the present. Yet the exchange rate is only one element in price competitiveness; nominal prices (in own currency) are the remaining elements, and, as discussed above, forward contracting (beyond perhaps a few months ahead) is likely to leave room for price revision. So we assume that, while exchange risk can be avoided (an assumption retained in other chapters), price risk cannot and gives rise to price expectations. Here we make no attempt to impose 'rationality', since, while it is not hard conceptually to envisage rational expectations about the exchange rate (cf. chapters 6–8) *conditional* on known traded goods prices or even merely known home goods prices, it is extremely hard to imagine traders solving a model of traded goods price determination unconditionally. Such a model would be highly complex and costly, to say nothing else: traded goods prices, it is argued below, depend on own home goods prices as well as others' traded goods prices (which in turn depend similarly on their home goods prices as well as others' traded goods prices), while home goods prices will depend on domestic monetary conditions and other (e.g. productivity) factors. However, it is a commonplace of forecasting methodology (see Box and Jenkins [1970]) that one may forecast competently, if not as well or better than with more elaborate methods, by employing generalised rational lag transfer functions, and in particular the autoregressive function; the reason for the success of such methods lies presumably in the existence of lags and the collinearity or interdependence between lagged own values and lagged values of exogenous variables. Consequently, we assume here that expected future price competetiveness depends on current and lagged values of itself. While the lag-structure may contain negative terms (and be auto-extrapolative), it is more likely that price competitiveness will regress towards a (trend-dominated) equilibrium so that all terms would be positive; we report below, but generally pass over, results with negative weights. Hence in formal terms we have (disregarding non-price variables):

		Type of structure
$XD = \sum_{i=t}^{D} d_i O_{-i}$	XD, deliveries, as a function of orders, O.	All weights positive, possibly two peaks reflecting 1) consumer goods, 2) capital goods.

		First weights may be zero.
$O = \sum_{i=0}^{A} a_i \bar{O}_{-i}$	Adjustment lags; actual orders a distributed lag function of past equilibrium orders.	All weights positive.
$\bar{O} = B\bar{P}$	Equilibrium order, O, as a function of expected price, P. B is the price elasticity of demand.	
$\bar{P} = a \sum_{i=0}^{M} m_i P^0_{-i} + b \sum_{i=0}^{N} n_i \Delta P^0_{-i} + K(M > N) = \sum_{i=0}^{M} g_i P^0_{-i} + K$	Expected price, $\bar{P}$, a function of both weighted past levels and weighted past rates of change.	First weight positive. Subsequent signs may be positive or negative but expected to be positive. As $b \to 0$ all weights $\to$ positive.
$P^0 = \sum_{i=e}^{F} f_i P_{-i}$	Information filter; P^0 is prices observed by the buyer, P is actual prices.	All weights positive. Possibly a fixed lag. First weights may be zero.

Combining all these gives an overall lag structure of:

$$XD = B \sum_{c}^{D} d_i \sum_{0}^{A} a_j \sum_{0}^{M} g_k \sum_{e}^{F} f_l \, P_{-i-j-k-l} + BK =$$

$$B \sum_{i=c+e}^{A+D+F+M} w_i P_{-i} + BK \quad (3.1)$$

where the first non-zero weight must be positive and the succeeding weights could in principle be positive or negative depending on the strength of the extrapolative term. But we expect them to be positive. The shape should build up towards one (or possibly two) humps before dying away with a reasonably long tail; this suggests the use of a polynomial of up to fourth order as discussed in more detail below. The total lag length is the sum of all the individual lag lengths, and the minimum lag length is the sum of the individual minimum lags (because the lags are not added but nested).

We now treat this as being loglinear and add the non-price variables to obtain the demand function for exports (by foreigners) in full as:

$$\ln XD = a_0 + \sum_{i=0}^{m} a_{1i} \ln M_{-i} + \sum_{i=1}^{n} a_{2i} \ln \left(\frac{PW}{R \cdot PX} \right)_{-i} + $$

$$+ \sum_{i=0}^{g} a_{3i} \ln WBC_{-i} + UD, \tag{3.2}$$

where UD is an error term.

3.3.2. *Supply*

1. General: Definitionally, total sales of the exportables industries can be subdivided into home and export sales:

$$S = XS + D \tag{3.3}$$

However, we are interested in the ex ante supply of exports. We assume that exportables industries operate under imperfect competition, which we define, using the definitions of Chamberlin [1932], as a condition of long run free entry combined with product differentiation. This implies, without the need to specify the exact degree of imperfection (from 'polypoly' to 'oligopoly with free entry'), that 1) exportables industries' supply is a function of price in the long run; 2) we can account for (frequently observed) price-discrimination between home and foreign markets, though the phenomenon is in fact irrelevant to our model as we argue below. On the demand side, we make the usual assumption that consumers are competitive.

It follows that we may specify ex ante supply and demand functions for exportables, S and D respectively. Thus we may rewrite the identity as

$$XS = S - D \tag{3.3'}$$

First abstracting from relative price effects, we suppose that, at constant relative prices, supply would grow exponentially at a constant rate, reflecting the rate and pattern of productivity growth. We also note that D is the domestic demand for current deliveries. This is equal, we assume, to orders placed v periods before where v, the domestic order–delivery lag, is a well-documented phenomenon (see again Zarnowitz). These orders we suppose to be related, again at constant relative prices, to domestic expenditure in that period.

Turning to price effects, exportables – namely those goods and services which are exported – may substitute in domestic supply and demand with non-traded (home) goods and services, and also with imports and importsubstitutes. There is a large and growing literature dealing with the problems and implications associated with the large amount of inter-industry trade, in other words the overlap between the traditional 'exportable' and 'importable'; see for example Linder [1961], Grubel [1967], Kravis and Lipsey [1971] and Grubel and Lloyd [1975]. For our purposes here, where we are pursuing the analysis at a high level of aggregation, it is sufficient to note the inevitability of considerable overlap; accordingly we acknowledge this by including import prices on the net supply side of the analysis. We have no separate data on home and import-substitute prices, and so we have to use a combined index of home prices of manufactures.

We would expect the ratios of exportable prices of each of the other categories to influence both S and D. We suggest that the production frontiers and indifference curves involved are long-run relationships into which adjustment costs both on the demand and supply side introduce a distributed lag.

For convenience we use a log-linear form of the supply function based on the argument that

$$XS = S - D \tag{3.4}$$

can be approximated, by first order Taylor series expansion, in logarithmic form as:

$$\ln XS = \frac{S_a}{XS_a} \ln S - \frac{D_a}{XS_a} \ln D + k, \tag{3.5}$$

where S_a, D_a, XS_a denote fixed points, $k = \ln XS_a - \frac{S_a}{XS_a} \ln D_a$

and $\frac{D_a}{XS_a} = \frac{S_a}{XS_a} - 1.$

We assume S_a, D_a, XS_a to be such that this approximation is as close as possible, so that S_a/XS_a can be interpreted as an 'average' value of S/XS over the period.

We write the demand and supply functions on the basis of our earlier arguments as:

$$\ln S = \ln S_0 + rt + \sum_{i=0}^{s} \varepsilon_{1i} \ln\left(\frac{PX}{PD}\right)_{-i} + \sum_{i=0}^{b} \varepsilon_{2i} \ln\left(\frac{PX}{PW/R}\right)_{-i} + US_1 \tag{3.6}$$

and

$$\ln D = \ln D_0 + d \ln DE_{-v} - \sum_{i=0}^{w} \varepsilon_{3i} \ln\left(\frac{PX}{PD}\right)_{-i} - \sum_{i=0}^{x} \varepsilon_{4i} \ln\left(\frac{PX}{PW/R}\right)_{-i} + US_2 \tag{3.7}$$

where S_0, D_0, are values of S,D in the base period, t is time, DE an index of real domestic expenditures, PD an index of domestic prices, PW/R (defined as before) in this context proxies import prices of manufacturers converted into sterling terms and US_1, US_2 are error terms.

Substituting these expressions into the supply function, we obtain:

$$\ln XS = b_0 + b_1 t + b_2 \ln DE_{-v} + \sum_{i=0}^{y} b_{3i} \ln\left(\frac{PX}{PD}\right)_{-i} + $$

$$+ \sum_{i=0}^{z} \ln\left(\frac{PX}{PW/R}\right)_{-i} + US \tag{3.8}$$

where

$$b_0 = k + \frac{S_a}{XS_a}\ln S_0 - \frac{D_a}{XS_a}\ln D_0;\ b_1 = \frac{S_a}{XS_a}r;\ b_2 = -\frac{D_a}{XS_a}d;$$

$$b_3 = \frac{S_a}{XS_a}\varepsilon_1 + \frac{D_a}{XS_a}\varepsilon_3;\ b_4 = \frac{S_a}{XS_a}\varepsilon_2 + \frac{D_a}{XS_a}\varepsilon_4;$$

$$\text{and } US = \frac{S_a}{XS_a}US_1 + \frac{D_a}{XS_a}US_2.$$

3.3.3. Export Pricing

We noted that there may be price-discrimination between home and foreign markets; this could occur either because the cost functions are different for the home and foreign versions of the product or because the elasticities of demand differ in the two markets. We assume as an approximation that over time the ratio of the home to the foreign price remains constant; this amounts to assuming that the elasticities of foreign and home demand and foreign production change in the same proportion. Hence in this time series work we can refer to a single price index of exportables.

In standard microeconomic theory, whether with Walrasian or Marshallian dynamics, it is assumed that the market clears in each time period, in the sense that price and quantity sold converge on the point of intersection of the demand and supply curve (in price-quantity space); the difference in dynamics noted above involves merely the very short term process of reaching the point of intersection, though the Marshallian process is usually also extended to supply-rigidity in commodity markets, as in the cobweb theorem. By contrast with these standard approaches, in this quarterly model the position, in price-quantity space, of the export supply curve is determined positively by capacity, negatively by domestic expenditure, that of the foreign export demand curve is determined positively by world income; while we have argued that the response of both international and domestic demand to export price changes is likely to be small in the short run.

In these circumstances, unless there is non-synchronisation of the home and

Table 3.2
Price indices for UK manufactures: Export and home sales.

	(1) Manufactured export prices	(2) Manufactured wholesale prices (Home Sales)	Ratio of (1) to (2)		(1)	(2)	Ratio of (1) to (2)
54–1	88.9	99.1	0.897	63–1	102.9	121.1	0.850
2	88.5	99.8	0.887	2	103.4	121.3	0.852
3	88.6	100.1	0.885	3	104.3	121.4	0.859
4	88.7	100.4	0.883	4	104.9	121.7	0.862
55–1	89.0	101.5	0.877	64–1	104.8	123.0	0.852
2	89.8	102.5	0.876	2	105.4	123.4	0.854
3	90.8	103.6	0.876	3	106.5	123.8	0.860
4	92.0	105.0	0.876	4	107.1	124.5	0.860
56–1	92.4	106.6	0.867	65–1	108.1	126.0	0.858
2	92.6	107.6	0.861	2	108.9	126.7	0.860
3	93.8	108.3	0.866	3	109.7	127.3	0.862
4	94.3	108.9	0.866	4	110.7	127.7	0.867
57–1	94.7	110.9	0.854	66–1	112.2	129.0	0.870
2	95.3	111.3	0.856	2	114.0	130.4	0.874
3	97.0	112.2	0.865	3	114.9	131.0	0.877
4	97.4	113.6	0.857	4	115.0	130.6	0.881
58–1	97.4	113.6	0.857	67–1	115.6	130.6	0.885
2	97.3	113.4	0.858	2	115.9	130.6	0.887
3	97.4	113.3	0.860	3	116.9	131.6	0.888
4	97.2	113.5	0.856	4	118.2	132.5	0.892
59–1	96.7	113.8	0.850	68–1	123.2	135.2	0.911
2	97.0	114.2	0.849	2	126.0	136.6	0.922
3	96.7	114.2	0.845	3	128.5	136.9	0.939
4	98.3	114.5	0.859	4	129.1	137.4	0.940
60–1	98.6	115.0	0.857	69–1	130.4	138.5	0.942
2	98.9	115.8	0.854	2	130.3	139.8	0.932
3	99.3	116.4	0.853	3	130.7	141.4	0.924
4	99.6	116.9	0.852	4	132.2	143.3	0.923
61–1	99.8	118.4	0.843	70–1	134.2	146.3	0.917
2	100.5	119.2	0.843	2	137.3	150.0	0.915
3	101.0	119.4	0.846	3	139.6	152.6	0.915
4	101.0	119.6	0.844	4	143.0	155.9	0.917
62–1	101.4	120.1	0.844	71–1	147.2	160.0	0.920
2	101.0	120.3	0.840	2	149.9	163.0	0.919
3	101.6	120.8	0.841				
4	102.3	121.0	0.843				

(1) Sterling Export unit value index, manufactures (Sections 5–8). Base weighted: 1954 weights, 1954 to 1960. 1961 weights, 1961 to 1971. Indices linked on annual value 1961. Index not adjusted for overvaluation. Up to 1960, excludes re-exports.

(2) Wholesale prices for home sales of manufactures other than food, drink and tobacco, from 1957; up to 1956, home sales of manufactures other than fuel, food and tobacco. Base weighted: 1949 weights, 1954 to 1956. 1954 weights, 1957 to 1962. 1963 weights, 1963 to 1971. Indices linked on annual values 1956 and 1963.

world cycles to a certain rather exact degree, it is likely that often market-clearing in the standard sense will not be possible without violent swings in relative export prices. Two possible situations are illustrated in Figure 3.1.

Figure 3.1
Possible price fluctuations for an exportable industry

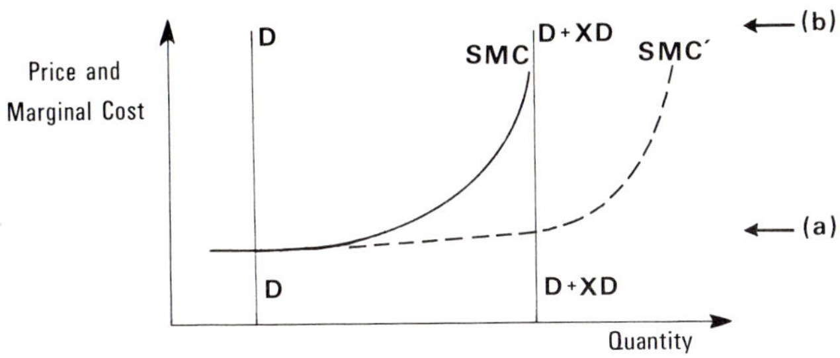

If capacity is greater than total demand (as with the short run marginal cost curve *SMC′*) then prices would fall to the level of marginal cost at (a); if less (*SMC*), prices could rise to (b). Yet we do not observe such swings in UK export prices, as col. (3) of Table 3.2, which gives the ratio of export prices to domestic wholesale prices from 1954 to 1971, clearly shows.

We suppose, therefore, that market clearing for exportables takes place, not in the standard way, but by the adjustment of stocks, queues, or output. Export prices, within this framework, are kept reasonably stable around equilibrium on the grounds that the costs to the firm of the price instability necessary to clear its market are greater than the costs of quantity instability. These phenomena of imperfect competition have been well documented and explained by industrial economists (see for example Scherer [1970]). But it is of interest – and confirms the rationality of this behaviour – that the behaviour we postulate here for firms corresponds to that of rational speculators in a perfectly competitive commodity market, in that they too would stabilise the price around equilibrium and operate a quantity buffer stock.

Hence our hypothesis is that *PX*, the exportables' price, is set at its equilibrium value, so that

$$\ln \overline{XS} = \ln \overline{XD} \tag{3.9}$$

where the bar superscript denotes the equilibrium value. Substituting from equations (3.2) and (3.8) above, ignoring lags and errors, and setting all variables at their equilibrium values, we obtain:

$$a_0 + a_1 \ln \overline{M} + a_2 \ln \frac{\overline{PW}}{R.PX} + a_3 \ln \overline{WBC} = b_0 + b_1 t + b_2 \ln \overline{DE} \qquad (3.10)$$

$$+ b_3 \ln \frac{\overline{PX}}{PD} + b_4 \ln \frac{\overline{P}}{PW/R}$$

We suppose that $\ln \overline{M}_t$ and $\ln \overline{DE}$ grow at constant exponential rates, s and q respectively, and that $\ln \overline{WBC} = 0$. In this case, we may collect terms so that

$$\ln PX = \ln \overline{PX} = \frac{1}{a_2 + b_3 + b_4} (a_1 s + b_2 q - b_1)t \qquad (3.11)$$

$$+ (a_2 + b_4) \ln \overline{PW/R} + b_3 \ln \overline{PD} + a_0 - b_0$$

We express $\ln \overline{PW/R}$ and $\ln \overline{PD}$ as distributed lags of recent $\ln PW/R$ and $\ln PD$, to reflect imperfect information (it is assumed that actual PW/R and PD are also set at equilibrium values).

3.3.4. Deliveries

As we have seen, market clearing by instantaneous price adjustment is ruled out in this model. For a good which is both perishable and related to a non-postponable demand, deliveries, Q, will necessarily be equal to whichever is the lower of demand and supply; excess demand will be frustrated without causing a carryover queue, while excess supply will either cause a cut in output or, if produced, perish.

Hence,

$$Q = \min(XD, XS) \qquad (3.12)$$

or, introducing a more general notation,

$$Q = Z(XS) + (1 - Z)(XD) \qquad (3.13)$$

where

$$Z = 0 \text{ if } XD > XS$$
$$\quad 1 \text{ if } XD < XS$$

This is in fact one model analysed by Fair and Jaffee [1972], whose work we consider further under Estimation.

For other goods, however, faced with an excess of demand or supply, the firm clearly has a number of options which may well be viewed as essentially a question of portfolio management, where the assets are stocks of exportables, export queues and home queues, and the constraints are stockholding costs, waiting costs of customers in each queue, as well as current and expected levels of export and domestic demand and capacity.

Exposition of our concept of market-clearing is greatly simplified if we make the following restrictive assumptions (which we do *not* make in our analysis and estimation):

1. export and domestic demand grow at a constant exponential rate but fluctuate cyclically around this trend;
2. capacity growth exactly equals the trend growth of total demand;
3. output is always at capacity because marginal cost at that point slopes very steeply;
4. uncertainty is absent;

and 5. the export cycle is symmetrical, as illustrated (in detrended form) below:

Figure 3.2

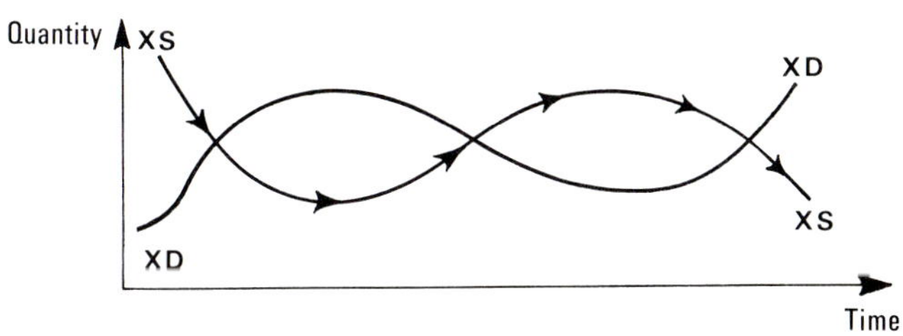

In this simplified framework, the firm maximizes profits by equating the marginal costs to itself of stockholding and of waiting in each queue.[2] We are interested in the extent to which export demand is 'cushioned' in times of excess demand, by stocks held over from the excess supply period or by increasing home queues; to the extent that the cushioning is inadequate, export queues build up in excess demand periods and are run down in excess supply periods.[3] Clearly, the greater the cushioning, the more export deliveries will correspond to export demand; while the smaller it is, the more they will correspond to export supply. Equally clearly, we are dealing with an aggregate, UK exportables, the relevant cost functions for which we cannot generate a priori; hence theory does not predict the extent of this cushioning effect. We therefore choose between different possible models on empirical grounds; we appeal partly to 'plausibility' (that is, evidence we suppose to be well known), but mainly to the results of our own experiments with this data.

To give the analysis maximum clarity, we tie together the concepts of 'cost' and of 'decay' in stocks and queues. So we suppose that the sole cost of carrying stock is depreciation so that the stock will as time passes satisfy a decreasing proportion of the demand it would originally have satisfied; similarly the sole cost of 'carrying' queues is their 'decay' (the result of the waiting cost of those in the queue) so that the queue falls of with the passage of time. It follows that stocks and queues will only carry over fully to future periods if they have zero cost (zero decay); they will not carry over at all if they have infinite cost (perish immediately).

Finally, we note that stockholding costs and home waiting costs play exactly the same role in relation to the cushioning of export demand; so we refer only to stockholding costs in what follows, but this should be interpreted to include home waiting costs.

We begin with a taxonomy of possible models, with some explanation of each. This is most easily read in conjunction with Figure 3.3.

1. $Q = XD$: total cushioning of export demand.

In this case, stockholding costs are zero while foreign waiting costs are large; stocks survive fully to satisfy export demand in excess demand periods.

[2] Subject to the usual constraint that stocks and queues cannot be negative. Since they may be zero, the problem can be dealt with by linear programming; for a fuller discussion of the issues involved see Holt, Modigliani, Muth and Simon [1960].

[3] Zarnowitz produces evidence that in the aggregate US manufacturing industry produces to order and therefore holds queues rather than stocks, though the aggregate conceals a variety of industries which produce to stock. It may well be that the UK pattern is similar, in which case the discussion that follows should focus primarily on home queues versus export queues.

2. $Q = XS$.
In this opposite case foreign waiting costs are negligible, while both stock and home waiting costs are large.

Figure 3.3
Stylised illustrations of various outcomes.

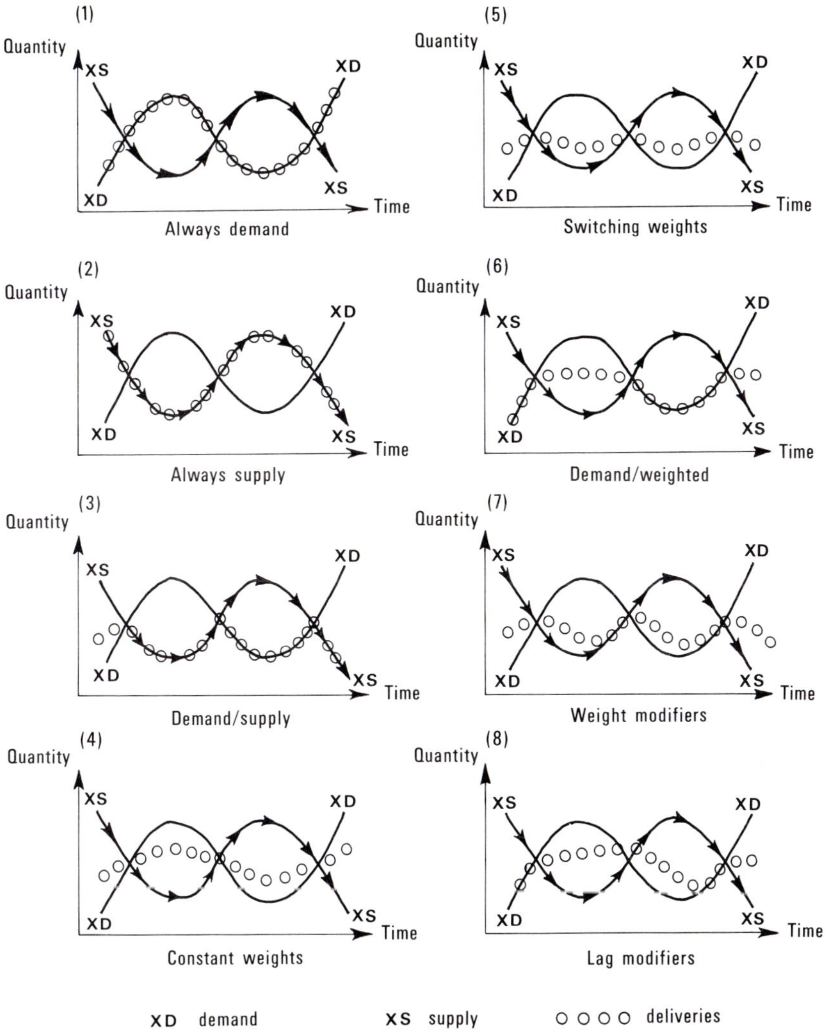

3. $Q = \min(XD, XS)$.
This is the case of complete perishability discussed above, where holding and waiting costs are infinite.
4. $Q = WXD + (1 - W)XS$.
Here stock (or home waiting) costs and foreign waiting costs are negligible, since there is no decay in either. Export queues from excess demand periods survive fully into excess supply periods, and stocks from excess supply periods (or the building up of home queues) survive fully to offset excess demand. This case is of some interest as it reduces to the conventional model with a pressure variable added to the demand schedule.

Thus

$$\begin{aligned} Q = WXD + (1 - W)XS &= XD - (1 - W)(XD - XS) \\ &= XS + W(XD - XS) \end{aligned}$$

$(XD - XS)$, excess demand for exportables, corresponds to the usual notion of pressure of demand in the export sector. It is also of interest to note that a supply schedule modified to include a pressure variable is equivalent to this conventional model, although this approach has not been adopted in empirical work to our knowledge.

In all the above cases 1–4, stock or waiting costs are either zero or very large; they are therefore the extreme cases. We now turn to cases where at least one cost is non-zero and non-infinite.
5. $Q = \min(WXD + (1 - W)XS, WXS + (1 - W)XD)$ $0 < W < 0.5$
Here the weight switches in bias towards the lesser of demand or supply. Both stocks and queues are used partially to offset excess demand or supply but both are subject to decay. Hence both the costs of stockholding and foreign waiting are positive but non-infinite.
6. $Q = \min(XD, WXS + (1 - W)XD)$.
This case in which deliveries are determined by the demand curve in excess supply periods but by a weighted average of the two curves in excess demand periods, implies the use of stocks partially to offset excess demand, but that export queues have no significant effect in offsetting excess supply. Hence stocks have a positive cost (and decay partially), but foreign queues decay totally (infinite cost).

More complex models are possible, if the weights on XD and XS are variables rather than parameters. In particular some writers (e.g. Bispham

[1970]) have produced some evidence that relative delivery dates may be an important quasi-price argument in the demand schedule, so that the time-profile of demand might be shifted according to some cumulant function of excess demand over previous periods. To some extent our use of *WBC* accommodates this possibility, insofar as during the periods of excess supply of UK exportables (when exports are demand determined in case 3 above) high pressure of demand in the industrial countries of *OECD* will lengthen their delivery dates relative to those of the UK and hence give the UK this form of competitive advantage. Cases 7 and 8 are two examples of such 'variable-weight' models. Others could be enumerated but estimation would appear to present equal or greater difficulties than cases 7 and 8, where they proved insuperable.

7. $Q = Z\,XS + (1 - Z)XD$

$$\text{where } Z = \frac{CU(U) - CU}{CU(U) - CU(L)}$$

where $CU(U)$ and $CU(L)$ are, respectively, the upper and lower limits on the capacity utilization series. This model embodies the same (general) cost assumptions as case 5 but it allows the weight to vary with the degree of excess demand and supply, with deliveries completely demand- or supply-constrained at the limits of observed capacity utilization. Again, we can substitute $(XD - XS)$ for CU to make the specification consistent with the other cases. (This model could also be regarded as an aggregated version of case 3, where aggregate deliveries are determined according to the distribution over component parts of conditions of excess demand/supply: at average levels of capacity utilization, half the firms are in conditions of excess demand, the rest in excess supply.)

8. (Lag modifiers). The work of Trivedi [1970] and Bispham [1970] suggests another use of modifiers again embodying the cost assumptions of case 5. They related the length of the distributed lag between orders and deliveries of engineering goods to capacity utilization. Thus

$$Q = \sum_{i=0}^{n} W_i XD_{-i}$$

$$W_i = a_i + b_i CU_{-i}$$

By dropping the constraint that $\sum_i^n W_i = 1$, we can permit permanent loss of deliveries in periods of excess demand (high *CU*). The supply schedule in this formulation is implicit in the relationship between *CU* and $(XD - XS)$, but it will be noticed that even in periods of excess demand, deliveries are still ultimately demand-determined though modified in amount and delivery time by supply constraints.

The use of modifiers in cases 7 and 8 has some attractions, though the estimation difficulties can be considerable. A particular advantage of both cases is that the implied buffering effects of stocks and queues is strictly temporary, and thus is likely to be of greater significance over short cycles than over long. Asymmetry as between stock and queue effects could also be introduced, through a non-linear version of the relation between W_i and *CU*, in case 8, and in case 7 by having a non-linear modifier. The difficulty in case 8 arises especially in the identification of the lag modifiers (the a_i and b_i) as distinct from the separate lag distributions of the determinants of demand, *XD*. Problems of collinearity are also inherent in case 7, since the determinants of *XS*, the supply of exportables, are also important determinants of *CU*, the modifier.

On the other hand, cases 1 and 2 are over-simple; the longevity respectively of stocks and queues over periods of several years (and hence zero cost assumption) is quite implausible.

In case 4, with constant weights, export queues have to have, as in cases 1 and 2, an implausibly long life in order to have a continuously positive effect in the excess supply periods. Hence cases 1, 2 and 4 can effectively be ruled out as over-restrictive.

Case 5 is attractively general while simple to estimate. The restriction in case 6 that foreign queues perish very rapidly also seemed a real possibility, since frustrated foreign buyers could well be successful in 'shopping around'. This in fact is also the case considered by Henry [1970], who argues: 'This alternative formulation does not specify so precise a rationing mechanism as (our case 3) but embodies instead the more general hypothesis that the net result of high pressure on domestic capacity is a reduction in the export share of the country in question.' The addition of the further restriction, in case 3, that the costs of both stocks and home waiting are infinite, seems by contrast likely to be over-restrictive. We did however also investigate this case.

3.4. Estimation

3.4.1. Introductory

The relative absence of simultaneity problems allows direct estimation of the structural equations by ordinary least squares. It is true that there would be a simultaneous relationship between export prices and export volume, if both 1) the coefficient of volume response to price change and 2) the coefficient of price response to capacity utilisation, are non-zero in the current quarter. But on a priori grounds we think that neither of these coefficients is likely to be non-zero; and below we present evidence (admittedly based on ordinary least squares estimation) which supports this a priori view. Note, too, that if only one of these coefficients is zero, then the equations are recursive which would be adequate for our purposes.

Also, on the demand side, there is a possible source of simultaneous bias in any feed-back from Q to M, total manufactured exports by the main manufacturing countries. For no bias, the necessary assumption is either that UK exports are perfect substitutes in the short run for competitors' exports or that any disturbance to UK exports not matched by an equal and opposite disturbance to other countries' exports is taken account of in our 'prior adjustments' for special factors (such as dock strikes), so that the total volume of world exports is independently determined. The first assumption is clearly in conflict with the assumption of finite relative price elasticities; the second assumption relies heavily on the wisdom of the Department of Trade and Industry's prior adjustments. Here we follow the conventional course of assuming the bias to be small, given the share of UK exports in the total (about 10%) and the small observed residual standard error (under 2%): the tendency is to overestimate the elasticity of UK exports with respect to world trade.

Of the sections that follow, 3.4.2 discusses the estimation of the export volume equation, 3.4.3 that of the export price equation, and 3.4.4 summarises the resulting point estimates of the model's structural parameters.

3.4.2. Export volume equation

(1) General methodology. Methods of estimation of disequilibrium models like those proposed in this chapter are still developing – for some recent work

see Fair and Jaffee [1972], Fair and Kelejian [1974], McGee and Carleton [1970] and Quandt [1972]. The principal problem is finding the divisions of the time-series into periods of excess demand and excess supply. Three types of solution have been proposed:

1. Data from outside the model may provide an independent classification of model data. In our case the obvious candidate is a measure of capacity utilisation in manufacturing industry.
2. Disequilibrium behaviour may be predicted by the model, and data on this used as evidence on the nature of the disequilibrium. Thus Fair and Jaffee and Fair and Kelejian make extensive use of the direction of change of relative prices, since a simple Walrasian adjustment would imply falling relative prices in periods of excess supply and vice-versa in other periods. Further, the extent of price change may be related to the extent of excess demand/supply, as well as to other variables.
3. An iterative procedure may be adopted to find the division of the periods which satisfies some criterion. We elaborate further on this below.

Solution 2 we may rule out on a priori grounds. It is possible, as we have indicated, that some (partly instantaneous) relative price adjustment takes place in the market for manufactured exportables, though insufficient to clear the market; however, we find no empirical evidence of such short-run influences on the relative prices of exportables and therefore we cannot rely on this method.

Our procedure was to adopt method 1 as a means of evaluating the feasibility of alternative model specifications, and then to proceed to a version of method 3 when satisfied that satisfactory results were possible.

The cases experimented with were cases 3, 5, 6, 7 and 8. Cases 1 and 4 (apart from being implausible) we considered already covered in the literature cited, while case 2 was considered as quite implausible.

We report here in detail the results of our estimation of case 6. The practical difficulties mentioned above proved too great to allow estimates of 7 and 8. In case 7 the collinearity of the modifier with DE (the domestic demand for exportables) and t (time) resulted persistently in quite unacceptable values for the coefficients of these variables. In case 8, although the use of the Almon procedure outlined in Bispham does reduce the number of coefficients to be estimated, the relevant lag structures could not satisfactorily be disentangled.

The estimation problems associated with cases 3, 5 and 6 are identical and are set out below. However, 3 was rejected because statistically it was apparent that demand variables (particularly world trade) had an impact in the excess demand periods. Case 5 was rejected because the supply variables were insignificant in excess supply periods.

The estimation of case 6. Fair and Jaffee building on work by Quandt [1958] and acknowledging help from Smallwood, propose the following algorithm for the solution of models like case 3 and case 6. The model is, for case 3,

$$Q = Z(bVS + US) + (1 - Z)(aVD + UD) \tag{3.14}$$

where $Z = \begin{matrix} (0 \text{ if } XD < XS) \\ (1 \text{ if } XD > XS) \end{matrix}$; aVD, bVS are the non-stochastic elements in XD, XS.

They propose that maximising the likelihood involves choosing values of Z to minimise the following expression:

$$J = \sum^{n} (US)^2 + \frac{1}{\lambda} \sum^{m} (UD)^2, \tag{3.15}$$

where $\lambda = \sigma^2_{UD}/\sigma^2_{US}$ is chosen by experimentation to minimise the expression. An iterative procedure is suggested for choosing Z by reallocating observations between supply and demand determined periods such that for each t, US^2 is less than $1/\lambda \;\; UD^2$ for supply periods and vice versa for demand periods. Each reallocation is followed by the re-estimation of new $\widehat{US}$'s and $\widehat{UD}$'s by least squares until a stable set of $\widehat{US}$, $\widehat{US}$ and $\hat{Z}$ results. The logical difficulty with this procedure is that, is a stable solution is reached, some observations will be classified as belonging to, say, a demand determined period even though the estimated demand and supply schedules show the period to be in excess demand – i.e. a supply determined period. Fig. 3.4 illustrates the problem.

The dotted line AA is the locus of points, for each t, such that

$$\lambda(XD \quad A)^2 = (A - XS)^2 \tag{3.16}$$

$$\text{therefore } A = \frac{\sqrt{(\lambda)}XD + XS}{\sqrt{(\lambda)} + 1} \tag{3.17}$$

Figure 3.4

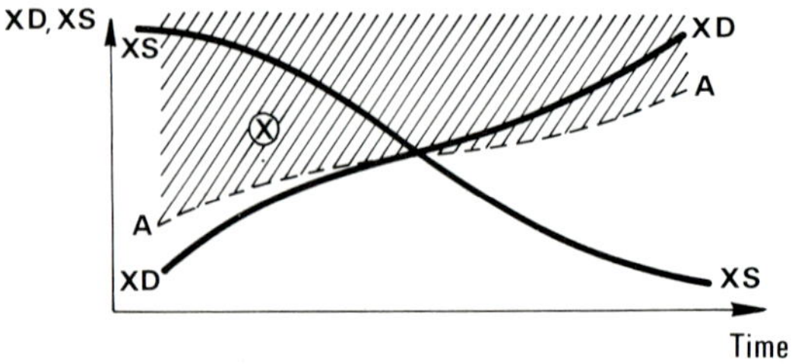

Any observation falling in the hatched half-space above AA will be inconsistently classified by Fair and Jaffee's criterion. The model specifies that any observation in a period of excess supply must be demand-determined, so all observations to the left of B, the cross-over point, must be demand-determined; and conversely for observations to the right of B. As a concrete example, Fair and Jaffee would allocate the observation marked X to the supply schedule, whereas we would allocate it to the demand schedule. Thus Fair and Jaffee's *M.L.* criterion is inconsistent with the model, whereas a procedure to minimise the residual sums of squares constrained by the requirement that the allocation to periods results in a consistent classification into excess demand and excess supply periods, may more closely approximate a true *M.L.* procedure.[4]

According we have adopted the following basic procedure:

1. Choose initial values of Z. To do this we used the series on capacity utilisation in manufacturing, classifying as demand periods all observations with $CU < 95$ $(Z = 0)$, and the rest as supply periods $(Z = 1)$. Call this initial vector Z^0.
2. Using the $Z^0 = 0$ observations, estimate the XD^0 schedule by O.L.S., and similarly estimate XS^0 using the $Z^0 = 1$ observations.
3. Set new values for Z, Z^1 as follows:
   if $XD^0 < XS^0$, $Z^1 = 0$; if $XD^0 > XS^0$, $Z^1 = 1$.
4. Repeat step 2) for Z^1, and hence obtain Z^2, etc.
5. If $Z^i = Z^{i-1}$ for all t, stop.

[4] A paper by Maddala and Nelson [1974], unavailable when this work was undertaken, sets out maximum likelihood methods for this type of model. Although the method used here is different, tests have been applied as if it were M..; the reader may prefer to interpret them merely as descriptive statistics.

This procedure is applicable to case 3. For case 6 step 2 is slightly modified because in periods of excess demand ($Z = 1$) the model is

$$Q = W\,XS + (1 - W)XD. \tag{3.18}$$

The demand schedule, XD, is uniquely determined from $Z = 0$ observations; hence W and XS can be subsequently determined from the $Z = 1$ observations.

Another difficulty with Fair and Jaffee's procedure is that it does not readily permit any observation to be classified as in equilibrium (e.g. at point B in Fig. 2), and hence doubly useful in that it can be used to estimate both demand and supply schedules. In their other estimation procedures, Fair and Jaffee could and did make this use of such observations (e.g. in periods when relative prices did not change), and this may have contributed to the greater success they reported for these other methods. Our procedure, however, readily lends itself to the use of equilibrium points, the only difficulty being to decide how close XD and XS should be for an observation to be so classified. Expressing the model in log-linear terms, case 6 can be written:

$$\ln Q = Z.W.\ln XS + (1 - Z.W)\ln XD \tag{3.19}$$

$$\text{where } Z = \begin{cases} 0 \text{ if } \ln XD < \ln XS + \theta \\ 1 \text{ if } \ln XD > \ln XS - \theta \end{cases}$$

θ is the proportionate tolerance of excess demand or supply around equilibrium. The supply demand-determined periods may therefore appear to overlap slightly.

With $\theta = 0$, we did not obtain convergence. By trial and error we decided on a value of $\theta = 0.02$, as this resulted in rapid convergence (after 4 iterations), and approximately makes the odds of misclassification even (as between $\ln XD = \ln XS$, and $\ln XD \neq \ln XS$).

One other minor qualification is necessary. 1958 (2), the first observation used in estimation, was classified as a period of excess supply in spite of the estimated excess demand in the final iterations: capacity utilisation was low at 89.4, in the middle of a trough, and the estimation of excess demand and supply is bound to be less certain at the extremes of the period of estimation.

(2) The estimation of the distributed lags. Because of the switching between excess demand and excess supply periods, the estimation of the distributed lags in the demand schedule poses special problems.

The first problem is that any technique involving lagged values of the dependent variables as regressors is ruled out (since they will often belong to the other regime). Consequently, lag structures must be directly estimated.

We use the method of polynomial approximation because it allows direct estimation of a large class of finite lag structures in an efficient manner. The restriction that there be no 'infinite tail' does not seem to us to cause difficulty; we have allowed the total lag length to range up to 25 quarters and we find it difficult to rationalise any lag weights beyond that. The restriction on the class of structures (to polynomials) can be held to cause more difficulty. While a polynomial of sufficiently high degree can approximate any given lag structure, it can only do so inefficiently because of the degrees of freedom lost in the higher degree. There are of course a very large number of possible lag structures that are not polynomial and the question we have to answer is: will we reach a significantly wrong conclusion about the structure if it is one of these?

We report in Table 3.3 the results of a standard F-test for the appropriateness of the polynomial. However, in addition, we can make out a case on a priori grounds. In the earlier section on the expected shape of the lag structure, we concluded that all the weights should be positive and that the first few weights should be zero or small. Because of the order-delivery lags dichotomy between consumer and capital goods, there might be twin peaks. These points taken together suggest the following likely shapes:

Figure 3.5

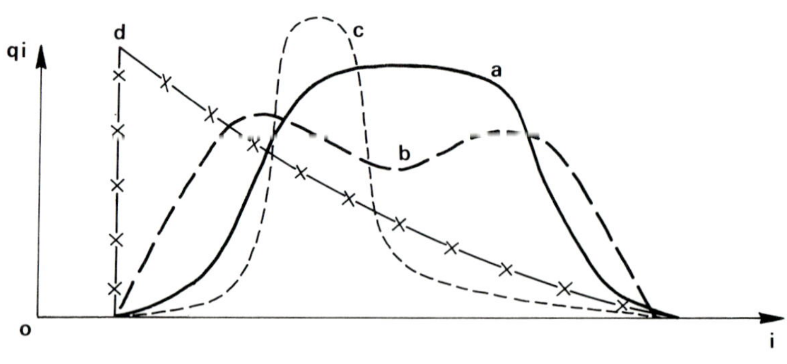

It is fairly clear that a can be well approximated by a quadratic, b by a fourth order polynomial, and c by a third order; d (the most unlikely of the four, because it allows little for the longer lag weights we would expect to find for capital goods) can be approximated by a second or third order polynomial with the first few weights set to zero. We conclude provisionally, therefore, that the polynomial method should be adequate for this sort of lag, and in the section on estimation we consider polynomials up to the 4th degree. The particular polynomial weighting scheme used was the method proposed by Almon [1965] and with all polynomials constrained to zero in the quarter following the final lag.

A straightforward application of the Almon method is possible, given the division of the periods, by eliminating supply period data after computing the artificial variables as described by Almon. However the second problem encountered was that full iteration as described above could also involve experimenting with lag-length and the order of the constraining polynomial at each stage of iteration. We therefore adopted the short-cut procedure of initially fixing the relative weights in the lag distributions by using the Almon method on what appeared at the time to be the longest demand period. The procedure adopted, then, was 1) provisionally fixing the lag structures before iteration 0; 2) discarding variables which in iteration 0 turned out insignificant; 3) once convergence had been achieved, the equations were re-estimated on this division, using the modified Almon method to determine the final form of the lag distribution.

The lag weights provisionally fixed (prior to iteration) were as follows:

Lag (quarters)	Prices[5]	World Trade[6]	WBC
0	0	0.67	1
1	0.013	0.54	
2	0.024	0.06	
3	0.033	−0.27	
4	0.041		
5	0.048		
6	0.053		
7	0.056		
8	0.059		
9	0.061		
10	0.061		
11	0.060		

Lag (quarters)	Prices[5]	World Trade[6]	WBC
12	0.058		
13	0.058		
14	0.055		
15	0.052		
16	0.048		
17	0.044		
18	0.039		
19	0.029		
20	0.024		
21	0.019		
22	0.014		
23	0.009		
24	0.004		

[5] This lag structure is appreciably longer than those conventionally used in this sort of work. Originally, like others, we looked at lag lengths of up to 3 years. The main feature of these results was that the estimated price elasticity turned out at well under unity, as will be seen later; this was unacceptable on the basis of other people's work done at the micro-economic level as well as on a priori grounds. Longer lags were tried at the suggestion of Donald MacDougall (see his [1957] pp. 331–2 for a discussion of long lags in the US trade context). Investigation showed that longer lags, apart from leading to more acceptable price elasticities, gave better results statistically, as shown below. The lag structure shown here was estimated over the period 1962(3) to 1969(1), though the lagged price terms go back to 1956 of course.

[6] Fitted over the period 1966 (3) to 1971 (2).

(3) Export volume – Estimation results. Satisfactory convergence occurred after 4 iterations, starting from the division of the periods based on the index of capacity utilisation. A value of CU of 95 was taken as an overlap point: hence for $CU \geqslant 95$, periods were supply-constrained, and for $CU \leqslant 95$ they were demand-constrained. The figure of 95 was arrived at by some experimentation with higher and lower figures and different overlaps: the criterion was the minimisation of supply influences in demand-constrained periods, and the minimisation of demand influences in supply-constrained periods.

Iteration proceeded as explained above, and the starting allocations were as follows (all periods shown inclusive; each starting allocation except for iteration 0 is the ending allocation of the previous iteration, e.g. iteration 1 starts with the division of periods produced by iteration 0):

	Demand	Supply	Demand	Supply	Demand	Supply
0	58(2)–59(3)	59(4)–61(2)	61(1)–63(3)	63(4)–66(3)	66(4)–68(3)	68(4)–69(4)
1	58(2)–60(1)	60(1)–62(3)	62(2)–64(2)	63(4)–67(1)	66(3)–68(2)	68(3)–69(3)
2	58(2)–59(3)	59(4)–62(4)	62(3)–63(4)	63(4)–66(4)	66(3)–68(2)	68(3)–69(3)
3	58(2)–59(4)	59(4)–62(4)	62(3)–63(4)	63(4)–66(4)	66(3)–68(2)	68(3)–69(3)
4	58(2)–59(3)	59(4)–62(4)	62(3)–63(4)	63(4)–66(4)	66(3)–68(2)	68(3)–69(3)
0	69(1)–71(2)					
1	68(4)–71(2)					
2	68(4)–71(2)					
3	68(4)–71(2)					
4	68(4)–71(2)					

Iteration 4 produced the same division of periods as the starting division of iteration 3, resulting in a solution oscillating between 3 and 4. The only difference between 3 and 4 lies in whether 1959 (4) is allocated to both demand and supply periods or solely to the supply period; iteration 4 (given below) shows a marginal improvement in fit on 3.

It is clear from the table that the final division of periods differs substantially from the initial division only for the period 1961–1962, when iteration suggests that supply constraints were effective for at least six quarters longer than the index of capacity utilisation would indicate.

Using the division of periods shown in the table, the initial results for iteration 0 were as follows (with standard errors in brackets below coefficients):

Initial results:
Iteration 0 (Division of periods based on Capacity Utilisation)

$$\ln XD = 2.89756 + \underset{(0.02528)}{0.61975}\,(L) \ln M + \underset{(0.29182)}{0.97260} \ln WBC - \underset{(0.24083)}{1.39614}\,(L) \ln P \tag{3.20}$$

$R = 0.99600$ $\quad$ SE of Estimate $= 0.02056$

F – values of omitted variables:

t	0.33215
$\ln XS$	4.61098 (sign: +)
$\ln DE_{-2}$	4.19059 (sign: –)

$$\ln Q = 7.76715 + \underset{(0.25345)}{0.55751} \ln XD + \underset{(0.00562)}{0.01410t} - \underset{(0.34164)}{0.96054} \ln DE_{-2} \quad (3.21)$$

$R = 0.99223$ $\quad SE$ of Estimate $= 0.02033$

F – values of omitted variables:

$\ln M$	(0 lag)	0.08715
$(L) \ln M$	(weighted lag)	1.14282
$\ln WBC$		0.21353
$\ln P$	(0 lag)	0.01849
$(L) \ln P$	(weighted lag)	2.25174

The supply schedule conditional on the demand schedule is

$$\ln XS = 17.55328 + 0.03187t - 2.17076 \ln DE_{-2} \quad (3.22)$$

Final results:

Having reached a division of the periods that gave convergence (or near convergence), we used this to investigate the appropriate lag structures in more depth, as well as to try out other variables discarded at an earlier stage.

Table 3.3 shows the standard errors obtained on the demand equation estimated, with various lag structures on prices, over the demand-constrained periods used for iteration 4. Experimentation with lag structures for M and WBC showed that the best results (for the best lag structures on prices) were obtained when M, M_{-1}, M_{-3}, WBC_{-1} and $(WBC_{-3} - WBC_{-4})$ were included separately as independent variables (polynomial approximation yielded no improvement with such short total lags). In addition, seasonal dummies were tried out on the grounds that ships, aircraft and precious stones, which were subtracted from seasonally-adjusted manufactures to give our dependent variable, were not themselves seasonally adjusted; the second quarter seasonal dummy ($D2$) turned out significant and was alone included, the others being totally insignificant and virtually zero. The standard errors reported in the Table are all for equations using this set of independent variables apart from prices. The lowest standard error is obtained with a total lag on prices of 21 quarters, a zero weight on the current quarter, and a quadratic (symmetric) distribution around 11 quarters (the average lag). The price elasticity is −1.5; it is important to note that shorter lag lengths lead to a reduction in the estimated elasticity, and this provides a further (a priori) reason for accepting the long lag.

Table 3.3
Standard errors of demand equation (and price elasticity)$^{+}$ using different lag structures on relative prices – estimation for demand periods only.[a]

Total lag length \ Polynomial degree*	2(0)	3(0)	4(0)	2(1)	3(1)	4(1)
7	0.02233 (−0.657)	X0.01627 (−0.679)	X0.01630 (−0.733)	X0.01933 (−0.560)	X0.01673 (−0.703)	X0.01641 (−0.702)
12	0.01878 (−0.855)	0.01806 (−0.887)	X0.01549 (−0.688)	X0.01724 (−0.807)	X0.01738 (−0.729)	X0.01595 (−0.656)
20	0.01629 (−1.415)	0.01662 (−1.490)	0.01691 (−1.699)	0.01684 (−1.449)	0.01720 (−1.649)	X0.01753 (−1.662)
21	*0.01625*† (*−1.524*)	0.01661 (−1.548)	0.01693 (−1.762)	0.01661 (−1.526)	0.01699 (−1.667)	X0.01756 (−1.725)
22	0.01628 (−1.638)	0.01663 (−1.584)	0.01722 (−1.751)	0.01684 (−1.649)	0.01723 (−1.667)	X0.01763 (−1.692)
25	0.01700 (−2.043)	0.01670 (−1.625)	X0.01707 (−1.486)	0.01702 (−1.937)	X0.01730 (−1.478)	X0.01770 (−1.470)

[a] *Notes:* † *F*-test for polynomial restriction:
We also estimated the equation with all the lagged and the current price variables (0 to 21) entered separately. The residual sum of squares was 0.0006, compared with 0.00607 on 2(0) above for the 21-quarter lag, and this gives

$$F_{21,2} = \frac{(0.00607 - 0.0006)/21}{0.0006/2} = 0.86.$$

This falles well short of the 5% critical value of 19.45.

\+ Standard error is in natural logarithms. Price elasticity is bracketed.

* (0) indicates current quarter weight is constrained to zero.
(1) indicates no constraint on current quarter weight.
All polynomials constrained to zero in the quarter after maximum lag.

X indicates that some lag weights had the wrong sign; this lag structure is accordingly ruled out on a priori grounds.

Final results were (division of periods as for Iteration 4):

$$\begin{aligned}\ln XD = 2.90574 &+ \underset{(0.13321)}{0.47826}\ln M + \underset{(0.14196)}{0.43272}\ln M_{-1} - \underset{(0.10104)}{0.32239}\ln M_{-3} \\ &+ \underset{(0.28222)}{0.62688}\ln WBC_{-1} + \underset{(0.38548)}{1.05094}(\ln WBC_{-3} - \ln WBC_{-4})\end{aligned}$$

$$+ \underset{(0.00691)}{0.01722D2} + \sum_{i=1}^{21} w_i \ln P_{-i} \qquad (3.23)$$

$$R = 0.99785 \quad \text{S.e.e.} = 0.01625$$

where the w_i *were:*

Lag	(0)	1	2	3	4	5	6	7	8	9	10
w_i	(0)	−0.018	−0.034	−0.049	−0.062	−0.073	−0.083	−0.090	−0.096	−0.101	−0.103
Standard error	(0)	0.002	0.004	0.006	0.007	0.009	0.010	0.011	0.012	0.012	0.012

Lag	11	12	13	14	15	15	16	18	19	20	21
w_i	−0.104	−0.103	−0.101	−0.096	−0.090	−0.083	−0.073	−0.062	−0.049	−0.034	−0.018
Standard error	0.012	0.012	0.012	0.012	0.011	0.010	0.009	0.007	0.006	0.004	0.002

The sum of the coefficients was − 1.524 (standard error: 0.183)

$$\ln Q = 7.26785 + \underset{(0.13553)}{0.48332} \ln XD + \underset{(0.00353)}{0.01434t} - \underset{(0.26725)}{0.83764} \ln DE_{-2} \qquad (3.24)$$

$$R = 0.99162 \qquad \text{S.e.e} = 0.01895$$

The supply schedule, conditional on the demand schedule, is

$$\ln XS = 14.06644 + 0.02775t - 1.6212 \ln DE_{-2} \qquad (3.25)$$

The total length is appreciably longer than was thought, at least until the post-Smithsonian experience, by many economists; thus, according to Branson [1972], the prevailing view on lags in early 1972 was that they did not extend beyond two years. However, longer lags, as found here, were suggested by MacDougall [1957] and have been successfully fitted to a variety of data by Junz and Rhomberg [1965, 1973] which, apart from the few industry studies mentioned by Branson, is apparently the only previous work available on price response lags in international trade. Since formal theory in its present state imposes no restriction on total lag length, this appears to be an area where empirical regularities appropriately may precede theory; the evidence here favours the hypothesis of longer lags.

We looked again, at this point, at relative exportable price variables for the supply equation; these were *PX*/*PD* (with domestic prices) and *R.PX*/*PW* (with import prices). Almon lags were fitted to them, both together and separately, for the supply-constrained periods with the rest of the model as above. Neither was significant and the lag coefficients mostly had the wrong sign; the results are not worth reporting here. While at first sight surprising, they can be explained quite easily. *R.PX*/*PW* varied considerably during supply-constrained periods; and the fact that it failed to contribute to the explanation of exports in these periods is consistent with the natural hypothesis that exportables and imports are not substitutes to any significant extent. *PX*/*PD*, on the other hand, hardly varied (see Table 3.2) up to devaluation and after devaluation (when it rose) there are only five supply periods (1968(3) to 1969(3)), all of them within two years of devaluation. The lag before resources can be shifted out of other domestic sectors into exportables is likely to be longer than that. So this result does not contradict the view that relative profitability has a significant long run effect. We discuss later the implications of this for the structure of the price equations.

The division of periods that resulted from these final results was:

Demand	Supply
58(2)–59(3)	59(3)–62(4)
62(4)–63(4)	63(4)–67(1)
66(3)–68(2)	68(3)–69(4)
68(4)–71(2)	

The difference from starting division in demand periods is solely one observation – 62(3) is included in the starting but excluded in the ending division. For supply periods, three additional observations are included; 59(3), 67(1), 69(4). It seemed unlikely that further iteration was justified by such marginal alterations in the period division and at this point a sensitivity test was performed; the coefficients were re-estimated for this new period division to see if there was a significant difference. It turned out that the differences were quite insignificant; the process was therefore stopped at this stage, and the previous results allowed to stand.

Serial correlation of residuals:

We have taken no account in estimation of possible serial correlation of the residuals, but present Durbin-Watson statistics for demand and supply schedules adjusted for discontinuities in the residual series. It is the discontinuities which would make the joint estimation of serial correlation coefficients very expensive in degrees of freedom, since to take account of first order serial correlation alone would mean the loss of an observation for each change of regime. The evidence of the *D-W* statistics suggests that the loss of efficiency from this source is not obviously greater than that resulting from the loss of three or four observations for each schedule.

The *D-W* statistic for each schedule was computed by pooling the data from each set of consecutive observations. For the demand schedule, there are four sets of consecutive observations on the residuals, so the formula is

$$DW = \frac{\sum_{i=1}^{4}\sum_{t=2}^{ni}(e_{it} - e_{it-1})^2 \dfrac{n}{n-3}}{\sum_{i=1}^{4}\sum_{t=1}^{ni} e_{it}^2} = 1.438 \tag{3.26}$$

where ni is the number of observations in the ith set of consecutive observations.

The supply residuals are more difficult, as the observed residuals are from a weighted average of supply and demand schedules. The residuals during supply periods take the form

$$v = wUS + (1 - w)UD \tag{3.27}$$

If $$US = \rho_1 US_{-1} + a_1 \tag{3.28}$$

and $$UD = \rho_2 UD_{-1} + a_2. \tag{3.29}$$

where a_{1t} and a_{2t} are independent random variables, then

$$v = w\rho_1 US_{-1} + (1 - w)\rho_2 UD_{t-1} + wa_1 + (1 - w)a_2 \tag{3.30}$$

v is not generated by a first-order autoregressive process (unless $\rho_1 = \rho_2$). But we have a point estimate of the first-order autocorrelation coefficient of v, derived from the DW statistic from the mixed equation.

This provides an estimate of

$$\rho = Ev\,v_{-1}/Ev^2$$
$$= \frac{E[\{w\rho_1 US_{-1} + wa_1 + (1 - w)\rho_2 UD_{-1} + (1 - w)a_2\}\{wUS_{-1} + (1 - w)UD_{-1}\}]}{E\{wUS + (1 - w)UD\}^2}$$

which, assuming a_1, a_2 are independent,

$$= \frac{w^2\rho_1 EUS^2 + (1-w)^2\rho_2 EUD^2}{w^2 EUS^2 + (1-w)^2 EUD^2} \tag{3.31}$$

The DW statistic for the mixed equation for supply-modified periods, calculated in the same way as just explained for the demand equation, is 1.480, implying an estimate of $\rho = 1 - (0.5 \times DW) = 0.26$. From the demand residuals we have a point estimate of ρ_2 as 0.28, and from the estimate of the mixed equation we have an estimate of 0.52 for w. An estimate of the denominator is provided by the residual variance of the mixed equation (0.000359); $E(UD^2)$ is estimated by the residual variance of the demand equation (0.000264) and $E(US^2)$ is obtained from the denominator as 0.001105. Solving ρ_1 gives an estimated value of 0.255.

The evidence therefore suggests little serious serial correlation in either of the underlying schedules, while the DW statistics for the estimated equations lie in the indeterminate region at the 5% level of significance.

3.4.3 The export price equation

The price equation to be estimated is:

$$\ln PX = \alpha t + \beta \ln(PW/R) + \gamma \ln PD + \delta(L)\ln R + \varepsilon(L)\ln CU \tag{3.32}$$

where $(L)\ln R$ and $(L)\ln CU$ are lag-weighted terms testing respectively for temporary exchange rate effects (R) and any significant cylical effect (CU = capacity utilisation). The constraints to be satisfied are $\beta + \gamma = 1$, $\Sigma\delta(L) = 0$. However, the equation was estimated freely in order to test these constraints; the procedure followed was that of searching for a set of (free) estimates that would satisfy the constraints, without a significant worsening of fit.

We first estimated it without any allowance for serial correlation in the error term. The results, as so often with time series price equations, revealed very significant serial correlation. It also began to be clear that neither (L) $\ln R$ or (L) $\ln CU$ had a part to play. A typical equation was:

$\ln PX_t =$ Coefficients: *Lag*	$\ln PW - \ln R$	$\ln PD$	$\ln R$	$\ln CU$	t
0	0.287(0.098)	0.143(0.294)	0.069(0.123)	0.014(0.086)	0.00014
1	0.165(0.062)	0.193(0.177)	0.026(0.052)	0.014(0.061)	(0.01849)
2	0.058(0.059)	0.245(0.174)	0.006(0.040)	−0.008(0.057)	
3	−0.018(0.065)	0.258(0.187)	0.004(0.047)	−0.032(0.035)	
4	−0.043(0.069)	0.190(0.224)	0.013(0.042)	−0.037(0.053)	
5			0.029(0.028)		
6			0.045(0.018)		
7			0.055(0.027)		
8			0.055(0.036)		
9			0.039(0.030)		

$R^2 = 0.997$ S.e.e. $= 0.0076$ $DW = 0.38$

[polynomials of degree 3, constrained to zero in quarter after last lag, in all cases] (3.33)

$\delta(L)$ were mostly insignificant and $\Sigma\delta(L)$ was non-zero; the weights $\varepsilon(L)$ were all insignificant. In addition $\beta + \gamma$ was much greater than 1. The extreme smallness of the Durbin-Watson coefficient also suggested that the first order serial correlation coefficients could be close to unity, and a first difference transformation was therefore tried.[7] The results varied with the length of lags and the degree of polynomial; best results were obtained when $(L)R$ and $(L)CU$ were dropped. The equation finally selected was

$$\begin{aligned}\Delta \ln PX = {} & \underset{(0.04747)}{0.14457}\,\Delta \ln(PW/R) + \underset{(0.04936)}{0.12883}\,\Delta \ln(PW/R)_{-1} \\ & + \underset{(0.15904)}{0.32133}\,\Delta \ln PD + \underset{(0.15293)}{0.36844}\,\Delta \ln PD_{-1} + \underset{(0.00098)}{0.0017} \end{aligned} \tag{3.34}$$

$$R^2 = 0.68025 \quad \text{S.e.e.} = 0.00492 \quad DW = 1.79012$$

(The lags in this equation were estimated freely.)

[7] The fact that we obtain satisfactory results with first differences here contrasts with our failure in chapter 2 with inter-fibre substitution. The reason must be that the lags here are properly specified, at least as revealed by the robustness of the coefficients. There the lags we suspected to be operating could not be identified in spite of extensive experimentation and so we used only current relative prices as the explanatory variable; the mis-specification involved is, as argued there, likely to vitiate the first-difference results more seriously than the level results.

3.4.4. *The structure of export price and volume model*

The export volume equation is in structural form and we therefore have directly estimated the following structural coefficients (long run).

1. *Demand for UK exports:*	*Coefficient*	*Estimated value*
World trade elasticity	a_1	0.6
Relative UK/competitors' prices elasticity	$-a_2$	−1.5
World business cycle elasticity	a_3	0.6
2. *Supply of UK exports:*		
Growth rate	b_1	0.0278
Domestic demand for exportables elasticity	$-b_2$	−1.6

We have no direct estimates from this equation of b_3, because of insufficient variation in the data, but b_4 was insignificant and is set at zero. We may, however, derive b_3 from the export price equation.

We have to scale up the sum of the estimated coefficients on $\ln PW - \ln R$ and $\ln PD$ from 0.95 to unity, the a priori constraint; this gives us 0.28 and 0.72 respectively. We then have:

$$\beta = 0.28 = \frac{a_2 + b_4}{b_3 + b_4 + a_2} = \frac{1.5}{b_3 + 1.5}$$

from which $b_3 = 3.9$.

We would also like to derive an estimate of r, the growth rate of supply in manufactured exportables, and d, the elasticity of exportables with respect to domestic expenditure. We have

$$b_1 = \frac{S_a}{XS_a} r = 0.028, \; b_2 = d\left(1 - \frac{S_a}{XS_a}\right) = -1.68$$

but $\dfrac{S_a}{XS_a}$ is unknown so that we cannot solve for r and k. However, we have an outside estimate of r from official statistics: the gross capital stock of manufacturing at 1963 replacement cost, as estimated by the *CSO* and recorded in *National Income and Expenditure*, rose from £183,000 million in 1958 to £293,000 million in 1970: this represents an exponential growth rate of 3.92% p.a.

We assume that exportables are a sufficiently large proportion of manufacturing output for this to be approximately the growth rate of exportables capacity. Hence r, which has the dimension of ln per quarter, can be set at approximately 0.01.[8] Hence we obtain

$$\frac{S_a}{XS_a} = 2.8$$

and $d = 0.93$.

The below-unity elasticity for manufactured goods is plausible, considering that services absorb an increasing proportion of *GNP* in advanced economies. While since S_a/XS_a is an average of S/XS for the estimation period, then the implication of this estimate, that about one-third of manufactured exportables are exported, is not inconsistent with what we know from official statistics; in 1963 the share of exports in total net manufacturing output was 27%, or one-quarter of capacity given that capacity utilisation was 98% in that year (*CU* was 93 against a 'full' capacity level of 95), and at least some of UK manufacturing capacity must be in importable and home goods, though we do not know how much.

3.5. Conclusions

We have set out a model of the UK (manufacturing) export sector, in which supply influences enter in a constraining manner whenever (and only when) the demand for exportables from home and foreign buyers is greater than or equal to the available capacity. We then explored the role of lags in price competitiveness within the demand-determined periods and found evidence that the price elasticity, taken with an appropriately long lag structure, is of a size ($1\frac{1}{2}$) consistent with the results of microeconomic investigation. World trade and the world business cycle are handled in a traditional manner but with particular attention to the (relatively short) lags involved; we found here

[8] 0.01 in natural logarithms is 1% for small changes; so 0.01 ln per quarter is equal to 4% per annum approximately.

that rate-of-change effects are important, probably because of the precise composition of UK markets by commodity and area. Given these 'demand' factors, the estimates of the growth in UK exportables capacity and the effect of expansion in domestic demand are plausible and statistically significant.

We also explored the implications of this model for export price formation. We argued that prices would be set so as to ensure long run equilibrium in the exportables sector, given the competition of other domestic sectors on the one hand, of overseas producers on the other. We found that this approach yielded plausible results; the evidence suggested that domestic competitiveness was the predominant factor, with a high implied elasticity of domestic transfer between exportables and other sectors. However, a large exchange rate change would also have a significant effect through the coefficient on overseas competitors' prices; this was the case for example after the 1967 devaluation.

Our period is importantly affected by this devaluation and our results can partly be regarded as an attempt to explain the effects of that devaluation within the confines of traditional trade theory. We do not allow any (arbitrary) quantitative or qualitative difference for exchange rate as against 'ordinary' price changes determining relative price competitiveness though we explicitly allow supply constraints to militate against the demand effects of an exchange rate change (this non-linearity being the reason usually put forward for differentiating it). Our results suggest that it is not necessary to depart from the theory in an ad hoc manner in order to explain the facts. They also indicate that the period of time needed for full adjustment to an exchange rate change to take place is considerably longer than has often been thought. Finally, they illustrate the principle (set out clearly by Johnson [1961]) that at 'full' employment an exchange rate change can only increase exports by displacing domestic demand while below it the conventional trade model can operate unconstrained.

Appendix 3.A: Data

In this appendix we list the data used, together with its sources. Estimation in all cases was done for the period 1958(2) to 1971(2). Data is however shown for all periods for which we have it (up to mid-1971).

Notes on variables

M – World Trade. Source is *UN* Monthly Bulletin of Statistics.

WBC–World business cycle. This is Exp $\Sigma_i w_i(\ln IP_i - \ln IP^*_i)$ where *IP* is industrial production, *IP** is trend industrial production 1955–71, w_i is share in UK exports in 1963, and *i* ranges over main industrial countries. Series for industrial production from *OECD*; trends fitted by ordinary least squares.

PW – Competitors' export prices. Unit values ($ terms) of manufactured exports for main competitors, weighted by 1963 trade shares.
Source: *UN* Monthly Bulletin.

PX – UK export prices. Unit value (£) of UK manufactured exports, not corrected for over-valuation. 1961 weights. For 1952 and 1953, values are estimated on basis of UK wholesale prices of manufactures. This is the same series as in Table 3.2, except that it has 1963 = 100.

R – Dollar-Sterling exchange rate. Average of end-month parity.

$\frac{R.PX}{PW}$ – Ratio of UK to competitors' prices (in $s.)

DE – Domestic demand for exportables. This is $\text{Exp}(0.423 \ln C + 0.420 \ln FI + 0.157 \ln PAC)$ where *C*, *FI*, and *PAC* are volume indices (1963 prices, Source: Economic Trends) respectively of private consumption, gross domestic fixed capital formation, and public authorities' consumption. The weights for each expeniture category are calculated as $\Sigma_i w_i q_i$ where *i* ranges over UK manufacturing industries, w_i is the industry share in UK exports in 1963, q_i is the share of the expenditure category (both direct and indirect) in the industry's output, also in 1963.

PD – Domestic wholesale prices of UK manufactures. Source as in Table 3.2.

CU – Capacity utilisation in manufacturing. Index based on Wharton School method (trend fitted through cycle peaks). Source: Taylor, Winter and Pearce, *Bulletin of Oxford Institute of Statistics*, May 1970. For figures from 1970, a similar series (source: Treasury) has been linked on.

X – Volume of UK manufactured exports, adjusted: value of UK exports of manufactures (*SITC* 5–8), seasonally adjusted, *less* ships, aircraft and precious stones (not seasonally adjusted), *plus* prior adjustments (for strikes etc.), deflated by the average value deflator for manufactured exports. Source: Department of Trade and Industry, March 1972. Before 1960, series were seasonally adjusted within Treasury.

	M	*WBC*	*PW*	*PX*	*R*	$\frac{R.PX}{PW}$	*DE*	*PD*	*CU*	*Q*
1952–1			97.80	88.30	2.8	0.903				
2			96.90	87.80	2.8	0.906				
3			95.90	86.60	2.8	0.902				
4			94.10	86.30	2.8	0.917				
1953–1			93.20	85.80	2.8	0.921				
2			92.20	85.60	2.8	0.928				
3			92.20	85.20	2.8	0.924				
4			92.20	85.30	2.8	0.925				
1954–1			91.30	85.60	2.8	0.937				
2			91.30	85.20	2.8	0.933				
3			90.40	85.30	2.8	0.943				
4			90.40	85.40	2.8	0.944				
1955–1		1.021	90.40	85.70	2.8	0.948	608.5			
2		1.031	90.40	86.40	2.8	0.956	620.8			
3		1.042	91.30	87.40	2.8	0.957	630.8			
4		1.040	93.20	88.50	2.8	0.950	630.8			
1956–1	10.21	1.022	94.10	88.93	2.8	0.945	630.2	106.6	94.9	
2	10.62	1.040	95.33	89.12	2.8	0.935	632.7	107.6	95.0	
3	10.97	1.046	96.63	90.28	2.8	0.934	637.8	108.3	93.5	
4	11.23	1.043	97.81	90.76	2.8	0.928	643.5	108.9	92.7	
1957–1	11.39	1.036	98.73	91.14	2.8	0.923	653.3	110.9	93.5	
2	11.45	1.029	99.29	91.72	2.8	0.924	653.3	111.3	93.2	
3	11.43	1.020	99.44	93.36	2.8	0.939	655.2	112.2	92.8	
4	11.36	0.991	99.23	93.74	2.8	0.945	655.9	113.6	91.6	
1958–1	11.28	0.974	98.74	93.74	2.8	0.949	660.5	113.6	91.2	
2	11.22	0.966	98.10	93.65	2.8	0.955	656.6	113.4	89.4	81.20
3	11.21	0.963	97.51	93.74	2.8	0.961	659.2	113.3	88.2	79.90
4	11.30	0.963	97.15	93.55	2.8	0.963	667.8	113.5	89.6	80.96
1959–1	11.49	0.962	97.18	93.07	2.8	0.958	671.2	113.8	88.1	79.76
2	11.80	0.978	97.71	93.36	2.8	0.955	692.3	114.2	91.7	84.69
3	12.22	0.979	98.75	93.07	2.8	0.942	697.1	114.2	91.9	87.44
4	12.72	0.986	100.13	94.61	2.8	0.945	725.6	114.5	95.4	90.92
1960–1	13.62	1.000	100.61	94.90	2.8	0.943	732.2	115.0	95.9	92.94
2	13.50	1.001	100.60	95.09	2.8	0.945	731.4	115.8	95.3	88.94
3	13.67	0.996	100.20	95.57	2.8	0.954	738.8	116.4	95.4	90.02
4	13.97	0.993	99.88	95.86	2.8	0.960	753.0	116.9	95.1	91.29
1961–1	14.12	0.973	99.97	96.05	2.8	0.961	770.5	118.4	94.9	92.85
2	13.81	0.969	101.21	96.73	2.8	0.956	776.7	119.2	95.0	89.84
3	14.18	0.983	101.14	97.21	2.8	0.961	789.2	119.4	94.4	91.01
4	14.28	0.991	101.16	97.21	2.8	0.961	783.7	119.6	92.9	91.01

	M	*WBC*	*PW*	*PX*	*R*	$\frac{R.PX}{PW}$	*DE*	*PD*	*CU*	*Q*
1962–1	14.78	0.980	100.77	97.69	2.8	0.969	782.1	120.1	92.5	91.14
2	15.08	0.976	99.42	97.30	2.8	0.979	793.1	120.3	93.2	95.97
3	15.38	0.981	99.91	97.88	2.8	0.980	793.1	120.8	93.6	98.20
4	15.22	0.974	99.68	98.56	2.8	0.989	789.2	121.0	91.2	95.68
1963–1	15.11	0.964	100.37	99.13	2.8	0.988	755.2	121.1	89.1	96.06
2	16.03	0.980	100.04	99.61	2.8	0.996	815.7	121.3	92.6	100.18
3	16.74	0.985	99.38	100.48	2.8	1.011	830.5	121.4	94.6	103.33
4	17.26	0.989	99.41	101.06	2.8	1.017	841.3	121.7	96.0	104.38
1964–1	17.60	1.002	99.51	100.87	2.8	1.014	860.9	123.0	97.4	106.17
2	17.93	1.000	100.34	101.44	2.8	1.011	873.9	123.4	97.4	106.80
3	18.28	0.998	100.83	102.50	2.8	1.017	888.0	123.8	97.1	105.00
4	18.98	0.999	101.83	103.08	2.8	1.012	896.9	124.5	98.1	105.21
1965–1	19.10	1.002	102.69	103.95	2.8	1.012	897.8	126.0	98.4	107.23
2	20.00	0.997	102.50	104.72	2.8	1.022	900.5	126.7	97.2	110.06
3	19.99	1.010	103.03	105.49	2.8	1.024	904.2	127.3	97.1	114.09
4	20.72	1.009	102.81	106.45	2.8	1.035	921.5	127.7	97.4	113.07
1966–1	21.42	1.018	104.81	107.80	2.8	1.028	918.7	129.0	97.2	109.62
2	21.43	1.018	104.91	109.53	2.8	1.044	926.1	130.4	96.4	114.32
3	22.21	1.014	103.81	110.39	2.8	1.063	933.6	131.0	95.7	111.61
4	22.91	1.012	105.46	110.49	2.8	1.048	932.6	130.6	93.3	117.21
1967–1	23.25	0.996	106.51	111.26	2.8	1.045	948.6	130.6	93.0	120.06
2	23.48	0.985	106.12	111.55	2.8	1.051	976.5	130.6	93.0	117.21
3	23.07	0.981	106.75	112.51	2.8	1.054	975.5	131.6	92.4	113.52
4	23.54	0.987	107.65	115.00	2.575	0.983	976.5	132.5	93.7	110.06
1968–1	25.91	0.991	106.57	118.57	2.4	0.954	1013.3	135.2	94.2	115.01
2	25.55	0.986	107.70	121.27	2.4	0.965	987.3	136.6	94.3	123.10
3	27.85	1.002	108.03	123.63	2.4	0.981	998.2	136.9	94.9	129.28
4	28.56	1.016	109.50	124.19	2.4	0.972	1000.2	137.4	95.6	130.32
1969–1	28.54	1.021	110.41	125.54	2.4	0.975	993.3	138.5	95.0	129.54
2	30.61	1.034	110.95	125.42	2.4	0.969	989.3	139.8	95.0	139.07
3	31.39	1.033	111.61	125.76	2.4	0.966	999.2	1414	95.0	144.03
4	31.90	1.027	115.01	127.22	2.4	0.948	998.2	143.3	95.0	147.82
1970–1	32.50	1.032	116.69	129.13	2.4	0.949	986.3	146.3	94.3	147.38
2	33.73	1.031	118.37	132.07	2.4	0.956	1024.5	150.0	93.2	149.31
3	33.61	1.016	119.00	134.23	2.4	0.967	1022.5	152.6	93.2	148.71
4	34.59	1.005	119.21	137.57	2.4	0.989	1029.7	155.9	93.3	146.20
1971–1	34.99	1.002	120.90	141.65	2.4	1.004	1014.3	160.0	91.2	149.16
2	36.02	0.994	122.92	144.32	2.4	1.010	1031.7	163.0	90.8	157.28

Chapter 4

A MODEL OF THE UK FORWARD MARKET AND CAPITAL ACCOUNT, 1963–71[1]

4.1. Introduction

In the previous two chapters, we investigated substitution effects in the markets for traded goods. In this we examine substitution in the capital account of the balance of payments. We attempt to apply the theory of forward exchange and of capital flows (across the foreign exchanges) to UK experience in the middle and late 1960s. This may sound an over-large subject for a single chapter; the reason for its size, however, is that forward rates have an important effect on capital flows through the interest differential covered for exchange risk, and these flows in turn may react on forward rates through arbitrageurs' response to the spot rate. As a simultaneous system, therefore, it required a joint project.

4.2. Theory

In what follows the underlying theory is reviewed briefly; some small modifications are introduced for the purposes of this study.[2]

The capital account of the balance of payments records transactions in financial instruments – including titles to ownership (share capital), bonds of

[1] I gratefully acknowledge helpful comments from colleagues in the Treasury and Bank of England, and also individually from Michael Beenstock, Charles Goodhart, Marcus Miller and Lionel Price. John Hutton cooperated on this work at an early stage and contributed much valuable discussion in the later ones.

[2] For a good survey of theory and past empirical work in this field, see Hodjera [1973].

all maturities, trade credit and inter-company accounts, bank deposits and currency. Certain current account transactions carry with them the familiar assumption that they will be automatically financed by one of the transactors and are called 'real capital flows'; for example, if a US company affiliate imports an oil-rig into the UK sector of the North Sea in order to drill for oil, it will show up in the external accounts as an import offset by a capital inflow and would be classified as 'direct investment in the oil sector'. It may seem clear enough that the US company involved will not rearrange its portfolio of financial assets/liabilities merely because it has changed the physical location of its activity (e.g. from the Norwegian sector of the North Sea); yet it is not so clear. The US company may aim at zero exposure to 'country risk' (i.e. expropriation by government or other residents of the country) and so match its acquisition of a physical asset in the UK with a financial liability in the UK (e.g. by raising a UK loan). The point is that, even in this extreme example, there is no theoretical presumption that a direct capital import will be financed by a capital inflow. In principle the decision on the physical location of productive activity and the decision on the geographical source of its financing are separate. The location decision is taken in the light of 'real' economic factors (distance from markets and supplies, transport costs etc.); the financing decision is taken in the light of monetary factors (yields on various securities) and exposure to a spectrum of risks, including foreign exchange risk and expropriation risk.

In practice, of course, the separation is not so clearcut particularly if exchange controls are designed to prevent it: also institutional factors may introduce prohibitive transaction costs into a full separation (e.g. raising a UK loan may be a lot of trouble). But our expectation must be that capital flows which are the net result of the financial decisions taken will primarily reflect these financial factors. Given the size of portfolios of net assets, their disposition between assets of different countries is assumed, on the lines of the familiar analysis of Markowitz [1959] and Tobin [1958, 1965] to depend on relative returns and risks. The risks we are concerned with are the general category of 'exchange risks'; hence we abstract from domestic risks (e.g. of individual default) by assuming that all financial assets are identical in respect of these.[3]

[3] This grouping of assets is essentially that proposed by Solnik [1973], who demonstrates that, on the same assumptions as used here, investor choice can just as well be expressed in terms of a choice between portfolios of each asset group as of one between the original assets.

Figure 4.1
The asset distribution of international portfolios.

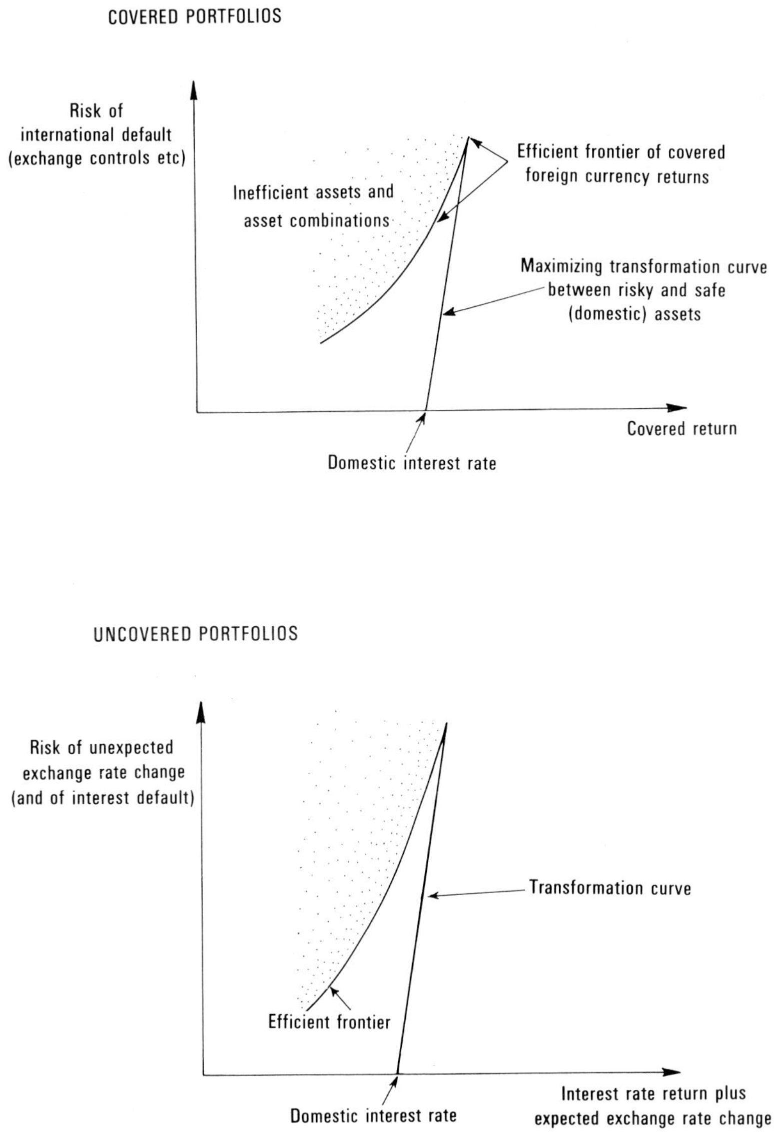

We have, however, to take an international portfolio approach that is somewhat more elaborate than that of Branson and Hill [1971]. They treat interest differentials as the relevant expected returns, while exchange risks include any gain or loss from change in exchange rates or international default. We maintain their assumption that interest rates are an adequate proxy for a spectrum of asset yields (shares, trade credits etc.) However, there are inadequacies with their concept of exchange risk. First anticipated exchange rate change is as much a part of the expected return on a foreign currency holding as the interest differentials. Secondly, exchange risk can be covered through the forward market. Third, international default is quite separate from exchange risk, being the residual risk that applies to covered or so-called 'arbitrage' transactions (as argued by Stoll [1968]).

We can deal with this by distinguishing covered transactions, in which the cost of cover provides the exchange rate return, and uncovered (or speculative) transactions, in which the expected exchange rate return is some measure of expected exchange rate change, that requires to be estimated. The *differentials* in return, covered or uncovered, are the same for portfolio holders wherever they are resident. However, the *risks* are loaded against foreign currency operations and hence bias portfolios, according to where the holder is resident, towards his domestic currency: hence the domestic currency is always the 'safe' currency.[4] This may be illustrated with an adaptation of the familiar Tobin diagram: see Figure 4.1. Portfolio holders in short face a choice of covered and uncovered assets. With covered assets, it is the residual risk of international default that places a limit on the (arbitrage) response to a change in the covered differential.[5] With uncovered assets, this risk combines

[4] This is, of course, a simplification which assumes that the domestic resident only consumes home goods whose price is invariant to exchange rate change. In practice there will be an element of risk in home currency because his consumption goods will rise in price if there is an unanticipated devaluation; eventually they would rise by the *full* devaluation precentage, but the lags involved are very long (according to simulations of the H.M. Treasury [1974] model used below, they are in excess of five years) and the initial effects small, so that when the risk is discounted to present value it is sufficiently small, compared with the foreign currency risk, to justify our simplification.

[5] While Officer and Willett [1970] argue convincingly that this is only one of a variety of complementary reasons why the covered arbitrage schedule should be upward-sloping, the others being non-monetary returns, non-unitary correlations of returns and risks in premature repatriation, it would appear to be the principal one for large international banks, such as typically operate in the market for sterling.

with that of *unexpected* exchange rate change to limit the (speculative) response to a change in the uncovered differential.

The portfolio holder could, in principle, achieve the same uncovered position by holding covered assets and taking an uncovered position in the forward market (e.g. instead of holding dollar assets uncovered, he could hold dollar assets covered and hold forward dollars as well). However, this is obviously an uneconomic operation because of the transactions costs involved in covering forward (selling forward dollars) *and* buying forward dollars, when the two operations cancel out. The assumption that speculation occurs in the spot market through uncovered portfolio holdings runs counter to one sometimes made in studies (e.g. Stoll) of forward rates, that speculation only occurs in the forward market. But assimilating such 'spot' speculation to a combination of forward speculation and arbitrage also runs into the problem that capital flows in the spot market are classified purely as arbitrage (which is wrong and will lead to the omission, in estimation, of all important speculative factors); this is operationally of no importance for single equation work on the forward market (where the double-counting fiction is harmless) but it is important in simultaneous equation work on this, just as it is for all work on the spot market and capital flows.

The main difference between short and long-term assets lies in the speed at which portfolios will be adjusted. With assets of three months' maturity which we use here as the indicative short term asset,[6] the lag in adjustment will not exceed three months (the length of the period in this study), because by the end of three months the asset must have been liquidated in any case and it will then automatically be transferred to the place of highest return. Hence, for this study, there is 'no' lag involved. With assets of longer maturity, clearly greater flexibility in speed of adjustment is possible and, specifically in the case of the 1-year market studied below, lags may extend up to four quarters.

There has been controversy over whether capital flows should be related to levels or changes in interest rates (see Branson and Hill). This revolves partly around the question of length of lags. Yet with a lag in adjustment this gives rise to a relationship with current and lagged levels of returns, in which the sign of the last lagged level should be opposite to that of the current level. Long lags in the changes can also be proxied by a relationship with the level

[6] The data used were chosen to fit as far as possible with this maturity criterion.

(because the level is equal to the sum of past changes plus a starting value). We should therefore look for a relationship with the current change in returns in the case of short-term flows (no lags) but with current and lagged levels in the case of long-term flows.

The level/change controversy also relates to the *growth* in portfolios as a factor determining the size of changes in holding. Branson and Hill introduce a scale variable. However, this leads to a considerably more complicated specification, with attendant problems. It is easier to proceed on the assumption that portfolios grow according to a constant linear trend. This can easily be shown to give rise both to a linear coefficient in the level of the covered differential and to a constant term, in the capital flows equation. So we may write the desired capital stock as:

$K^* = P[k(S - S^E) + k^*]$ (4.1) where P is the total world portfolio. The actual capital stock could adjust to this in a conventional manner so that:

$$K = (1 - \lambda)K^* + \lambda K_{-1} = (1 - \lambda) \sum_{i=0}^{\infty} \lambda^i K^*_{-i} \tag{4.2}$$

Hence:

$$\Delta K = \frac{1 - \lambda}{1 - \lambda B} [Pk(\Delta S - \Delta S^E) + k(S - S^E)\Delta P + k^* \Delta P] \tag{4.3}$$

which, provided ΔP is constant, may be approximated by a finite lag structure to give a relationship in the current and lagged values of both the level and rate of change of $S - S^E$, and where $k^* \Delta P$ is a constant representing the trend 'wealth effect' for portfolio growth (B is the lag operator).

In this study, we assume that speculators are concerned with sterling and the dollar as the two principal international currencies; other currencies, and assets denominated in them, are neglected. Given the prevalence of severe exchange controls on operations in most of these other currencies, this is perhaps not a serious over-simplification; the high R^2 of the results are consistent with such an interpretation.

4.3. Forward markets

Two markets are studied, the long term (1 year) and the short term (3 months). Forward markets with as long a maturity as one year have tended to be ignored on the grounds of their 'thinness'. Yet this property of a market is not a guide to the significance of the market price. In commodity markets, there are plenty of examples of grades (e.g. very fine or very coarse) in which dealings are thin; the price, nevertheless, bears a meaningful relationship to the prices of other grades, in which the bulk of business is done and with which it is closely substitutable. In short, its price, like other prices, is determined by underlying supply and demand in the market as a whole in the long term and by speculators' anticipation of other prices in the short term. In the case of the UK 1-year forward rate, dealings have until recently been limited by exchange control regulations to non-residents and the impression of some banks consulted (there are no figures for dealings) was that the market was thin. The exclusion of UK resident operators would indeed reduce the level of dealings. But the significance of the market price is that it is part of a network of forward rates, all of which are close substitutes (as in the commodity case). The factors influencing the price are thus in principle no different from those operating in shorter maturities; their relative weights may differ and this is what is explored in this paper.

The theory tells us that, whatever the maturity, operators in the forward market may be:

1. arbitrageurs, whose forward transactions are offset by equal and opposite current spot transactions:
2. speculators, who take forward positions without any current offset:
3. 'traders', by whom is meant anyone wanting to cover a future foreign exchange transaction in the forward market (this includes future lending and borrowing):
4. The Central Bank, who may intervene for policy reasons discussed below.

Arbitrageurs respond to the covered differential on bonds of the relevant maturity; as we have seen, they face the risk of default and this will place a limit on the elasticity of their response. Speculators respond to the difference between the forward rate and the spot rate they expect on the date when the forward maturity expires. For example, by buying forward at a lower rate than they expect to be able to sell spot, they make a profit; they do, however, carry the pure foreign exchange risk that the rate will differ from their expectation. This places a limit on the elasticity of their response.

Traders (i.e. the basic transactors in the balance of payments) are committed to a future foreign exchange transaction; the exchange risk may be taken on by either or both trading partners (through price adjustments), and it may or may not be covered in the forward market. A convenient analytic device is to treat them all as covering forward (risk-averters) *and* as speculators obeying the same forces as non-trading speculators. So, for example, if traders fear a depreciation greater than is implicit in the forward rate, exports will, let us say, not be covered because foreign exchange receipts are felt likely to yield a gain in terms of domestic currency, but imports, say, will be covered; analysis here would treat this as a risk-averting or basic demand for forward £s equal to net exports and a speculative supply of forward £s equal to imports plus net exports.

The following table illustrates the relationships of arbitrage, spot speculation, forward speculation, basic transactions and the reserves.[7]

Table 4.1
Transactions in £s (flows, – equals sale).

Time:	0	0	+1	+1
Market:	Spot	Forward	Spot	Forward
Arbitrage	–100	+100	–100	+100
Spot speculation	–100	–	–100	–
Forward speculation	–	–200	–	–200
Basic transactions	–	+100	–	+100
Past forward speculation	?	–	+200	–
Reserves	?		–	

Arbitrage represents an equal and opposite flow in spot and forward markets. Current spot speculation is simply a flow in spot markets. Basic transactions ('trade') are simply a flow in the forward market. Traders, say, are net exporters so they buy forward £s (+100); when they receive foreign exchange in the next period, they hand it over to the forward speculators who sold them the forward £s, and hence they do not go into the spot market. The forward speculators, who sold forward £s to both arbitrageurs and traders,

[7] Kenen [1965] discusses a trichotomy of trader-arbitrageur-speculator in similar terms.

do have to go into the spot market in the next period in order to buy these £s spot and satisfy their forward customers. So past forward speculation against the £ equals a current spot transaction in favour of £s, representing the inflow from past arbitrage against the £ and from current traders' receipts of foreign exchange.

In addition there are the complications of forward markets, and basic transactions, of different maturities. In this study only two maturities are examined, three months and one year. In this case, the table becomes (one period = three months):

Table 4.2
Transactions in £s (–, sale).

	0	0	0	+1	+1	+1	+4	+4	+4
Market	Spot	3 mths fward	1 year fward	Spot	3 mths fward	1 year fward	Spot	3 mths fward	1 year fward
Arbitrage:									
3 months	–100	+100	–	–100	+100	–	–100	+100	–
1 year	–100	–	+100	–100	–	+100	–100	–	+100
Current Speculation: (spot and forward)	–100	–200	–200	–100	–200	–200	–100	–200	–200
Basic Trade:	–	+100	+100	–	+100	+100	–	+100	+100
Past Forward Speculation:									
3 months	?	–	–	+200	–	–	?	–	–
1 year	?	–	–	?	–	–	+200	–	–
Other maturities	?	–	–	?	–	–	?	–	–
Reserves	?			?			?		

For analysis of capital flows, transactions are regrouped in the spot market by breaking down past forward speculation into its components, past arbitrage and current basic trade. Past arbitrage and current capital transactions are then grouped with capital flows, which must therefore be regarded as an amalgam of net arbitrage, current speculation in the spot market, and other (exogenous) capital flows. The current balance is regarded as an exogenous variable.

For analysis of the forward markets chosen there is the problem of measuring basic transactions of the given maturity. Quite clearly, there are no data so we have to make assumptions. One possible assumption is that the balance on these transactions is insignificant in its effect and can be treated as zero. The other assumption is that it is related to the current balance out-turn during the quarter in which the maturity occurs; hence we 'lead' the current balance by the appropriate number of quarters, to test this hypothesis against its alternative. It does not appear to matter, for this purpose, whether we treat the current balance as an indicator of the net stock or of the net flow, of forward liabilities; both should move in the same direction, just as desired trading stocks are a function of the expected flow of orders. This merely suggests the possibility of a slightly longer lead in order to use the current balance flow as a stock indicator.

4.4. Government/Central Bank reaction functions

This is an area of potentially enormous complexity, since we need to specify not only official objectives but also the inter-relationships between the instruments for achieving them, which in this context are short term interest rates (or domestic credit), the spot exchange rate (which can move within the parity limits) and the reserves (or spot intervention)[8]; real income or long-term interest rates and prices are treated as predetermined, and so by implication is fiscal policy, in this study. One cannot cut this knot by assuming that these instruments are predetermined because the simultaneity is quite manifest in the quarterly data; we could move to using monthly or even weekly data for forward markets but this would have the disadvantage that we could not analyse capital flows, for which such data are not available, and the interactions between capital flows and forward markets would be lost. One could also not guarantee, even with weekly data, to get around the simultaneity, since during the period the Government dealers were active on a daily basis in the gilt-edged and spot markets.

[8] Spot intervention (defined as currency flow, *DR*) was distinguished from forward intervention, on which data was obtained from the Bank of England on a confidential basis; forward intervention, however, did not appear to contribute significantly to the forward rate equations and the variable was, therefore, not included in the model's final version.

The ideal solution would be an attempt (see, for example, Hutton [1977]) to set up a model taking account of the interplay between objectives and instruments in a way that allows for the role of monetary policy in management of the domestic economy. However, in this study the simplification is made that monetary policy was assigned (in the sense popularised by Mundell – see for example his [1962]) wholly to the balance of payments during this period. We, therefore, assume that the authorities' three instruments, the short-term interest differential, the spot rate and currency intervention. are used in some combination exclusively to eliminate the excess demand or supply of foreign currency. Each instrument is assumed to be a linear function of this excess demand only; the interest differential and spot rate functions are then expressed as linear relationships of the directly observed currency intervention and excess demand. The justification for such a crude approach has to be that our primary interest in this study was not in the reaction functions but in private sector behaviour; but further refinement must be an area for potential research.

4.5. Specification and estimation

The theory as set out above gives the broad limits within which the specification of the estimating equations can lie. The final specification is the result of some interaction with the data; the model's formal structure is shown in Table 4.3, the estimated results in Table 4.4, and the actual/predicted values are plotted in Figures 4.3–8.

The work began with forward rates, on the grounds that these would provide clues to the movements in 'confidence' which in turn are so important to capital flows. All rates of exchange were first normalised by expressing them as percentage deviations from parity. This is natural because Government commitment to a parity sets it up as the major speculator in the market, in the three senses that it has access, through its reserves and central bank co-operation, to large amounts of funds for spot intervention; that it can also intervene to as large an extent as it wishes in forward markets, and that it can use domestic policy instruments for the defence of the rate. However, there is a limit to the size of central bank co-operation (because of the risk of default) as there is obviously to the size of reserves; there is also a limit to the willingness of the authorities to intervene in spot and forward

Figure 4.2
Spot, 3-month, and 1-year forward rates – *S,FS,FL* ($s per £, as % deviations from parity).

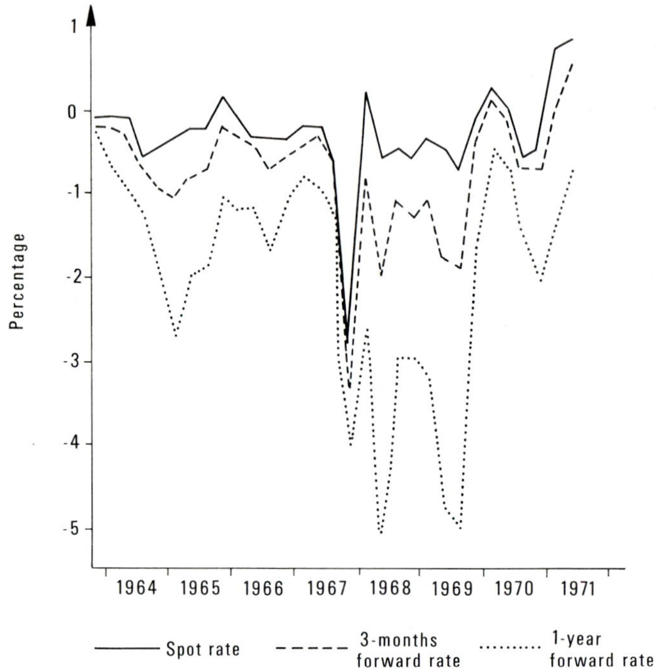

markets because of the exchange risk of capital losses, which are also, when the transactions are with non-residents, losses of real resources to the economy; and finally the willingness to use domestic instruments is limited by domestic interests. Hence exchange rate change in a fixed rate market depends, apart from the margins, on the possibility that these limits will be reached and the parity will be changed; the parity, therefore, acts as a point of reference.

Expressed in this way, the spot, 3-months and 1-year forward rates showed considerable variation, and were fairly well, though not nearly perfectly, correlated as is evident from Figure 4.2.

The devaluation quarter, 1967(4), stood out as an extreme observation with an obvious explanation in the political events of the time (talks with central bankers, Mr. Callaghan's 'noncommittal' statement in the House, etc.) and a dummy variable seemed called for to prevent it from influencing the relationships prevailing in normal times. In the same spirit, I allowed for

Figure 4.3
1-year forward rate, actual and estimated – *FL* ($s per £1; % deviations from parity).

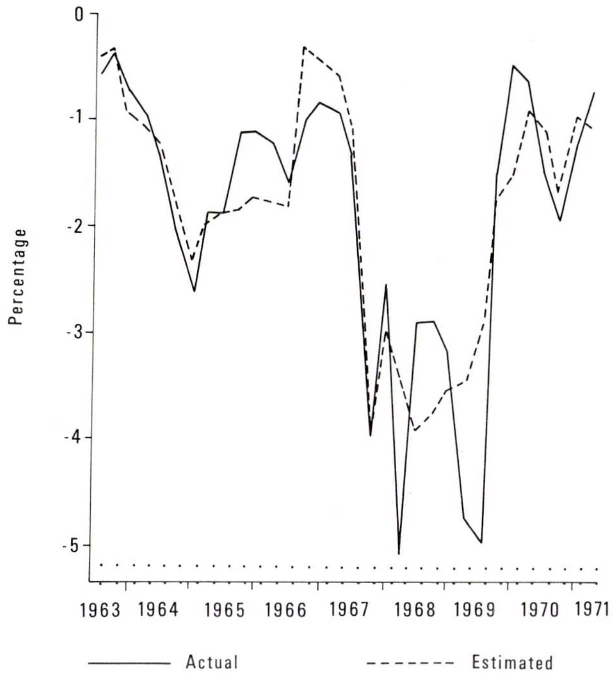

abnormal variations in election quarters with a dummy equal to 1 in these quarters. In Chapter 7, it is shown formally how such extreme conditions will influence the capital flows relationships.

On the question of exchange rate expectations,[9] it is assumed that speculators are profit-maximising and that therefore they search for a good predictive model of the spot rate; the model they actually use may not be the true one, but it is assumed that it is based on previous experience of the fixed rate market and is then solved (in the manner of rational expectations) for the future exchange rate. In Chapter 5, we show how the expected rate is obtained from what seems to have been the 'popular' model of the period; and we call the resulting expression a 'semi-rational' expectation. In the

[9] For a previous application of (fully) rational expectations to the foreign exchange market, see Black [1973].

case of the UK where net exogenous capital flows are relatively unimportant in the balance of payments, this turns out to consist of a weighted average of recent values of the current balance. It is clear enough that the worse this trend in the current account, first, the more pressure there is on the actual spot rate within the margins and also on the reserves; and secondly, the more likely is the government to devalue towards the equilibrium, because the pressure on the spot rate and the reserves brings closer the limits on intervention referred to earlier.

Thus, the expected spot rate was represented by a distributed lag in the visible trade balance. This appeared to be the most significant confidence indicator, perhaps because it is published promptly, generally little revised and (unlike the reserves) incapable of manipulation by the authorities. Preliminary results showed that such a lag gave a good explanation in the one-year forward rate equation. It also appeared that a pure expectations theory would account for this forward maturity, since the effect of the spot rate adjusted for the interest differential was statistically quite insignificant. A further result was that the current balance four (and five) quarters ahead, indicating the covered position of traders, was insignificant. This made it possible to treat the long-term forward rate as equivalently the spot rate expected in one year's time, and also as a (recursively) predetermined variable in the other equations.[10] Equation (4.9) was the result, and as Figure 4.3 shows, the fit was reasonably good.

The three-months forward rate, equation (4.11), seemed to fall neatly into place in relation to this long-term expected rate and the spot rate adjusted for the interest differential. It was found that the weights of speculative expectations and of arbitrage were roughly equal, at 0.50; this finding is not dissimilar to that of Stoll. As with the 1-year rate, the current balance one (and two) quarters ahead was insignificant.

Capital flows were divided into short term (four items)[11] and long term (the rest of the capital account). The approach was boldly (some might say, rashly) aggregative; in this respect (and in some others) it is similar to that of

[10] The finding that speculators dominate the 1-year forward market implies that the 1-year forward rate is not a biased indicator of the expected rate. For there to be bias, as e.g. asserted by Solnik [1973], it is required that arbitrageurs influence this forward market.

[11] The items were: Overseas Sterling Area private £ balances, All Non-Sterling Area £ balances, Banks' foreign currency transactions (other than lending for overseas investment), and the Balancing Item.

Helliwell and Maxwell [1972] in their work on Canadian capital flows,[12] and see also Branson [1968].[13] The purpose of the study is to explain aggregate endogenous capital flows; and this immediately restricts the interest in disaggregation. The relevant question here is: are relationships at the aggregate level more stable than those at the disaggregated? We have a general theory applicable to (short and long term) endogenous capital flows, in which the explanatory variables are common. Thus our model could be disaggregated as:

$$Y_1 = a_1 X + u_1, \tag{4.4}$$

$$Y_2 = a_2 X + u_2, \tag{4.5}$$

where Y_1 and Y_2 would be the parts of Y, X is the common explanatory variable, and u_1, u_2 the disaggregated errors. And our aggregate version is

$Y = aX + u$ (4.6) where $Y = Y_1 + Y_2$, $a = a_1 + a_2$, $u = u_1 + u_2$.

The relevant question is therefore: will the variance of $(\hat{a}_1 + \hat{a}_2)$ be greater or less than the variance of $\hat{a}$? We have

$$\text{var}\,(\hat{a}_1 + \hat{a}_2) = \frac{\text{var}\,u_1 + \text{var}\,u_2}{\sum X^2}, \tag{4.7}$$

and

$$\text{var}\,\hat{a} = \frac{\text{var}\,u_1 + \text{var}\,u_2 + 2\,\text{covar}\,u_1 u_2}{\sum X^2}. \tag{4.8}$$

[12] Though in that piece they do not attempt to explain long-term capital, flows; for their work on these see Helliwell et al. [1971].

[13] Branson's [1968] work on US capital flows is more disaggregated and generally more extended. There are nevertheless considerable similarities of general approach; e.g. the use of simultaneous estimation, the integration of forward markets, and the use of flexible Almon lag structures. In Branson, monthly exchange rate equations are estimated as reduced form functions of current and lagged trade flows, interest differentials, and the expected exchange rate where this is generated by the same second-order autogressive process as the actual exchange rate (i.e. expectations are rational); the monthly capital flow equations distinguish six categories, assets and liabilities of short term maturity, long term maturity and related to direct investment, the arguments being changes in trade flows, in interest differentials, in national incomes, and in lagged dependent variables.

Table 4.3
The structure of the model.[1]

Nature of equation		Dummies	Equation no.
Long-run speculation (one year forward rate is proxy)	$FL = \sum_{i=1}^{14} a_i \, VIS_{-i} + k_1$	D	(4.9)
Long-run capital flows	$DKL = \sum_{i=0}^{4} b_i RL_i + \sum_{i=0}^{4} c_i FL_{-i} + k_2$	$D, EL, D1, D2, D3$	(4.10)
	(simultaneous block)		
Short-run forward rate	$FS = \frac{d}{d+e} SS + \frac{e}{d+e} f(FL) + k_3$	D	(4.11)[2]
Short-run capital flows	$DKS = g \, \Delta CDS + h \, \Delta\overline{VIS} + k_4$	$D, EL, D1, D2, D3$	(4.12)
Spot-rate/intervention trade-off	$SD = j \, DR + k_5$	D	(4.13)
Interest rate/intervention trade-off	$RS = k \, DR + k_6$		(4.14)
Intervention identity	$DR = BB + DKS$		(4.15)
Spot-rate arbitraged to 3 months ahead	$SS = SD - RS$		(4.16)
Covered differential	$CDS = FS - SS$		(4.17)
Basic Balance	$BB = CB + DKL$		(4.18)
Trade balance confidence factor	$\overline{VIS} = \sum_{i=1}^{14} a_i (VIS_{-i} / \sum a_i)$		(4.19)

where:

FL = 1 year forward rate, \$/£ (% deviations from parity)
VIS = Visible balance (£ million)
DKL = All capital account flows except DKS (£ million)
RL = Long-term \$/£ interest differential (% per annum)
FS = 3 months forward rate, \$/£ (% deviation from parity)
SD = Spot rate, \$/£ (% deviation from parity)
DKS = Short-term capital flows (£ million)
RS = 3 months \$/£ interest differential (% per quarter)
CB = Current Account Balance (£ million)
EL = Election-devaluation dummy (1 in Election quarters and in 1967(4)
D = Special Devaluation dummy (1 in 1967(4)

$D1$, $D2$, $D3$ = Seasonal dummies

Notes: [1] The model is block-recursive. Equations (4.9) and (4.10) are determined recursively, FL and DKL in that order. Then equations (4.11)–(4.19) solve simultaneously for the other endogenous variables. Of these only (4.11)–(4.14) are behavioural equations; the rest are identities.

[2] (4.11) derived from $d\ (FS-SS) + e\ (FS-fFL) = 0$, the equilibrium condition in the 3 months forward market. fFL is the spot rate expected in 3 months.

The difference depends on the covariance of u_1 with u_2; if it is positive, then disaggregation will give a gain (to set against the additional costs of work involved), if it is negative then aggregation will be preferable.

In the case of capital flows, theory suggests that there is widespread substitutability between different sorts of flows, since each represents a different instrument or channel for achieving the same results, whether covered arbitrage or spot speculation. Furthermore, the practice of statistical classification suggests that substitutability could also arise on this score. These considerations suggested the aggregative approach as offering the highest likelihood of good results. However, the only way of testing which approach is better, is to try the disaggregated; one cannot test for error correlation without fitting disaggregated equations. This is therefore an appropriate area for further research. Meanwhile it is worth noting that even if disaggregation would give better results, a good aggregate result is a worthwhile return to initial effort.

Figure 4.4
Long term capital flows, actual and estimated – *DKL* (£ million per quarter).

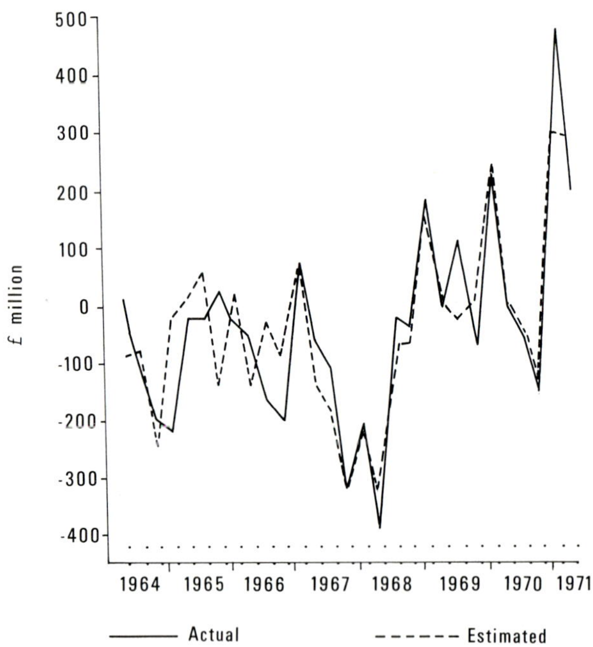

Long-term capital flows, equation (4.10), appeared to be well explained by the long-term interest differential, *RL*, and the long forward rate, both current and lagged levels. Further investigation showed that *RL* was not influenced by the predetermined variables in our model and could therefore be treated as itself predetermined. Hence long-term flows could also be regarded as (recursively) predetermined.

Short-term flows, equation (4.12), have been previously investigated by Hutton [1977] and found to be responsive to changes in the short-term interest differential and the cost of short-term cover as well as various confidence variables. These results are apparently improved by amalgamating these two into the covered differential and incorporating speculative expectations as suggested by the forward market results. Both the long-term forward rate and the lag-weighted visible balance were used as proxies for expectations; the latter performed best. This suggests that the error term in the long-term forward equation is not related to short-term confidence

Figure 4.5
3-month forward rate, actual and estimated – *FS* ($s per £; % deviations from parity).

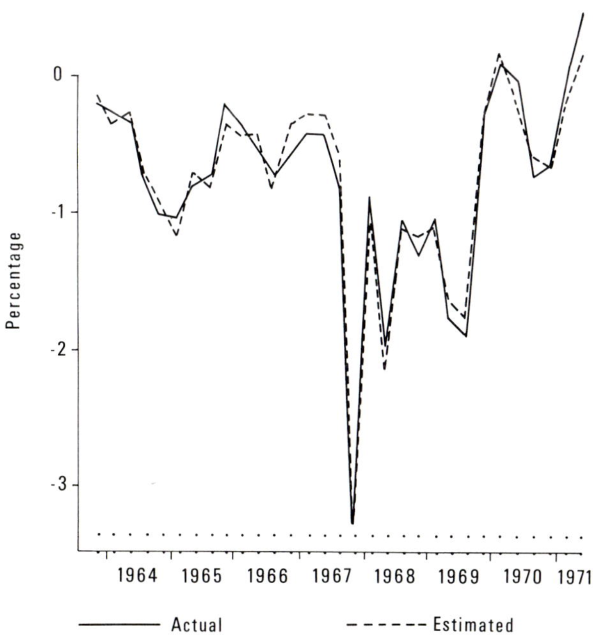

Table 4.4 Empirical results.[1]

	$\bar{R}^2$	See	DW	Estimator	Equation no.
$FL = \underset{(0.500)}{0.768} + \sum_{i=1}^{14} a_i VIS_{-i} - \underset{(0.755)}{2.548}\, D$	0.73	0.732	1.85[1]	*OLS*	(4.9)
(2) $a_i =$ 0.00719, 0.00536, 0.00397, 0.00296, 0.00227, 0.00184, 0.00162, (0.00112) (0.00072) (0.00053) (0.00049) (0.00049) (0.00049) (0.00049)					
0.00154, 0.00154, 0.00157, 0.00156, 0.00146, 0.00121, 0.00074 $(i = 1\ldots14)$ (0.00051) (0.00055) (0.00060) (0.00063) (0.00061) (0.00052) (0.00032)					
$DKL = -\underset{(139.4)}{502.4} + \underset{(60.2)}{233.5}\, D1 + \underset{(62.2)}{143.8}\, D2 + \underset{(62.3)}{146.5}\, D3$	0.76	104.2	2.51[1]	*OLS*	(4.10)
$+ \underset{(148.0)}{190.8}\, D + \sum_{i=o}^{4} b_i RL_{-i} + \sum_{i=o}^{4} c_i FL_{-i}$					
(2) $b_i =$ 119.1, 157.8, 61.2, −66.6, −121.7 $(i = o,\ldots,4)$ (78.0) (54.5) (53.5) (33.8) (51.0)					
(2) $c_i =$ 67.7, 18.7, −12.1, −25.1, −20.9 $(i = o,\ldots,4)$ (26.5) (11.2) (15.5) (11.1) (15.0)					
$FS = \underset{(0.040)}{0.142} + \underset{(0.071)}{0.493}\, SS + \underset{(0.021)}{0.335}\, FL - \underset{(0.217)}{0.516}\, D$	0.97	0.122	1.36	*TSLS*	(4.11)
$DKS = \underset{(56.7)}{3.3} + \underset{(75.7)}{193.3}\, D1 + \underset{(83.4)}{119.4}\, D2 - \underset{(78.0)}{163.3}\, D3 + \underset{(173.8)}{74.4}\, D$	0.61	142.7	1.59	*TSLS*	(4.12)
$- \underset{(93.3)}{165.7}\, EL + \underset{(1.71)}{3.65}\, \Delta \overline{VIS} + \underset{(106.0)}{364.7}\, \Delta CDS$					
$SD = -\underset{(0.049)}{0.200} - \underset{(0.288)}{2.223}\, D + \underset{(0.000133)}{0.000606}\, DR$	0.79	0.269	1.26	*TSLS*	(4.13)
$RS = \underset{(0.046)}{0.156} - \underset{(0.000119)}{0.000261}\, DR$	0.06	0.254	1.18	*TSLS*	(4.14)

Notes: [1] $\bar{R}^2 = R^2$ corrected for degrees of freedom. See = Standard error of estimate. DW = Durbin Watson statistic. OLS = ordinary least squares. $TSLS$ = two-stage least squares. Standard errors parenthesised below coefficients.

[2] Third-order Almon polynomials on the lagged variables; first weight unconstrained, weight after the maximum lag tied to zero.

factors, even though it *is* related to the three-months forward rate; the explanation for this is unclear.

The capital flows equations predicted surprisingly well, in view of the popular supposition (alluded to in chapter 1) that capital flows are highly unpredictable. As one might expect, short-term flows ($\bar{R}^2 = 0.61$) were more unpredictable than longterm ($\bar{R}^2 = 0.76$); but Figure 4.6 shows that the predictions of short-term flows were usually in the right direction, the (less serious) error being in the size of swing. Given that there is little, if any, trend in either capital flows series, the $\bar{R}^2$ are standard for relationships in which forecasters typically place confidence; they can be compared, for example, with a good equation in first differences such as equation (3.34) for export prices ($R^2 = 0.68$).

The Government reaction functions, equations (4.13) and (4.14), are written as trade-offs between foreign exchange intervention and respectively the spot rate and the short-term interest differential. The spot rate equation

Figure 4.6
Short term capital flows, actual and estimated – *DKS* (£ million per quarter).

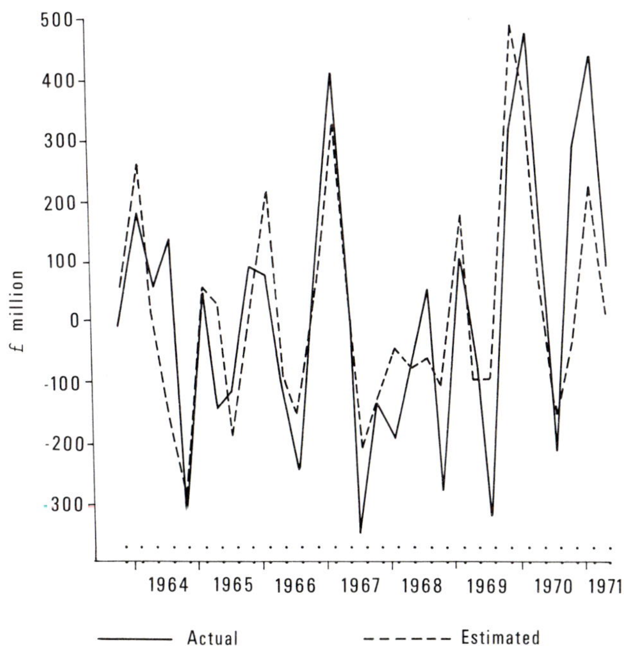

is reasonably successful; the $\bar{R}^2$ of 0.69 is misleading since the 1967 devaluation dummy does a great deal of work, but Figure 4.7 shows that the equation picks up the direction of change well. The short-term interest differential is poorly explained but intervention is a significant determinant. This suggests, as one might expect, that monetary policy in the UK is influenced by domestic as well as external factors. But it is also likely that the trade-off with current intervention is too simple – for example it may be nonlinear or there may be a trade-off with expected future intervention. (See Hutton).

This last interpretation is supported by the familiar pattern (see Figure 4.8) of high Bank Rate responding to sterling crises at the ends of 1964 and 1967. The high UK differential at end-1970 seems to be explained by the anxiety of the UK authorities to achieve their *IMF* loan repayment schedule (again an external factor); though interest rates overseas had slipped to low levels in the recession, UK rates were not allowed to match these falls.

Figure 4.7
Spot rate, actual and estimated – *SD* (\$s per £; % deviations from parity).

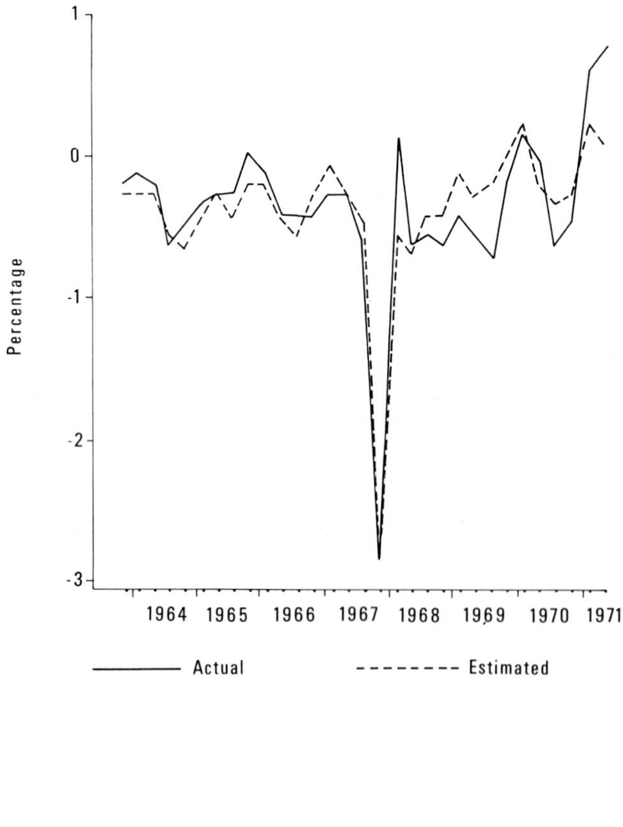

Figure 4.8
3-month interest differential, actual and estimated – *RS* (UK local authority – Euro-$ deposit; % per quarter).

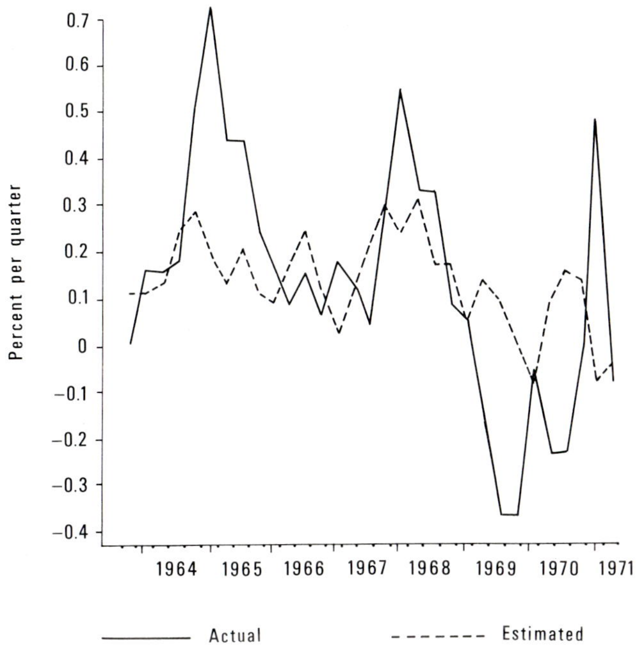

4.6. Conclusions

This chapter attempts to explain both movements in the capital account of the UK balance of payments and the related behaviour of UK forward rates, short and long term. The basic hypotheses are:

1. Capital flows respond to interest differentials adjusted for the cost of covering against possible exchange rate change (forward cover), as well as to speculative anticipation of changes in the rate.

2. Forward rates, in turn, which combine with the spot rate to set the cost of forward cover, are determined by the interplay of arbitrageurs (who sell forward when the forward rate is higher than the spot rate, allowing for the interest differential) and speculators (who sell forward when they expect the future spot rate to be less than the prevailing forward rate).

Appendix 4.A: Data[a]

	DKL	VIS (−1)	FL	RL	BB	FS	DKS		RS	SD	DR	EL	D
1960 (1)	52												
(2)	115	−50											
(3)	250	−115											
(4)	163	−124											
1961 (1)	−271	−117											
(2)	−185	−69											
(3)	27	−60											
(4)	84	−5											
1962 (1)	99	−18											
(2)	−7	−24											
(3)	−27	−11											
(4)	−9	−43											
1963 (1)	−120	−24		1.750									
(2)	80	4	−0.693	1.380									
(3)	−103	−8	−0.482	1.200									
(4)	−44	−24	−0.368	1.370	−45	−0.146	17	1963 (4)	0.035	−0.096	−28	0.0	0.0
1964 (1)	−156	−52	−0.668	1.590	−207	−0.218	208	1964 (1)	0.182	−0.068	1	0.0	0.0
(2)	15	−132	−0.914	1.770	−51	−0.300	63	(2)	0.187	−0.125	12	0.0	0.0
(3)	−105	−93	−1.246	1.870	−281	−0.704	155	(3)	0.200	−0.532	−126	0.0	0.0
(4)	−188	−143	−2.000	2.090	−271	−0.936	−311	(4)	0.515	−0.400	−582	1.0	0.0
1965 (1)	−209	−151	−2.600	2.300	−231	−0.979	65	1965 (1)	0.730	−0.279	−166	0.0	0.0
(2)	−22	−40	−1.954	2.580	−27	−0.768	−139	(2)	0.457	−0.196	−166	0.0	0.0
(3)	−21	−84	−1.793	2.400	−96	−0.682	−100	(3)	0.457	−0.186	−196	0.0	0.0
(4)	27	−64	−1.032	1.920	77	−0.168	98	(4)	0.265	0.111	175	0.0	0.0
1966 (1)	−13	−49	−1.093	2.070	−27	−0.279	75	1966 (1)	0.175	−0.039	48	0.0	0.0
(2)	−56	−73	−1.175	2.300	−81	−0.471	−82	(2)	0.110	−0.304	−163	1.0	0.0
(3)	−157	−69	−1.579	2.550	−238	−0.654	−250	(3)	0.180	−0.350	−488	0.0	0.0
(4)	−185	−44	−0.979	2.250	18	−0.496	38	(4)	0.090	−0.339	56	0.0	0.0
1967 (1)	82	113	−0.800	2.080	95	−0.379	414	1967 (1)	0.202	−0.179	509	0.0	0.0
(2)	−57	−39	−0.854	1.950	−96	−0.371	84	(2)	0.150	−0.196	−12	0.0	0.0

(2)	−393	−164	−3.040	2.270	[illegible]	[illegible]	[illegible]	(2)	[illegible]	[illegible]	[illegible]	[illegible]	[illegible]
(3)	−26	−212	−2.887	2.560	−84	−0.979	60	(3)	0.360	−0.442	−24	0.0	0.0
(4)	−37	−148	−2.833	2.510	−63	−1.238	−283	(4)	0.122	−0.554	−346	0.0	0.0
1969 (1)	190	−119	−3.096	2.750	157	−0.967	115	1969 (1)	0.062	−0.300	272	0.0	0.0
(2)	−1	−127	−4.617	3.300	157	−1.717	−75	(2)	−0.155	−0.471	82	0.0	0.0
(3)	125	−48	−4.875	3.160	275	−1.862	−322	(3)	−0.332	−0.629	−47	0.0	0.0
(4)	−66	35	−1.471	2.560	99	−0.283	337	(4)	−0.352	−0.100	436	0.0	0.0
1970 (1)	219	−1	−0.446	2.250	426	0.104	489	1970 (1)	−0.040	0.225	915	0.0	0.0
(2)	−5	65	−0.617	2.580	144	−0.038	83	(2)	−0.222	0.038	227	1.0	0.0
(3)	−46	−41	−1.458	2.530	6	−0.708	−208	(3)	−0.207	−0.525	−202	0.0	0.0
(4)	−166	−74	−1.921	3.330	38	−0.608	309	(4)	0.0	−0.379	347	0.0	0.0
1971 (1)	477	57	−1.800	3.390	512	−0.008	461	1971 (1)	0.510	0.704	973	0.0	0.0
(2)	201	−70	−0.650	3.160	540	0.462	94	(2)	0.070	0.796	634	0.0	0.0

[a] *Notes on variables:*

DKL	All capital account flows except *DKS* £ million. Not seasonally adjusted. Source: Economic Trends.
VIS (−1)	Revised visible balance, lagged one period. £ million. Seasonally adjusted. Source: Economic Trends.
*FL**	1-Year Forward Rate, $/£ (value of £ in $s). % deviations from parity. Source: Bank of England.
*RL**	Differential (UK-US) between U.K. 20-year Govt. Bonds Redemption Yield. (Source: B of E Bulletin) and U.S. Long Term Bonds(10 years or more) Redemption Yield; % annum. Source: International Financial Statistics.
BB	Current Balance plus *DKL*; £ million. Not seasonally adjusted. Source: Economic Trends.
*FS**	3-Months Forward Rate, $/£ (value of £1 in $s). % deviations from parity. Source: B of E Bulletin.
DKS	Short-term capital flows, as defined: OSA private £ balances, NSA £ balances, Banks' foreign currency transactions (other than lending for overseas investment), Balancing Item. £ million. Not seasonally adjusted.
*RS**	3-Months Interest differential (UK-Euro $) between U.K. Local Authority and Euro-$ deposits. % per quarter. Source: B of E Bulletin.
*SD**	$/£ spot rate ($s per $1). % deviations from parity. Source B of E Bulletin.
DR	Currency Flow, £ million. Not seasonally adjusted. Source: Economic Trends.
EL	Election-devaluation dummy.
D	Special devaluation dummy.

* Quarterly average of end-month values.

3. The authorities react to losses in reserves by letting the spot rate move (to a small extent because the margins were narrow) and by moving short term interest differentials in favour of the UK (through monetary policy).

These theories are reasonably consistent with the facts. In particular, the one year forward rate is, it appears, dominated by speculative expectations, as proxied by the trend in the current balance. The three months' maturity forward rate seems to be determined in roughly equal proportions by the spot rate (minus the three months' interest differential) and speculators' expectations (as measured by the one year forward rate). The response of short-term capital flows to a 1% per annum change in the covered three months' interest differential is estimated at £90 million. Long-term capital flows respond strongly to changes in the long-term interest differential and the expected long-run exchange rate, as measured by the 1-year forward rate.

More generally, we have found that substitution effects are a powerful force in external financial flows just as they were in trade flows, and we have estimated the structural coefficients through which speculation operated on the capital account during the fixed rate period. These estimates, of substitution and speculation mechanisms, will form the raw material from which we will try in succeeding chapters to build up a model of the external account and the exchange rate, not only for the fixed rate regime but also for the floating exchange rate regime under which the world is currently operating.

PART II

EXCHANGE RATE BEHAVIOUR

Chapter 5

A MODEL OF THE UK FLOATING EXCHANGE RATE[1]

5.1. Introduction

In Chapter 6, a model of a floating rate will be discussed in which the equilibrium exchange rate is determined as in the monetary approach, but the path to equilibrium is determined by structural equations in the second tradition. Such a model is of interest since many authors of large-scale models will, if pressed, agree that their models ought at least to tend asymptotically to a 'monetary' solution, even if they do not actually do so (or only within an excessively long period); for example, Eckstein et al. [1974] discuss the *DRI* model for the *U.S.A.* in the light of such long-term desirabilia, and see also Ando [1974]. It is true that predictions from the two approaches will differ in practice, as long as there are differences in dynamic formulation and residual unwillingness on both sides to carry out the necessary model adaptation. Nevertheless, some recent work appears to be showing the necessary practical convergence – Jonson [1976], Parkin [1974] and Dornbusch [1975] are examples.

In Chapter 6, we will assume that exchange rate expectations are fully rational, but argue that attainment of this condition will occur as the result

[1] I am grateful to colleagues at the Treasury, particularly Michael Beenstock, Bryan Hopkin and Arnold Lovell, to members of the International Business Workshop at Chicago, especially Robert Aliber, and of the Manchester Inflation Workshop, in particular Tapan Biswas, Dennis Coppock, Jack Johnston and Michael Parkin, for helpful discussions. I am also grateful to Sam Moore for useful discussion of several points with bearings also on other chapters.

of a learning process. Here we discuss both the actual model that appeared to be working in the UK in the 1960s and the nature of the learning process by which it should tend to the fully rational model.

5.2. Expectations and adaptiveness

Much empirical work has been done in the area of expectations on the assumption that they 'adapt' to the forecasting error in the most recent period.[2] This assumption leads to the convenient Koyck [1954] transformation, but apart from grounds of convenience, it has also been justified as capturing the true learning process. It may indeed be possible by simulating search situations, to establish that the adaptive process would under certain circumstances lead the user to the right answer in the end.[3] However, it seems unlikely that such a process will be the most efficient except when there is total ignorance of the models underlying the forecast variable, simply because the process would not be utilising all available information (viz. from the models themselves). It is possible, as discussed earlier (chapter 1), that the cost of information about variables other than the forecast variable is prohibitively high relative to the forecasting benefit. However, this is unlikely in the context of exchange rate speculation where the forecaster's livelihood depends on the forecast's accuracy; it seems also that, quite generally, much information is available at low cost to forecasters of most economic variables. This suggests that here at least adaptive schemes are too restrictive.

We have in mind therefore a 'model-learning' process, whereby the speculator begins by using one model or model combination for his forecast; in subsequent periods, he is assumed to adjust the weights on each model according to its predictive success. It is assumed that the process converges on the true model; this indeed has to be so since, as the sample tends to infinity, estimated coefficients of the true model will tend to their true values while those of the false models will tend to zero. More practically, since structural change can prevent the sample from becoming at all large, we suppose that the 'true' model here considered is not subject to significant structural change. Specifically, as will be argued below, the speculator was

[2] Or previous periods also; the process is generalisable in various ways.

[3] It has also been shown by Muth [1961] that, under certain assumptions about the model and the error process, adaptive expectations are rational.

unaware of the existence of significant lags in price elasticities until very recently, when there was powerful evidence available from both the sterling 1967 and the dollar 1971 devaluations. Finally, we assume that all speculators have access to the state of knowledge about the model, and therefore use the same model, assuming that all other speculators are also using it. Thus, we may call this speculative process 'semi-rational', because it is rational in every respect except that speculators are solving the wrong model. It is natural to suppose that a shift from a fixed rate to a floating rate would have some effect on the formulation of exchange rate expectations. Certain modifications are easily carried out and discussed below in this chapter. However, possible modification of the parameter, h, the response of capital flows to a change in the expected rate, is more complex, and a full discussion is deferred until chapter 7, where we propose some tentative modification under both fully and semi-rational assumptions and examine the implications for the behaviour of the floating exchange rate. At this stage, however, we merely note that this modification is sufficiently tentative for it to be reasonable to assume, as a working hypothesis, that the original parameter estimate may stand unmodified. This we do in what follows and leave it to chapter 7 to put this assumption in perspective.

5.3. The model as estimated for the 1960s fixed-rate regime in the UK

We begin with a brief description of the balance of payments sector of the model (much of it recapitulating earlier chapters); we will revert to the domestic sector.

5.3.1. The balance of payments sectors

The import equations (see Rees and Layard [1971] for a full treatment) are disaggregated by broad end-use categories and most of the equations are specified in terms of demand factors (relative prices or costs, income and trend terms) modified by pressure-of-demand variables.

The export equations (see chapter 3) consist of foreigners' demand for UK manufactured exports (with a long lag on relative prices distributed symmetrically over five years and a price elasticity of 1.5) and the domestic supply of manufactured exports, related to domestic demands suitably weighted and a trend representing capacity in exportables industries. Provided supply exceeds demand, exports are determined by the demand equation; if demand exceeds supply, exports are determined by a weighted average of demand and supply, corresponding to diversion of exports to the home market. Exports of other goods are exogenous.

Export prices of manufactures (see chapter 3 again) have an elasticity of $\frac{2}{3}$ to domestic costs and $\frac{1}{3}$ to foreign export prices of manufactures (converted into £s). This is supposed to reflect the long-run equilibrium at which the overall supply of exportables is just distributed between foreign and home demand; the relative weight on domestic as compared with foreign prices reflects the relative size of the elasticity of domestic resources transfer (i.e. traded versus non-traded goods) compared with that of foreign demand. All import prices and export prices of non-manufactures are exogenous.

These sectors, given certain critical assumptions about the domestic economy to be discussed in the next section, give rise to a reduced-form relationship from the exchange rate to the current account of the balance of payments. This, as would be expected, has the appearance of the now well-known 'J-curve', whose existence was more casually inferred by many British economists from the experience of the UK 1967 devaluation and by many US economists from the US experience since the Smithsonian agreement. The total length of the lag (in a static economy) is about ten years in the model because the price effects of the exchange rate change takes about four years to work out and then the trade effects of the price change take about another five; but by the end of sixth year the marginal changes are very small and can be effectively ignored.

The exchange rate in question is the effective (i.e. some weighted average) rate, though during the estimation period, the distinction between dollar and effective rate was not important, and they could be justifiably treated as the same. However, in simulations for the period since mid-1971 they are of course different.

With such long lags, the exchange rate market would react perversely to exchange rate changes in the absence of equilibrating capital flows. This point was first made formally by Britton [1970] and it has been pounced on popularly as a 'proof' that floating exchange rates would be unstable, it being assumed that capital flows can but be disequilibrating or at best unresponsive when trade is so slow to respond.

Yet this assumption appears to be incorrect. In the capital flows sector of the model (see chapter 4) it was found that not only did short-term capital respond positively to the change in the covered differential (and hence negatively to the spot exchange rate) as well as directly to the change in exchange rate expectations but that a more powerful relationship partly in levels held for other (long-term) capital. Forward rates at three-months and one-year are determined, in accordance with the conventional theory of forward exchange, by the expected future spot rate and the current spot rate adjusted for the interest differential. Expectations of the future spot rate were hypothesised to be determined (semi-rationally) by some weighted average of past current account balances.

This expectations function is derived (the Appendix 5.A shows the formal derivation) on the assumption of a 'popular' model, whose principal difference from the 'true' model is that there is rather a short lag before exchange rate effects on the nominal current balance are fully felt (for convenience, the lag is omitted in this model); it is suggested here that this was the generally accepted model during the 1960s and was not significantly modified during the period.

Branson [1972] recorded that by that time lags were thought to be spread over only two years; this in itself is short relative to what is proposed in chapter 3, but may well have been longer than the view in the mid-60s before the big UK and US devaluations of 1967 and 1971.

Reducing these relationships to 'quasi-reduced' form, we obtain a four-equation system in the nominal current balance, C; the capital balance, ΔK; the expected exchange rate (1 year ahead), S^{E+4}; the change in reserves, I; and the spot exchange rate, S. Either $S = S_0$ (the 'fixed' parity) or $I = O$ (the floating case) can be exogenously given; more generally a reaction function trading off S against I could be specified (the dirty float). So we have (in the fixed rate case):

Current Balance $$C = \sum_{i=0}^{23} b_i S_{-i} + k_1 \qquad (5.1)$$

where $b_0 = -8.34$, $b_1 = -0.07$, $b_2 = -0.97$, $b_3 = 2.45$, $b_4 = 5.23$,
$b_5 = 4.71$, $b_6 = 3.84$, $b_7 = 1.82$, $b_8 = 2.49$, $b_9 = 2.52$,
$b_{10} = 2.43$, $b_{11} = 2.38$, $b_{12} = 2.2$, $b_{13} = 1.27$, $b_{14} = 1.59$,
$b_{15} = 1.2$, $b_{16} = 1.33$, $b_{17} = 1.04$, $b_{18} = 0.96$, $b_{19} = 0.96$,
$b_{20} = 0.47$, $b_{21} = 0.5$, $b_{22} = 0.12$, $b_{23} = 0.26$, $\Sigma b_i = 30.39$.

$$\text{Capital balance} \qquad \Delta K = \sum_{i=0}^{4} h_i(S - S_0)_{-i} - \sum_{i=0}^{4} j_i(S^{E+4} - S_0)_{-i} + k_2 \qquad (5.2)$$

where $h_0 = 254$, $h_1 = -167$, $h_2 = -12$, $h_3 = -25$, $h_4 = -21$;
$j_0 = 294$, $j_1 = -207$, $j_2 = -12$, $j_3 = -25$, $j_4 = -21$.
$\Sigma h_i = \Sigma j_i = 29$.

$$\text{Expected exchange rate:} \quad S^{E+4} = -\sum_{i=0}^{14} a_i C_{-i} + S_0 + k_3 \qquad (5.3a)$$
(4 quarters a head)

where $a_0 = 0$, $a_1 = 0.007$, $a_2 = 0.005$, $a_3 = 0.004$, $a_4 = 0.003$, a_5 through $a_{11} = 0.002$, a_{12} through $a_{14} = 0.001$. $\Sigma a_i = 0.036$.
Average lag = 5 (quarters).

$$\text{Balance of payments identity:} \quad C + \Delta K + I = 0. \qquad (5.4)$$

The model is quarterly: C, ΔK, I are expressed in £ million per quarter, S, S_0 as percentage deviations from the initial parity, in this fixed rate case; k_1, k_2, k_3 are constants. (A rise in S is a depreciation in the exchange rate.) In the floating rate case, the model alters in two ways: (5.3a) becomes:

$$S^{E+4} = -\sum_{i=0}^{14} a_i C_{-i} + \sum_{i=0}^{14} \frac{a_i}{\sum_i a_i} S_{-i} + k_3 \text{ where the } a_i, b_i \qquad (5.3b)$$

where the a_i, b_i are given as before.

In addition, S can now be taken as percentage deviations from the parity before the float; since there is now no parity, $S_0 = 0$ and drops out, and we alter the constants as necessary.

5.3.2. The domestic economy

It is a familiar implication of the 'absorption' controversy of the 1950s (Alexander [1952] and Johnson [1961] who puts it in perspective) that certain assumptions about the domestic economy, that have the effect of not 'making room' for the expenditure-switching effects of exchange rate

Figure 5.1
Flow chart of the model's external side.

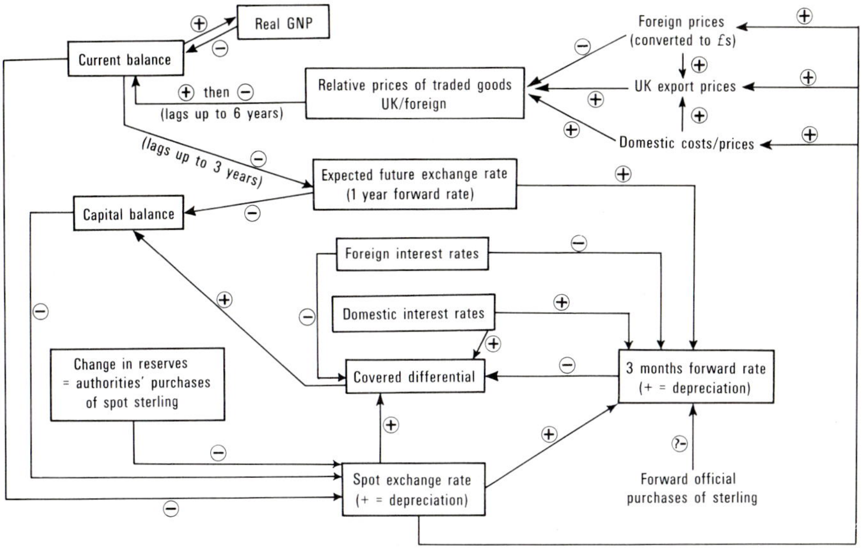

changes will cause them solely to change relative price levels, leaving the current balance unaffected; Meade [1951] has exhaustively considered the possibilities. The monetary approach in its simplest form, in which output is at constant full employment, there are no home goods and arbitrage is perfect, can be considered as a pure absorption approach, in which the demand for money relative to its initial supply determines absorption. For dynamic analysis this is clearly unsatisfactory; the study of dynamics is however at such a rudimentary stage relative to that of comparative statics that at this point of time dynamic formulation is largely a matter of taste. It seems fair to say that, for all the faults and myopia of the bulk of the work on large econometric models, it represents an honest and useful attempt to explore dynamic structures, if often with theory trailing behind the 'discovery' of empirical regularities.

For this reason the balance of payments sector has been linked up with the Treasury model of the UK economy (which is probably as good as others available for the UK at present). In simulations with this combined model, reported below, it has not been possible to constrain the model formally to generate exactly the equilibrium exchange rate that would emerge from a monetary approach; but it can be taken that the equilibrium exchange rate is broadly the same. What the simulations are intended to illustrate is the disequilibrium behaviour of the economy and the rate when subjected to shocks that do not affect the equilibrium exchange rate. The particular assumption made about monetary policy in response to such shocks is that it is, in the same spirit as Dornbusch [1975], 'coercive', that is, it causes absorption to 'make room' for the expenditure-switching effects induced by the rate change. This assumption is made for illustrative convenience, in that it is an extreme case; the other extreme being where monetary policy deliberately 'frustrates' the exchange rate change by causing absorption to be inflexible.

A brief sketch of the Treasury model on the domestic side is now given – but for a full description of it in a version close to that used see Evans, Shepherd and Riley [1973], and for more recent versions, see H.M. Treasury [1974, 1975]. The model is of the familiar multiplier-accelerator type. An aggregate consumption function (in real terms) provides the multiplier; real investment and stock equations disaggregated between main sectors (manufacturing, residential etc.) constitute the accelerator. Tax parameters modify these demand equations, while real public sector expenditure is an exogenous demand factor. In the version used here, monetary effects are imposed exogenously (this deficiency has been partly remedied, however, in recent unpublished work on the model).

The supply side of the model parallels the Okun's Law approach for the labour market and the Wharton approach for capacity utilisation. Hence, the supply of labour is given demographically while the demand for labour is a distributed-lag function of real *GDP*; unemployment reacts to changes in net supply with a coefficient of 0.5 reflecting marginal changes in participation. For capital stock, an index of capacity is created by linking peaks in a *GDP* index (these supposedly representing full capacity output); the actual *GDP* index is then related to this to obtain capacity utilisation. These two approaches are not necessarily consistent with each other or with the investment equation; further research is proceeding on integrated labour/capital demand and supply functions.

In principle, the interaction of the demand and supply sides should modify actual real expenditures. This modification is not built into the model for any of the domestic demand equations as yet though it is incorporated as an exogenous adjustment to them. However, it is built into the export and import equations discussed above.

Determination of domestic costs and prices is through a reduced form relating them to unit labour costs and import prices, with lags over a few quarters. Earnings respond to the rate of change of a labour demand pressure index (not a Phillips-type relationship but supposed to reflect overtime etc.) and (with an elasticity of unity lagged over three years) to retail prices.

5.4. Simulations with the model before learning takes place

Chapter 6 below considers the model's behaviour when full rationality has been acquired by speculators. We here consider the prior question of stability in the original semi-rational state; it is also the question of most immediate relevance to behaviour immediately after the shift to floating. We compare in particular the stability of fixed and floating rates. In what follows we set out the actual stimulated values that result from a single permanent shock to each system. The simulations are carried on for a large enough number of periods to exhibit the stability properties clearly. A formal derivation of the stability properties is difficult and inconvenient with such a large model, and is not attempted.

We give the model the same shock in both cases, adding £100 million to the current balance in each quarter throughout the 20-year simulation period. Such a 'permanent shock' is of course a strange fiction, used simply to bring out the dynamic responses within the model.[4]

In the fixed rate case, it is assumed that the rate is 'adjustable' and that it adjusts by 5% when reserve losses or gains have cumulated to £850 million (about $2 billion), the critical amount at which it is supposed that a 'one-way option' – or crisis – is produced.

The results are shown over a seven-year span in Table 5.1 and Chart 5.2.

[4] It may be thought of either as the result of a change in the true equilibrium rate which is not directly perceived by speculators given their model or as a serially correlated shock, where $\rho = 1$ and which is permanent, for illustrative purposes only; it is possible to derive the effects of shorter-lasting shocks from these 'permanent' effects in the floating case by simple subtraction, in the fixed case by rather more complicated calculations (because of the non-linearity introduced by the parity changes).

Table 5.1
Effects of permanent current balance shock with fixed (but adjustable) rate.[2]

Year	Quarter	S^{E} +4	S	C	$C + \Delta K$
1	1	0	0	−100	−100
	2	0.7	0	−100	−312
	3	1.3	0	−100	−321
	4	1.7	0	−100	−318
2	1	7.0	5	−142	−340
	2	7.5	5	−142	−400
	3	7.9	5	−147	−389
	4	13.3	10	−176	−418
3	1	13.8	10	−151	−443
	2	19.0	15	−174	−403
	3	19.4	15	−143	−414
	4	19.5	15	−112	−314
4	1	24.4	20	−48	−154
	2	23.9	20	−8	17
	3	23.2	20	49	172
	4	22.3	20	107	341
5	1	21.3	20	161	508
	2	15.1	15	255	698
	3	13.4	15	293	911
	4	6.9	10	377	1049
6	1	0.1	5	444	1258
	2	−6.8	0	494	1411
	3	−13.7	−5	536	1513
	4	−20.6	−10	550	1570
7	1	−27.1	−15	546	1538
	2	−33.4	−20	518	1444
	3	−41.1	−25	426	1792
	4	−44.7	−30	326	829
8	1	−44.3	−30	151	530
	2	−47.7	−35	68	−19
	3	−46.5	−35	−92	−217
	4	−44.9	−35	−242	−531
9	1	−41.5	−35	−301	−1195
	2	−33.9	−30	−476	−1348
	3	−25.3	−25	−605	−1891
	4	−16.9	−20	−695	−2086
10	1	−8.2	−15	−751	−2346
	2	0.3	−10	−777	−2450
	3	8.7	−5	−778	−2521
	4	16.1	0	−758	−2297

Year	Quarter	S^{E+4}	S	C	$C + \Delta K$
11	1	23.3	5	−719	−2202
	2	30.0	10	−664	−2004
	3	36.1	15	−595	−1749
	4	41.7	20	−514	−1490
12	1	46.7	25	−423	−1130
	2	51.0	30	−323	−797
	3	49.9	30	−149	−407
	4	52.7	35	−66	100

[2] *Notes:* $I = -(C + \Delta K)$ by the balance of payments identity. S = pegged exchange rate (% deviation from the initial parity); S^{E+4} = expected S; C = current balance (£ million per quarter); I = foreign exchange intervention (£m. per qtr.); ΔK = capital account balance (£m. per qtr.); the 'shock' to C is set at − 100 (£m. per qtr.) in each period from Year 1, quarter 1. Adjustable peg is shifted by 5% if cumulated I since the last peg change exceeds £850 million; shift takes place at the end of the quarter.

As with the floating rate, the 'fixed' rate is also cyclical; however, it is clear that the cycles are explosive and unstable in the long run since the rate moves progressively more rapidly during the period, until by the first quarter of the year it is dropping by 5% per quarter, after rising 20% in the first three years.

This result confirms the now-widespread view that a 'fixed-but-adjustable' parity was, given market and other conditions of the early 1970s, unmanageable at that time. If one compares this simulation with the international experience from mid-1971 (when the market first started to speculate on new parities) to spring-1973 (when de facto floating became the rule), there are some striking similarities.

The reason for this instability is that, when the current balance worsens with the shock, speculators interpret this as a deterioration in relative price competitiveness requiring a devaluation; they therefore move funds out of sterling. The authorities, instead of standing firm as under the old rules of the fixed rate game (enumerated in the Bretton Woods agreement), try to stabilise the market after a few quarters' losses of reserves by a small devaluation of 5%. However, this adjustment in the peg makes the current balance progressively worse for the succeeding three quarters and only makes up this worsening in the fifth. The capital outflow therefore gets worse. The authorities respond by a further devaluation, provoking a further worsening in the current balance and continued capital outflows on the previous scale. At this point, the effects of the earlier devaluations begin to improve the current balance but speculators, still impressed by the earlier deficits, continue to withdraw funds, precipitating a further drop in the rate. The turn-round in the current balance however is now occurring with such violence because of the overshooting in the exchange rate that the whole process is plunged into reverse. On the way back up, the peg is soon moving at the maximum speed of once per quarter; the market has by the middle of the seventh year become clearly quite uncontrollable. At this point, the rate has been revalued by 20% on its original starting point (and risen 40% in a year and a half), while the current balance is running at a surplus of £2 billion p.a. and total reserves accumulating at the rate of £6 billion p.a. In practice of course the authorities would have allowed the rate to float long before.

However, when we turn to the floating rate in this pre-learning situation we find that it too is both cyclical and unstable, as shown in Table 5.2 (also Chart 5.2)[5] It is apparent that it behaves in a very similar way to the 'fixed-but-adjustable' rate. As we shall see in chapter 6, not much importance is attached to this instability because of the model-learning process that we envisage. It is nevertheless of interest as providing some insight into the early stages of behaviour – the infancy, so to speak – of a floating rate system.

The instability occurs because, as the rate drops in response to the shock, the current balance worsens. Speculators respond 'naively' to this worsening and withdraw funds, so pushing the rate down further. However, they respond with more than naivety; believing that the response of trade to the exchange rate is rapid, they mentally adjust the current account figures for the improvement they should have seen. This of course makes the figures look correspondingly worse, so that their withdrawal of funds and the corresponding drop in the rate is the greater. As the rate drops, even though after a time the current account begins to improve, it is not improving fast enough to keep up with this mental adjustment, so that the rate continues to drop. The improvement only catches up with the adjustment after about $3\frac{1}{2}$ years (roughly the total lag on the trade equation minus that on the speculators, weights, the a_i in equation (5.3)), at which point the process as in the adjustable peg goes into strong reverse. By the middle of the seventh year it too is appreciating at about 5% per quarter. Hence similar instability to the

[5] I am grateful to Mrs Christine Moore of Manchester University for programming the floating-rate model and obtaining these results.

adjustable-peg case is induced here by speculators rationally applying the wrong model, there by the authorities attempting to placate the market by over-frequent adjustments.

This result must be qualified somewhat. The precise form of the pre-learning floating rate model was derived above, on the basis of arguments developed in Appendix 5.A. The crucial modification is the addition of a weighted average of past exchange rates, $\sum_i \frac{a_i}{(\Sigma a_i)} S_{-i}$, to eq. (5.3a) for the expected rate, S^{E+4} (the 'mental adjustment' just referred to). It could reasonably be argued – and was for some time by the author – that this modification was inappropriate. Speculators may learn, perhaps rapidly, about the length of the lags and so discount the effects of these past movements in the exchange rate more heavily; these movements could then be at least partly assimilated into the error term, v, and hence $\sum_i \frac{a^i}{(\Sigma a_i)} S^{-i}$ would drop out or have a smaller effect.

It is therefore of interest to compare the stability properties of the floating rate when this modification is dropped, that is the model is run with exactly the same parameters as in the pegged case ('unmodified'). The results for this floating case are shown in Table 5.3 (and Chart 5.2). The floating rate is mildly cyclical and overshoots somewhat. Thus the long-term equilibrium rate after such a permanent shock would be roughly 4% lower than before. However, the spot rate overshoots to a depreciation of 5.34% before cyclically returning to −0.9% (an appreciation); the length of this first cycle, trough to trough, is 25 quarters. The next cycle has a peak of 5.28%, a trough of −0.73%, and a length of 29 quarters; the next a peak of 5.15%, a trough of −0.62% and a length also of 29 quarters. This indicates that in this model the floating rate is cyclical and stable, but that the damping factor is close to unity so that the number of cycles required for convergence appears to be about 27, each cycle having about a seven year span – not far short of two centuries in all!

Nevertheless, this does show that the faster speculators learn about the system, the less its instability, even if they are still basing their assessment of the exchange rate equilibrium on a partially inappropriate indicator (namely a weighted average of past current balances). This is not a surprising, but it is a reassuring, conclusion. The rate is still cyclical and only very slightly damped because the indicator is inappropriate. Thus, as the rate drops in

Table 5.2
Effects of permanent current balance shock with floating rate (modified model).[a]

Year	Quarter	S^{E+4}	S	C
1	1	0	0.4	−103
	2	0.8	1.6	−114
	3	1.7	2.9	−125
	4	2.7	4.3	−136
2	1	3.8	5.7	−145
	2	4.9	7.2	−147
	3	6.1	8.7	−144
	4	7.4	10.3	−136
3	1	8.7	11.8	−124
	2	9.9	13.2	−108
	3	11.2	14.5	−86
	4	12.4	15.7	−60
4	1	13.4	16.6	−28
	2	14.3	17.2	9
	3	14.9	17.5	50
	4	15.2	17.3	96
5	1	15.1	16.6	145
	2	14.6	15.3	197
	3	13.7	13.5	249
	4	12.2	11.0	301
6	1	10.3	8.0	350
	2	7.8	4.4	394
	3	4.9	0.3	430
	4	1.6	−4.3	458
7	1	−2.2	−9.3	473
	2	−6.3	−14.5	475
	3	−10.6	−19.8	461
	4	−15.1	−25.1	430
8	1	−19.6	−30.2	380
	2	−23.9	−34.8	311
	3	−27.9	−38.9	222
	4	−31.4	−42.0	114
9	1	34.3	44.1	−13
	2	−36.3	−44.9	−156
	3	−37.2	−44.2	−315
	4	−36.9	−41.8	−484
10	1	−35.2	−37.6	−661
	2	−32.0	−31.4	−839
	3	−27.2	−23.2	−1014
	4	−20.8	−13.1	−1180

Year	Quarter	S^{E+4}	S	C
11	1	−12.6	−1.0	−1328
	2	−2.8	12.9	−1452
	3	8.6	28.4	−1546
	4	21.3	45.2	−1600
12	1	35.2	62.8	−1608
	2	49.9	80.9	−1564
	3	65.1	98.9	−1461
	4	80.2	116.2	−1296

[a] *Notes:* $\Delta K = -C$ since $I = 0$. Other notes as for Table 5.1; S = floating rate (% deviations from pre-float parity).

response to the current account deterioration, speculators move out funds and push the rate down further because they respond to the initial worsening of the current account; but their response is not a strong one and the lagged effects on trade soon catch up with the deepening 'J' effect, and the process reverses. In subsequent chapters we will trace the effects on the stability properties of the floating rate system first as speculators learn fully about the system and secondly as their behaviour adapts to its properties.

5.5. Conclusions

We have shown that the pegged rate system was, within the model we have estimated for the UK, unstable, given the 'fixed-but-adjustable' operating rules of the early 1970s. This will not surprise many. It has long been accepted by economists that within such a system the 'one-way option' phenomenon makes crisis endemic. Abandonment of it was inevitable, once it was recognised that for reasons of monetary independence national governments would no longer accept the de facto fixity of rates that prevailed in the fifties and early sixties.

More interestingly, we have found that the infancy of a floating rate system is prone also to exchange rate instability; in this 'modified' version of the model, this instability is as great as in the fixed-but-adjustable case. This conclusion is not at variance with the erratic behaviour of exchange rates since 1973, though this can also be accounted for in other ways (e.g. government pronouncements, or rumours provoked by the 'reform' of the

Figure 5.2
Effects of £ 100 m. per quarter reduction in current balance on exchange rate.

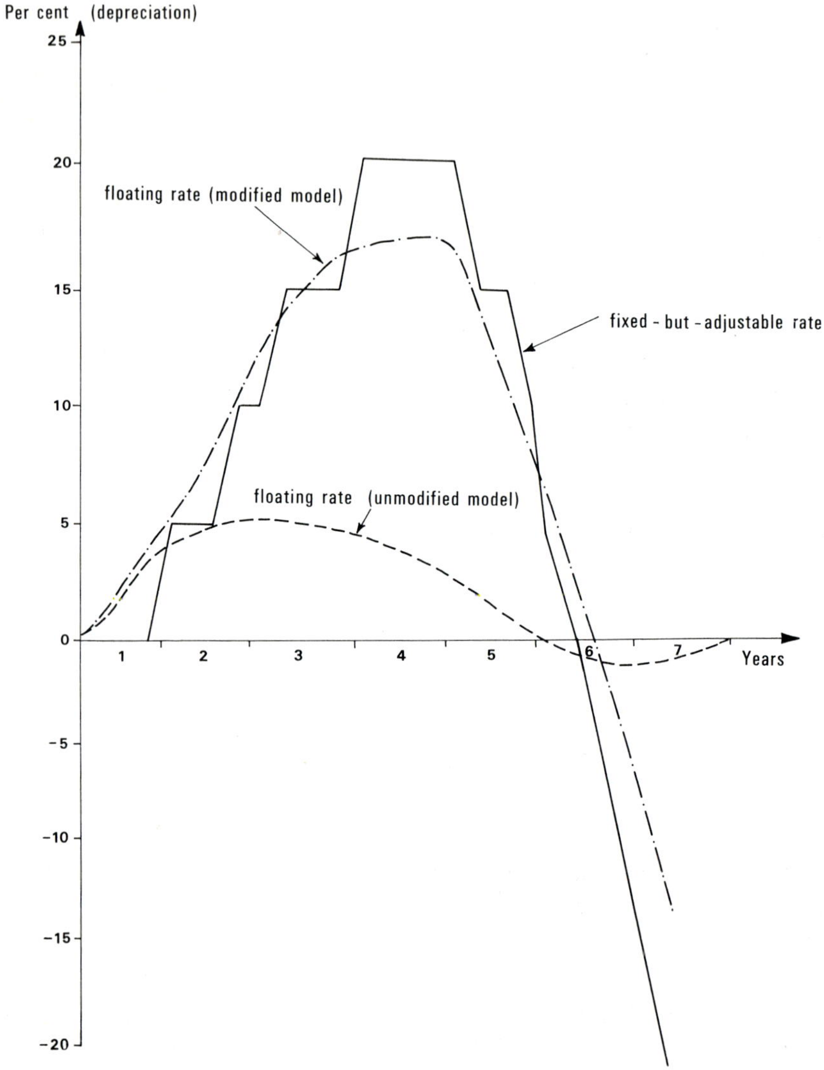

Table 5.3
Effects of permanent shock to current balance with floating rate (unmodified model).[2]

Year	Quarter	S^{E+4}	S	C
1	1	0.0	0.41	−103
	2	0.74	1.59	−113
	3	1.37	2.53	−121
	4	1.90	3.34	−128
2	1	2.34	4.06	−130
	2	2.69	4.63	−125
	3	2.93	5.03	−115
	4	3.07	5.26	−102
3	1	3.11	5.34	−87
	2	3.08	5.30	−71
	3	2.99	5.15	−54
	4	2.86	4.92	−37
4	1	2.67	4.59	−20
	2	2.43	4.17	5
	3	2.12	3.65	9
	4	1.70	3.00	22
5	1	1.28	2.33	33
	2	0.85	1.66	41
	3	0.43	1.01	46
	4	0.04	0.42	47
6	1	−0.29	−0.08	45
	2	−0.56	−0.47	39
	3	−0.74	−0.74	30
	4	−0.83	−0.86	18
7	1	−0.83	−0.84	4
	2	−0.74	−0.69	−11
	3	−0.57	−0.39	−29
	4	−0.32	0.02	−46
8	1	−0.23	0.53	−62
	2	0.36	1.12	−7
	3	0.76	1.76	−90
	4	1.17	2.42	−100
9	1	1.58	3.06	−107
	2	1.97	3.67	−110
	3	2.32	4.21	−106
	4	2.61	4.66	−106
10	1	2.83	4.99	−99
	2	2.97	5.20	−89
	3	3.03	5.28	−76
	4	3.01	5.21	−61

Year	Quarter	S^{E+4}	S	C
11	1	2.89	5.01	−45
	2	2.69	4.69	−28
	3	2.42	4.25	−12
	4	2.10	3.72	3
12	1	1.73	3.12	17
	2	1.33	2.49	29
	3	0.92	1.85	37
	4	0.52	1.23	43

[a] *Notes:* $\Delta K = -C$ since $I = 0$. Other notes as for Table 5.1; S = floating rate (% deviations from pre-float parity).

international monetary system). We go on to consider the asymptotic properties of the floating rate system once full-model-learning has occurred. Meanwhile, the option of 'managing' the infant floating rate is open, that is of central banks acting as stabilising speculators (but not as targets for speculation as in the pegged case). Given the requirement of flexibility because of monetary independence such transitional management could be an attractive way of limiting instability until the learning process has progressed beyond this stage.

We also found that, as speculators come to allow for longer lags, so the instability is reduced even though they continue to use past current balances as the indicator of exchange rate disequilibrium; in the 'unmodified' model, where the effects of past exchange rate movements are totally disregarded, the exchange rate is just stable.

The floating rate may perhaps start out life as the 'modified' model but its course of development is likely then to run through the 'unmodified' model all the way to full rationality with appropriately adapted parameters. To these subsequent developments we next turn.

Appendix 5.A: Semi-rational expectations in a structural payments model

1. The floating case. We suppose that S^{E+4}, 'semi-rational' expectations of the future exchange rate, is governed by the 'popular' model consisting of:

$$C = (\eta - 1)XS + u + g \tag{5.A.1}$$
$$\Delta K = h\,\Delta(S - S^E) \tag{5.A.2}$$

$$S^E = ES_{+1} \qquad (5.A.3)$$
$$C + \Delta K + I = 0 \qquad (5.A.4)$$

where E denotes the expectation taken within this model (and not within the true model). Here (5.A.1) differs from (5.1) in two respects. First, it has no lags; hence $(\eta - 1)X = \Sigma b_i$ (where η = the sum of the price elasticities in trade, X = the value of exports in the base year). Second, it has an error term, u, assumed to be random, and an exogenous variable, g, which is a composite of the systematic influences on trade other than the effects of the exchange rate.

(5.A.2) is a simplified version of (5.2), with no adjustment lags, no portfolio growth coefficient on the level of interest rates, and S^E replacing S^{E+4}.

(5.A.3) indicates that exchange rate expectations are now derived rationally on the basis of this model and the information available (i.e. 'semi-rationally' given that this is not the true model).

(5.A.4) is simply (5.4).

We first solve these equations for S^E as in the fully rational case described in Chapter 7. It is shown there that:

$$S^E = W_0 \sum_{i=0}^{\infty} \mu^{i+1} u_{-i} \quad \text{where} \quad W_0 = \frac{-1}{(\eta - 1)X + h(1 - \mu)} \qquad (7.10)$$

in terms of % deviations from equilibrium. To this we explicitly add S^*, the equilibrium rate, to obtain S^E in terms of the actual exchange rate; S^* will be a function of g (to be precise $S^* = g/(\eta - 1)X$). Hence, here:

$$S^E = W_0 \sum_{i=0}^{\infty} \mu^{i+1} u_{-i} + S^*. \qquad (5.A.5)$$

We wish to derive expression (5.3b) for the expected exchange rate four quarters ahead. So in fact we require:

$$S^{E+4} = W_0 \sum_{i=0}^{\infty} \mu^{i+4} u_{-i} + S^* \qquad (5.A.6)$$

We assume that $\sum_{i=0}^{\infty} \mu^{i+4} u_{-1}$ is small enough to be neglected. We further assume that speculators' semi-rationality extends to not knowing the true S^* (because they 'confuse' u and g). Therefore, conditional on their information:

$$S^{E+4} = ES^*, \tag{5.A.7}$$

where ES^* is their best estimate of S^*.

To derive an estimate of S^* from the popular model, it is assumed that $C = v + b\,(S - S^*)$ where v picks up random movements in S^*, national income, etc., and $b = (\eta - 1)X = \Sigma b_i$. Now $EC = b(S - ES^*)$ but the variance around the expected value can be reduced by taking a lag-weighted average up to N quarters back, $\sum_{i=0}^{N} w_i C_{-i}$ (where $\Sigma w_i = 1$ and the weights diminish because of the opposing forces of variance-reduction and up-to-dateness). So

$$ES^* = -\sum_{i=0}^{N} a_i C_{-i} + \sum_{i=0}^{N} w_i S_{-i} \quad \text{where} \quad a_i = \frac{w_i}{b} \tag{5.A.8}$$

is a good (i.e. low variance) estimate of the equilibrium exchange rate. This is therefore the expression for S^{E+4} which is used in the model of chapter 5. It is of interest that the popular model appeared to embody a correct notion of the long-run elasticity since $\Sigma a_i = 0.036$ which is roughly equal to $\dfrac{1}{\Sigma b_i} = 0.033$.

2. The pegged rate case. We proceed identically in this case. We solve the model set out in chapter 7 for the 'pegged' case, add S^* to allow for a non-zero equilibrium, drop the constant term which tends to zero, and derive:

$$S^E = A\alpha(1 - \delta)(1 - b)\left[\sum_{i=0}^{\infty} V_{i+1} + \sum_{i=0}^{\infty} \delta^{i+1} B^i \sum_{i=0}^{\infty} V_i\right] u_{\ i} + S^* \tag{5.A.9}$$

where the parameters are as defined in chapter 7 pp. 185–190.

Making the same assumption as in the floating case, we obtain $S^{E+4} = ES^*$. We now have:

$C = v + b\,(S_0 - S^*)$, where v picks up random movements in S^*, national income, etc., as before; from this

$$\sum_{i=0}^{N} w_i C_{-i} = \sum_{i=0}^{N} w_i v_{-i} + b(S_0 - ES^*) \tag{5.A.10}$$

so that

$$ES^* = \frac{-\sum_{i=0}^{N} w_i C_{-i}}{b} + S_0.$$

There is a complication in using this estimate immediately after a parity change, since clearly the C_{-i} from before the parity change should be excluded from the measure. This, however, is most conveniently handled by a post-parity-change dummy variable whose values decay at the same rate as the influence of these C_{-i} decays in the expression ES^*; given the speed of decline in the w_i, this variable would fall off quickly.

Chapter 6

STRUCTURAL AND MONETARY THEORIES OF THE BALANCE OF PAYMENTS: STABILITY AND RATIONAL EXPECTATIONS[1]

6.1. Introduction

The monetary theory of the balance of payments is familiar from the writings of Johnson [1973], Dornbusch [1973], Polak [1957] and of course David Hume [1752]; and developments continue, e.g. Parkin [1974 and 1977] and Jonson [1976]. The structural theory, as it might be termed, stems from Meade [1951], and has given rise to numerous studies of trade flows (e.g. Adams et al. [1969]), as well as a more recent interest in capital flows equations (for a good survey, see Hodjera [1973]). The approach attempts to explain the components of the balance of payments, separating especially the current from the capital account; structural equations are estimated for exports, imports and capital flows, each of which have the exchange rate as an independent variable as well as other macro-economic variables such as prices, real income and interest rates; when these equations are combined with the rest of the macro-economic model, the exchange rate may be regarded either as exogenous (the fixed rate case) or as endogenous, with the authorities not intervening (free floating) or following a flexible intervention policy ('dirty' floating). A model of this sort is currently in use in the Treasury for the UK, and for

[1] This chapter was stimulated by the proceedings of the Money Study Group Conference at Oxford, September 1974, particularly contributions by Bill Allen, Rudiger Dornbusch, Harry Johnson and Marcus Miller. I have also benefited from discussions in the Manchester Inflation Workshop on this general area, and particularly from points made by Malcolm Gray, David Laidler, Michael Parkin, Michael Sumner and George Zis.

an account of the basic model see H.M. Treasury [1974]; a more detailed account of the balance of payments sector is given in chapter 5, while particular equations are dealt with in Rees and Layard [1971] on imports, chapter 3 (exports), chapter 4 (capital flows). This model appears to be of interest in several respects:

(i) it explicitly embodies exchange rate expectations as a lagged endogenous variable, and so is capable of giving an empirical answer to the question of whether floating rates are stable or not.

ii) the same structural equations are used – with scope for modification of specific structural paramaters – to solve for all exchange rate regimes.

iii) the notorious 'J-curve' is produced, not from casual observation of 'Js' since 1967 or Smithsonian, but from the estimated equations themselves.

It is argued elsewhere (see, for example, Beenstock [1976]) that in long-term equilibrium the properties of the structural theory, properly specified, are those of the monetary theory. This is consistent with the observation by Johnson [1973] that the monetary theory is essentially a long-run theory of the balance of payments.[2] Thus if the structural model is stable without intervention or if intervention ensures stability, then the differences between the structural and monetary theories would solely relate to the features of the dynamic path to equilibrium.

It is the characteristics of this dynamic path that this chapter is concerned to explore. The monetary theory has not as yet been developed in this dynamic aspect. What we hope to show is that it can be substantially enriched in this respect by incorporating the essential features of the 'structural' approach. There would then seem to be no point in distinguishing the 'monetary' from the 'structural' approach; rather we should distinguish 'short-run' and 'long-run' responses within the same general framework.

Nevertheless, a prior question which has exercised many economists is that of the stability of the freely floating exchange rate. Within the monetary theory as specified in its simplest form the exchange rate is necessarily stable, as explored below. However the structural approach has been shown to give rise to prima facie instability under certain conditions. Britton [1970] demonstrated that, given a response lag of net trade volume to the exchange rate (the J-curve), the exchange rate will be unstable if exchange rate expectations are

[2] It is also of interest that some of Johnson's earlier writings (see Johnson [1961]) contributed to the advance of the structural theory.

sufficiently elastic. It is generally believed that, if exchange rate expectations are formed 'rationally' in the sense of Muth [1961], there will be exchange rate stability. Nevertheless even this proposition could be questioned (see for example Allen and Miller [1974]) on the grounds that at least one of the roots in the characteristic equation for the exchange rate will be greater than unity under rational expectations. In general this will cause an explosive solution unless the initial conditions coincidentally impose a zero coefficient on this root.

The first point is well taken and gives rise to a purely empirical question; are the parameter values in such a model such as to ensure stability? This question is discussed in chapter 5 and it was found that a model of this sort for the UK appeared likely (given that some modification of the pegged regime parameters was probably appropriate) to be unstable. This however assumes that speculators do not learn; and it was also argued there that speculators will follow a learning process (a 'model-learning' process) which would lead them asymptotically to fully rational expectations using the 'true' model. This evidence therefore merely suggests that in its *early* years the floating rate may be unstable.

The second point is more serious, both because it holds regardless of the empirical evidence and especially because the speculative learning process would itself converge, as argued, on fully rational expectations. In the rest of this chapter therefore, expectations will be assumed to be rational; and it will be argued that unstable roots can indeed be ruled out, as is generally believed, by imposition of a boundary condition suggested by the monetary theory of the balance of payments. We proceed within a deterministic framework in this paper, since we are concerned here solely with stability, and not stochastic, properties.

In the rest of this chapter, we explore the stability of the floating exchange rate within a variety of 'structural' and 'monetary' models of the balance of payments, assuming throughout that expectations are rational. We begin with simple models of each type (sections 6.2 and 6.3) and gradually relax their simplifications (sections 6.4–6.6) until we ultimately arrive (section 6.8) at a general model of the balance of payments, which incorporates both the structural and the monetary elements; it is in other words a general equilibrium model with a reasonably realistic dynamic structure. The basic point made is that monetary stability, defined as a money supply that is exogenous or at most reacts with a less-than-unit elasticity to the domestic price level, is a necessary condition for stability, since without it the equilibrium exchange rate is indeterminate. Furthermore, it is a recurring feature of these models, because of the rational expectations element, that they exhibit formal instability in the absence of boundary conditions. Such a 'stability problem' has begun to receive some attention in the literature; it is argued here (and has also been argued by others recently) that boundary conditions should be applied and are sufficient to ensure stability. Much of the discussion that follows considers some of the boundary conditions that are relevant to each model. Finally the general model's stability properties (its rate of approach to equilibrium and the extent of cyclicality) are considered in some detail. The practical conclusion is that one should expect rather slow convergence to equilibrium after a shock to the exchange rate – perhaps about 5 years – and that the path is likely to be cyclical and overshoot at least once before effective convergence.

6.2. Two simple models

The monetary theory, in its simplest form with a freely floating rate (though this has only recently been explored in the literature,[3] which generally assumes fixed rates) could be written as:

$$\begin{aligned}
&\text{Home Prices:} \quad && P = \frac{\bar{M}}{\bar{y}} && (6.1)\\
&\text{Home Goods Market:} \quad && \bar{y} - e = t && (6.2)\\
&\text{Foreign Exchange Market:} \quad && Pt + \Delta K = 0 && (6.3)\\
&\text{Foreign Prices:} \quad && P^* = \frac{\bar{M}^*}{\bar{y}^*} && (6.4)\\
&\text{Foreign Goods Market:} \quad && \bar{y}^* - e^* = -t && (6.5)\\
&\text{Traded goods arbitrage condition:} \quad && S = P - P^* && (6.6)\\
&\text{Speculative capital flows:} \quad && \Delta K = h(\Delta S - \Delta S^E) && (6.7)\\
&\text{Rational exchange rate expectations:} \quad && S^E - \bar{S}_{+1} && (6.8)
\end{aligned}$$

where M is money, P (an index of) prices of traded goods, e real spending, y real income, t the real trade balance, S the exchange rate (in percent deviations from the base for the price indices; a rise is a depreciation of the home currency), S_E the expected rate and ΔK capital flows; a bar over the variable

[3] See, for example, Dornbusch [1976] and Kouri [1976].

indicates that it is exogenous, the * superscript that it is foreign. In this model there are no bonds, no non-traded goods, no distribution effects (so that the terms of trade are constant) and no transfers of real income. Full employment in a stationary economy is assured by (instantaneously) flexible money wages and prices. This (non-linear) model consists of eight equations with eight unknowns (P, P^*, e, e^*, t, K, S, S^E).

Equations (6.1) and (6.4) reflect domestic demand and supply of money in each economy. The equations state that it is the price level that is determined by their interaction. With the assumption that prices mae instantaneously to achieve full employment ($\bar{y}$, $\bar{y}^*$) given the domestic money supply ($\bar{M}$, $\bar{M}^*$), an adjustment lag in the demand for money does not arise here (as it does in Dornbush [1973]). Hence these equations capture the important 'classical' notion that under floating rates (as in a closed economy) the domestic money supply determines the domestic price level.

Since there are no bonds in this model, capital flows take the form of incremental demand by foreigners for home money. However, by (6.1) and (6.4) they have no effect on prices, and consequently they do affect the balance of trade (t), through (6.3), and expenditure (e, e^*) through (6.2) and (6.5).[4] The (highly stylised) notion is that, for example, an expected appreciation induces a capital inflow, with foreigners offering their currency for £s across the exchanges. This induces a slight ('infinitesimal') current appreciation in the £ sufficient to induce the necessary arbitrage flows of goods (a trade deficit) in the opposite direction.

The current period's exchange rate in (6.6), because of assumed perfect arbitrage between traded goods, is determined by relative prices at home and

[4] Kouri [1976] by contrast allows these capital flows to affect prices, which are determined through the money market equation *including* these flows. This creates the possibility of divergent paths even within this model. He notes that the possibility would be eliminated by boundary conditions on the extent to which the money stock could be held by foreigners (or equally domestic residents could hold foreign money). He suggests a number of plausible ones (such as minimum domestic balances for tax payment). This 'stability problem' is quite analogous to the ones discussed later, as is the solution. This said, it seems nevertheless to be of restricted interest since those who engage in monetary speculation are a minority of the population; the rest use domestic currency as the medium of exchange, except in hyper-inflations, and it therefore seems appropriate to assume that the domestic price level is not *significantly* affected by the minority. Of course models such as this and Kouri's are so simple that it is not easy to judge whether the restrictions they place are 'appropriate' or not. Nor does it in fact matter very much, provided they are simply regarded as steps on the way to a fuller treatment, such as that attempted in this chapter.

abroad (the equation is linearised, as a convenient approximation for values close to equilibrium). The next period's exchange rate is written as exogenous because it is, by (6.6), equal to next period's relative prices. These in turn are determined through equations (6.1) and (6.4) by next period's exogenous money supplies (which are assumed here to be perfectly anticipated).

If $\overline{M}$ and $\overline{M}^*$ are constants then P, P^*, S and S^E are also constants; $\Delta K = 0$ through (6.7), $t = 0$ through (6.3), and income equals absorption at home and abroad through (6.2) and (6.5).

If there is a once-for-all rise in $\overline{M}$ (or fall in $\overline{M}^*$), then in the period *before* the change ΔS^E rises, and with $\Delta S = 0$ there is a capital outflow; correspondingly, there is a trade surplus and a reduction in absorption. In the next period, when the monetary change actually occurs, ΔS^E reverts to zero, but S now rises and causes a capital inflow equal to the earlier outflow, a trade deficit and a temporary excess of absorption over income. In the subsequent periods, there is equilibrium with new price and exchange rate levels and $\Delta K = t = 0$.

If this proportionate rise in $\overline{M}$ (or fall in $\overline{M}^*$) is repeated in each subsequent period, then the initial period's events (i.e. before the change) are the same. But in the period of the change instead of ΔS^E reverting to zero it remains at its higher value, equal to ΔS; there is now (moving) equilibrium with prices rising at home (or dropping abroad) at the rate of monetary expansion (or contraction), and the home currency depreciating to maintain purchasing power parity.

If the initial trade surplus and capital outflow provoked by this monetary policy is to be avoided, then the authorities must ensure that the policy is not anticipated. In this case, in the period before the change there will be no speculative capital outflow; and in the period of the change the moving equilibrium will be instantly achieved.

It is clear that the exchange rate is stable under such exogenous monetary policy regimes; a random shock to the rate will have no repercussions on the rate in future periods, simply because a change in the rate has no impact on policy. It is of interest however to enquire what degree of monetary policy responsiveness to the exchange rate is consistent with exchange rate stability, since absolute unresponsiveness would seem an over-strong condition for stability. Accordingly, letting M and M^* endogenously respond to S, we can distinguish degrees of 'monetary stability' by the coefficient $a = \frac{\Delta m_{+1}}{m} \cdot \frac{S_{-1}}{S}$ where

$m = \frac{M}{\bar{y}} - \frac{M^*}{\bar{y}^*}$; this coefficient is the elasticity of world monetary policy to exchange rate movement and we therefore write $m_{+1} = aS + \bar{m}$ where $\bar{m}$ is the exogenous element in m. We can conveniently recast (6.6), by using (6.1) and (6.4), as $S = m$, hence (6.8) as $S^E = S_{+1} = aS + \bar{m}$. Provided $-1 < a < 1$ (inelastic), the exchange rate is therefore stable; a random shock to the exchange rate will generate stabilising capital flows because S^E rises by less than S. Thus monetary stability ensuthes exchange rate stability in this simple model. In what follows, we assume exogenous monetary policy, but digress from time to time as here to consider the implications of monetary responsiveness.

There are numerous complications which may, and will, be introduced into this simple model. However, it is necessary to compare like with like and at this stage we move to a structural model of equal simplicity. In essence we do this by relaxing the assumption of perfect arbitrage that ensures each traded good has the same price everywhere, and write:

$$C + \Delta K = 0 \qquad (6.3.1)$$

$$C = Pt + \pi = X(\eta - 1)(S - P + P^*) \qquad (6.6.1)$$

where $\eta < \infty$ is the sum of the (compensated) elasticities of demand for exports and imports,[5] X is the value of trade in the base year (divided by 100 because of the percentage units of S, P, and P^*), C is the current balance in home prices, Pt is the volume balance expressed at current home prices, and π is the residual element (due to terms of trade changes). Secondly, we drop the bar over S_{+1}, since this is now endogenous. If P and P^* are normalised at 100 and treated as fixed, so that equilibrium S is zero and S can therefore be treated as being in percentage deviations from equilibrium, then it follows that: $(X(\eta - 1) + h\Delta - h\Delta F)S = 0$, (where F is the forward operator), one of the roots of which must be greater than unity in absolute terms. Thus, imperfect arbitrage in traded goods introduces the possibility of exchange rate instability, even if there is monetary stability.

[5] Not the conventional elasticities of pure trade theory but elasticities with respect to the price level of traded goods in country A relative to that in country B.

6.3. Boundary conditions imposed by the nature of arbitrage in traded goods and by limitation of speculative portfolios

This second conclusion is the essence of the argument for instability. Yet it is a fragile construct. Since theory rules out the possibility that a homogeneous commodity can enjoy a different price across a frontier, allowing for tariffs, transport costs, etc., the result relies on the existence of product differentiation within commodity categories, so that the products of each country have a finite elasticity of demand.

Yet, while product differences may influence choice over some range of price difference, this influence will tend to break down outside that range for two reasons:

(1) There tends, for most consumers with a preference for a certain mix of product qualities, to be a certain fixed premium byond which the preferred mix is not worth having as compared with the others, because within a product group the mix of product qualities is of minor importance.

(2) If (1) failed and a producer were enjoying a significantly higher price than his rivals, then they would produce a product mix to match his and so capture his market.

In this case the elasticity rapidly approaches infinity beyond some range; observed price differences would remain within it and would trace out a finite elasticity of the sort found in much empirical work. It follows that any unstable root would eventually drive the elasticity to infinity. At this point the model switches to the perfect arbitrage version. But if there is perfect arbitrage, the exchange rate cannot be out of equilibrium; therefore the exchange rate cannot be at or beyond the 'floor' or 'ceiling' at which this switch takes place. This point is similar to Sohmen's [1969] assertion that unstable exchange rate zones are bounded by stable ones, and rests on similar arguments. Though 'infinite' elasticities cannot be observed directly, they can be inferred from the existence of bounds on movements in relative prices. It has been found in a recent EEC study, Robinson et al. [1976], that the 'price competitiveness' of traded goods[6] for no major industrial country moved outside a range of ± 10 per cent from its 1970 level over the floating rate period, 1971 to mid-1976. This is a very plausible range for the boundaries we have in mind. This can be illustrated:

[6] Prices of traded goods relative to competing countries', in a common currency.

Figure 6.1

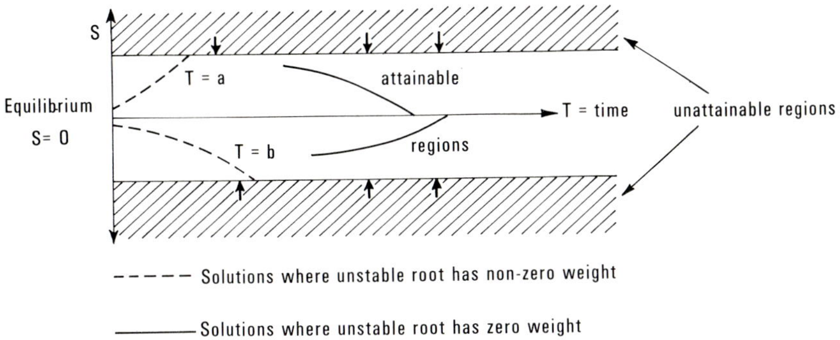

Now let the initial conditions be such that the coefficient on the unstable root is non-zero, so that the solution, like the dashed lines above, approaches the switchpoints. Consider a point like a (or, analogousy, b) and let the distance between a and the switchpoint tend to zero. The speculator knows that in the succeeding period, S can go no higher, so that $\Delta S_a^E = \Delta S_{a+1} < 0$: yet from the preceding path, $\Delta S_a > 0$. So $h(\Delta S_a - \Delta S_a^E) > 0$. However, at S_a, the trade balance, t, is positive (because the exchange rate is undervalued). Therefore $t_a + \Delta K_a > 0$ and S_a cannot be the market-clearing exchange rate (the rate must be lower).

But, if S_a cannot be the rate at $T = a$, nor can S_{a-1} since S_{a-1} can only be the rate if S_a is the rate in the next period. And so on for all $T < a$, so that in the end the whole path leading to S_a is unattainable.

It is possible to show, in a similar way, that any explosive path is unattainable. This result comes about because expectations are rational, so that the speculator knows at $T = 0$ that after $T = a$ the rate would hit the ceiling. Were the difference equation generating the rate based on, for example, an autoregressive expectations scheme, then the rate would hit the ceiling and stay on it until with new initial conditions produced by the ceiling constraint the equation pulled it off; this would be comparable to the behaviour of national income in Hicks' [1950] theory of the trade cycle.

It follows that all unstable roots must have a zero weight in the particular solution of the final form difference equation, which therefore has a stable path, all unstable roots being unattainable because of the floor/ceiling constraint.[7] In the simple case of the quadratic, this gives a particular solution exactly like that of a stable first order difference equation, where only one initial value is required to solve for the path of the rate.

The 'boundary' condition (or equivalently 'terminal' conditions) on the rational expectations model has been receiving increasing attention in the literature as pointed out by Shiller [1976] in a recent critique. In general, some boundary condition has to be imposed on these models in order to generate the types of stable solutions they are generally believed to imply. This fact may initially have been obscured by the simplicity of many of the models under debate (such as that in section 6.2 above). We have dwelt on the mechanics of the process in detail for this reason. It must be stressed that for the boundary condition to be effective in ruling out unstable roots, it must be recognised as part of the model by speculators. As Shiller noted in an early version of his [1976], 'if somehow the public ... got the idea that y (the vector of endogenous variables) would explode, then their expectations would be borne out'.

We have seen to this point that in the context of an exceedingly simple exchange rate model monetary stability is *necessary* for exchange rate stability, since without it a random shock would destabilise the *equilibrium* exchange rate. Monetary stability does not prevent the emergence of an exchange rate solution with one unstable root, unless the restriction of perfect traded goods arbitrage is imposed on the model, a restriction which seems excessively

[7] This point was recognised by Muth in discussing an inventory demand model with rational expectations of essentially the same structure as the one here. He noted (p. 326) that 'for a bounded solution the coefficient of the larger root (of a reciprocal pair) vanishes'.

It might seem that, because of the uncertainty introduced by the stochastic element in the balance of payments equation, the rational forecaster could have only a one-period time horizon; that is, he makes no forecast beyond the period ahead. However, rational expectations necessarily imply an infinite time-horizon (as pointed out, for example, by Sargent [1973] p. 441). The forecast for the next period hinges on next period's forecast for the subsequent period, S^E_{+1} and so on to infinity; according to the rational expectations hypothesis,

$$S^E_{+1} = E(E_{+1}S_{+2}) = E(ES_{+2} + \Phi(u_{+1})) = ES_{+2} = S^{E+2}$$

where E_{+i} denotes the mathematical expectation given information at time $t + i$, S^{E+2} is the rate expected to hold two periods ahead, and u is the error term in the payments equation. Thus the future one period forecasts are the implicit forecasts made today for all future periods, and the rational forecaster has to hold these expectations (i.e. make these forecasts) for his one-period forecast to be valid. It at once follows that with a ceiling and floor a forecast from a solution with an unstable root will be logically inconsistent in the way shown above, so that instability is ruled out.

severe for dynamic analysis. However, even without it, the existence, for economic reasons, of bounds to the exchange rate's movement suffices to rule out any unstable root in the general solution for the exchange rate path. It follows that monetary stability is also *sufficient* for exchange rate stability.

6.4. The monetary model and non-traded goods

The monetary theory has recently been extended by Dornbusch [1973] to allow for non-traded goods. Provided that the economy remains bondless, this extension causes no stability problem, given monetary stability. We take the original monetary model of 6.2 above but instead of (6.3) and (6.6) write:

$$P_t t + \Delta K = 0 \qquad (6.3.2)$$
$$P_t - P_t^* = S \qquad (6.6.2)$$

and add:

$$wP_t + (1 - w)P_h = P \qquad (6.9)$$
$$wP_t^* + (1 - w)P_h^* = P^* \qquad (6.10)$$

where P_t, P_h are prices of traded and non-traded ('home') goods respectively, and w is the share of traded goods in national output; the countries are assumed to be identical except for size. It is apparent that, since P and P^* are determined by $\overline{M}$ and $\overline{M}^*$ and since any movement of traded relative to home goods prices would cause a supply/demand imbalance in the home goods market, which is ruled out by relative price flexibility, therefore $\overline{M}$ and $\overline{M}^*$ determine $P = P_t = P_h$ and $P^* = P_t^* = P_h^*$ respectively. This both fixes the exchange rate and sets $\Delta K = P_t t = 0$ as before.

6.5. The monetary model, non-traded goods and bonds

However, the addition of bonds to the monetary model of section 6.4 as in Dornbusch [1975] brings with it a stability problem under floating rates exactly analogous to that already examined for the structural model.

In this section we follow the specification used by Dornbusch [1975] for the general case where the price level of non-traded goods is stabilised in each country, only we assume that monetary policy alone is used for stabilisation.

Monetary policy in this model is not necessarily either constant or stable (in the sense defined above that $|a| < 1$; these cases are considered in the following section.) However, it should not be confused with a 'permissive' monetary policy, in the usual sense of one that keeps real expenditure constant whatever the price level. Rather, the policy is one (a 'coercive' one) which makes the exchange rate change 'work'; so if there is a devaluation which raises the price level domestically, money supply has to be cut and vice versa, the opposite in general of a permissive policy.

In the monetary model in 6.4 above, we now write, in place of equations (6.1) and (6.4):

$$\frac{M}{P} = e^{-\beta r} e \qquad (6.1.1)$$

$$\frac{M^*}{P^*} = e^{-\beta r^*} e^* \qquad (6.4.1)$$

where r is the nominal interest rate, and add equations

$$e = \bar{y}\, e^{-\gamma r} \qquad (6.11)$$

$$e^* = \bar{y}^*\, e^{-\gamma r^*} \qquad (6.12)$$

these being the home and foreign expenditure functions, where e is the base of natural logarithms.[8] To allow for changes in r and r^*, we also add instead of (6.7):

$$\Delta K = h(\Delta S - \Delta S^E + \Delta r - \Delta r^*) \qquad (6.7.1)$$

and we add

$$t = \varepsilon X(P_t - \bar{P}_h) = -\varepsilon^* X(P_t^* - \bar{P}_h^*) \qquad (6.13)$$

[8] Future income and spending are assumed to be unaffected by today's capital flows. Within a growth model we would need to specify carefully the consumption/investment/foreign investment determinants; here we abstract from such issues. But we may note that the assumption would hold if foreign investment took place at the expense of domestic investment only (consumption is interest-inelastic); then the interest income (net of exchange rate loss) on foreign bond holdings would be approximately equal to the income foregone by not investing in domestic assets.

where ε is the total elasticity of net supply of traded goods to $(P_t - \bar{P}_h)$, and the bar over home goods prices indicates their exogeneity.

It can be shown that[9]

$$\varepsilon X = \frac{\bar{y}(\sigma_p + \sigma_c)(w)(1 - w)(m_h + m_t)}{m_h.\ 100}$$

where σ_p, σ_c are elasticities of substitution respectively along the production frontier and the indifference curve between traded and home goods, and m_h, m_t are marginal propensities to consume respectively home and traded goods.

Figure 6.2
Exchange rate appreciation, validated by monetary expansion.

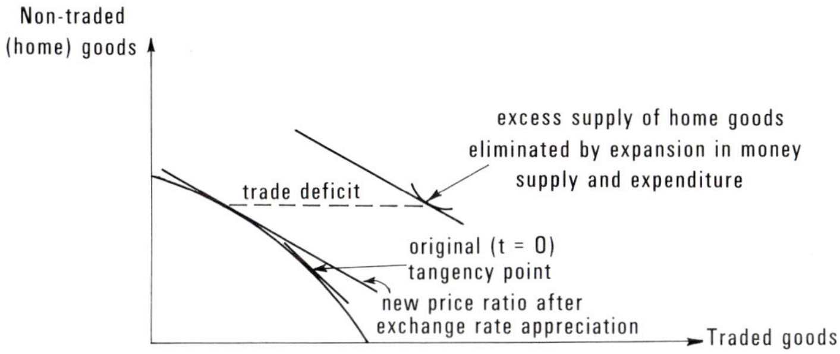

It follows from (6.6.2) and (6.13) that

$$\Delta P_t = \left(1 - \frac{\varepsilon}{\varepsilon^* + \varepsilon}\right)\Delta S$$

which because the countries are identical except for size

$$= \left(1 - \frac{\bar{y}}{\bar{y}^* + \bar{y}}\right) S \text{ which we write as } (1 - s)\Delta S.$$

9 Stabilisation of P_h requires that demand and supply for non-traded goods balance after the price change. Let $P' = P/100$. Hence $\Delta(P'_t - P'_h)(\bar{y})(1 = w)(\sigma_p + \sigma_c)w = -\Delta e \cdot m_h$, where the left hand side is the imbalance in net demand for non-traded goods resulting from the substitution effect, and the right hand side is the income effect required to offset this. The effect on the trade balance is $\Delta t = \Delta(P'_t - P'_h)\bar{y}\, w(1 - w)(\sigma_p + \sigma_c) - m_t \Delta e$. Substituting for Δe from above and dividing both sides by $\Delta(P'_t - P'_h)$, we obtain $\dfrac{\Delta t}{\Delta(P'_t - P'_h)} = \varepsilon X.\ 100.$

Equally

$$\Delta P_t^* = -s\Delta S.$$

Accordingly, we may rewrite (6.13) as

$$t = \varepsilon X(1 - s)S \tag{6.13.1}$$

where, for t close to zero, $t = P_t t$ and where P_h, P_h^*, are normalised at 100 and held constant, so that S can again be seen as measured in percent deviations from equilibrium.

Also $\Delta r = \dfrac{(1-s)(w)(1-w)(\sigma_p + \sigma_c)}{m_h \cdot \gamma} \Delta S$ and $\Delta r^* = \dfrac{-(s)(1-w)(w)(\sigma_p + \sigma_c)\Delta S}{m_h \cdot \gamma}$[10]

Substituting this into the payments equation (6.3.1) gives $\{\varepsilon X(1-s) + h\Delta - h\Delta F + h\sigma'\Delta\}S = 0$, where $\sigma' = \dfrac{(1-w)(w)(\sigma_p + \sigma_c)}{m_h \cdot \gamma}$; one of the roots of this equation must again be absolutely greater than unity, making the solution unstable.

The unstable root is only eliminated if ε and $\sigma' \to \infty$, as in the structural model if $\eta \to \infty$. However, this implies linearity in either the production frontier or the indifference curve between traded and non-traded goods, which is not in general to be expected.

6.6. Monetary stability with bonds and non-traded goods

In Section 6.5 the money supply was endogenous in a way fixed by the parameters of the model. We now consider how the same model would behave if the money supply was fixed or had a stable response ($a < 1$), to the exchange rate. We find that the stability problem remains regardless of the assumption made about money supply policy; money supply stability or even exogeneity will not eliminate the unstable root. We argue later that the problem is solved,

10 Since for example in the home country $\Delta r = \dfrac{\Delta \log e}{\gamma}$ (from 6.11), $\Delta \log e = \dfrac{\Delta e}{\bar{y}}$ and Δe is as derived above (footnote 9).

as before, by the imposition of boundary conditions whose rationale can be easily given.

That an exogenous money supply will not eliminate unstable roots from the formal difference equation solution can be most easily shown geometrically.[11]

Figure 6.3
Exchange rate appreciation, money supply exogenous.

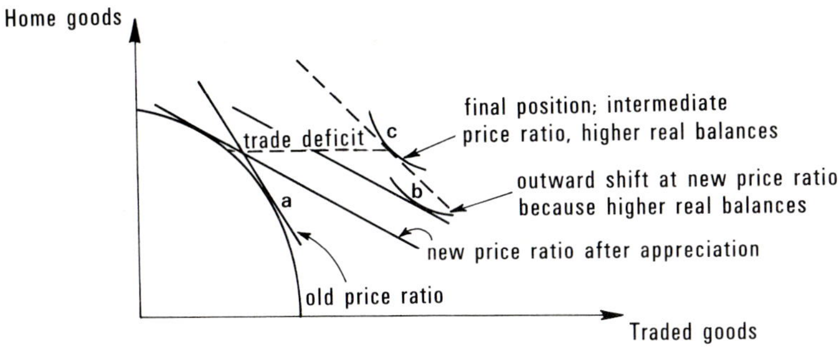

11 Algebraically, we may consider the effects of an appreciation on the home country. In equilibrium, we must have as before demand and supply for home goods in balance. Hence $\Delta(P_t' - P_h')\bar{y}(1 - w)(w)(\sigma_p + \sigma_p) = -\Delta e \cdot m_h$, as above (footnote 9); hence also $\Delta e/\bar{y} = \Delta \log e = \{-\Delta(P_t' - P_h')(1 - w)(w)(\sigma_p + \sigma_c)\}/m_h$. Also we have $0 = \Delta \log e + \Delta \log P - \beta \Delta r$ from the demand for money function. $\Delta \log P = w\Delta P_t' + (1 - w)\Delta P_h'$; $\Delta \log e$ as above; $\Delta P - = (1 - k)$ k is a parameter (to be found below) such that also $\Delta P_t^* = -k\Delta S$; and $\Delta r = \dfrac{-\Delta \log e}{\gamma}$ from the expenditure function. Substituting into $0 = \Delta \log e + \Delta \log P - \beta \Delta r$ from these we obtain:

$$\Delta P_h = (1 - k)\Delta S\left[\frac{-wm_h + (1 - w)(w)(\sigma_p + \sigma_c)(1 + \beta/\gamma)}{(1 - w)m_h + (1 - w)(w)(\sigma_p + \sigma_c)(1 + \beta/\gamma)}\right]$$

Provided $m_h > (1 + w)(\sigma_p + \sigma_c)\left(1 + \dfrac{\beta}{\gamma}\right)$ which will be the case unless σ_p and σ_c are implausibly low, ΔP_h will have the same sign as ΔS and be smaller than $\Delta P_t = (1 - k)\Delta S$. If, on the other hand, $m_h > (1 - w)(\sigma_p + \sigma_c)\left(1 + \dfrac{\beta}{\gamma}\right)$, then ΔP_h has the opposite sign to ΔS. Here note two limiting cases:

(1) As $\sigma_p + \sigma_c \rightarrow \dfrac{m_h}{(1 - w)(1 + \beta/\gamma)}$, so $\Delta P_h \rightarrow 0$ and $\Delta P \rightarrow w\Delta P_t$.

(2) As $\sigma_p + \sigma_c \rightarrow 0$, so $\Delta P_h \rightarrow \dfrac{-w}{1 - w}(1 - k)\,\Delta S$ and $\Delta P \rightarrow 0$.

Hence provided $\sigma_p + \sigma_c > 0$, there will always be a rise in real balances with an appreciation (ΔS negative), because ΔP will be negative; and there will be a trade deficit (since $\Delta P_h > \Delta P_t$). Note, finally, that $k = s$ from (6.6.2), the above expression for ΔP_h, and the analogous one for ΔP_h^*.

In the above diagram an appreciation causes P_t and so also the price level to fall, expanding real expenditure given a fixed money supply to reach a point such as b. Equilibrium in non-traded goods at the new exchange rate will occur at a point such as c where relative prices, P_t and P_h, have not returned to their original relationship. The price level, P, is generally lower, real expenditure is higher, and there is a trade deficit. The opposite occurs abroad. This implies that an expression for t, as a function of S, can be substituted as before into the payments equation, yielding the usual quadratic with one unstable root.

If the money supply is not fixed but reacts to the exchange rate change, then in order to prevent any trade imbalance resulting the money supply has to change by the same percentage and in the same direction as P_t changes in response to the exchange rate. Thus, an appreciation of $z\%$ will lower P_t by $z\%$ which will cause an excess supply of non-traded goods and a trade deficit; to eliminate this P_h must fall by $z\%$ also. Hence P falls by $z\%$, and to prevent real expenditure and the interest rate changing M must also fall by $z\%$. However, by equation (6.6.2) $P_t - P_t^* = S$, so that $\frac{M}{M^*}$ must rise by the same percentage as S, and therefore a in the expression defining monetary stability is 1. Thus, if $a < 1$ (monetary stability), t will respond to the exchange rate giving rise to the quadratic as before.

However, while $a = 1$ (monetary permissiveness) will succeed in keeping $t = 0$ if S changes, it will not give a stable solution for the exchange rate. In the payments equation we now have

$$h(\Delta S - F\Delta S) = 0$$

the single root of which is unity. The exchange rate is indeterminate, just as P and P^* are indeterminate. Any shock will fix domestic price levels and the exchange rate until the next shock comes along.

This repeats our earlier result, that monetary stability is required to ensure a determinate *equilibrium* exchange rate but that it is insufficient to ensure that all roots are stable. The introduction of bonds and non-traded goods into the monetary model will in general therefore cause a stability problem analogous to that of the structural model.

6.7. The analogous solution of the stability 'problem' for the monetary theory

However, this stability problem has an analogous solution to the early one. If S were to diverge from equilibrium, $(P_t - P_h) - (P_t^* - P_h^*)$ would also diverge, driving the output of the depreciating country towards total specialisation in production of traded goods, whereas the appreciating country would tend to the opposite specialisation; the trade balance would of course tend to the level of output of the depreciating country.

The absurdity of this result is apparent, as can easily be demonstrated. At the limit where the depreciating country is totally specialised, ε is obviously zero. If ε is zero then the root, ℓ, of the difference equation is given by $(-h\ell^2+2h\ell-h)=0$, and is unity, so that the exchange rate would change no further; if the two countries are of equal size, this is simultaneously a floor in the one and a ceiling in the other, but if they are of unequal size, then a floor or ceiling is reached when the smaller country becomes specialised. This floor/ceiling then makes the whole path unattainable by the same argument as in section 6.3 above.

6.8. The general case: the monetary/structural model

It was pointed out above that the monetary and structural models have the same long run equilibrium exchange rate. We have now seen that both the monetary and structural models share a stability problem, which is solved for each in a similar manner, so that the floating rate must converge.[12] The similarities between the models are therefore considerable and it is natural to explore a generalised model that 1) incorporates the common features; 2) of unshared features, takes from each model the assumptions that are least restrictive on short run behaviour (provided this can be justified); 3) adds certain new 'dynamic' aspects about which we have information. Such a model, which we might call 'structural/monetary', should be a superior model of short run behaviour than either, while retaining the long run features of both.

[12] Stability is assured usually by the existence of at least one stable root. But if (improbably) there is none and hence no attainable path from disequilibrium, stability is nevertheless achieved in the following 'degenerate' manner. Absence of any attainable path from a disequilibrium exchange rate means that the disequilibrium cannot occur. Therefore the rate must always be in equilibrium.

As a basis, we take the non-traded goods model of section 6.6 above but, since for dynamic analysis its assumptions of full employment and of 'coercive' monetary policy appear too restrictive, we relax these as follows. We retain the assumption that home goods prices are fixed in each economy, but this occurs because this is their equilibrium price level; firms allow output to change in short run disequilibrium because this is less costly than price instability.

The money supply is assumed to have an equilibrium level (which determines the equilibrium price level) but is assumed to be responsive to shocks. Instead of a coercive monetary policy, this responsiveness takes the form of stabilising the interest rate (the real and nominal rates are the same in this model)[13] at its 'natural' level, in order not to distort expenditure decisions; the natural rate of interest is assumed to be equalised in the two countries by free factor flows or by free trade.

It follows that a movement in S will not disturb the rate of interest or real expenditure, but will, because of the substitution effect above, shift net supply into or out of home goods and out of or into traded goods. This will cause a trade deficit and an equal contraction of home goods output, or a trade surplus and equal home goods expansion. Formally, we can write these into the model of section 6.6 by substituting for (6.2) and (6.5),

$$y = e + t, \tag{6.2.1}$$
$$y^* = e^* - t, \tag{6.5.1}$$

and noting that in (6.13) it is now the case that $\varepsilon X = e(\varphi + \sigma_c)w(1 - w)/100$ (the substitution effect only, derived as above); and instead of (6.7.1) we revert to the original (6.7), dropping Δr and Δr^* which are now zero by the assumption about monetary policy.

To this basis, we add, because of the effect of product differentiation in the relevant range of price differences, a finite elasticity, η, from the structural model. We consequently revert to (6.3.1) for the balance of payments identity, since now the terms of trade can change; however, now $C = P_i t + \pi$

Finally, we add two further aspects for which we have the relevant parameter estimates for the UK:

1) lags in the response of trade volumes to relative prices;

[13] For expositional convenience merely. We may allow for inflation components in the nominal rates; these will be balanced by an equilibrium rate of change in the exchange rate. Monetary policy would then be assumed to stabilise the real interest rate at its natural level.

2) more than one forward market (and future time period).

The aim in this section is to use the available parameter estimates to estimate the length of time to convergence and the nature of any oscillations by the exchange rate in a UK model with these features.

6.8.1. Non-traded goods and finite elasticity

The Dornbusch [1975] analysis assumes than η (hereafter the 'demand' elasticity)[14] is infinite, while ε (hereafter the 'supply' elasticity) is finite. Now we generalise and assume both to be finite for relevant price changes. This yields two separate expressions for t, respectively t_s (for the 'supply' of t) and t_d (for the 'demand' for t):

$$t_s = \varepsilon X(P_t - P_h) = t_s^* = -\varepsilon^* X(P_t^* - P_h^*)$$
$$t_d = \eta X(S + P_t^* - P_t) = -t_d^*$$

Setting $t_s = t_d$ and $t_s^* = t_d^*$ yields equilibrium values for P_t and P_t^* of

$$P_t = \frac{\eta(S + P_t^*) + \varepsilon P_h}{\eta + \varepsilon} \tag{6.14}$$

and

$$P_t^* = \frac{\eta(P_t - S) + \varepsilon^* P_h^*}{\eta + \varepsilon^*} = \frac{\eta s(P_t - S) + \varepsilon(1 - s)P_h^*}{\eta s + \varepsilon(1 - s)} \text{ since}$$
$$\varepsilon^* = \frac{(1 - s)}{s}\varepsilon \tag{6.15}$$

Thus equilibrium prices of traded goods are a weighted average of foreign traded goods' prices corrected for the exchange rate and home (non-traded) goods' prices, where the weights are the relative size of respectively the demand and the supply elasticities. It has been argued by Beenstock and Minford [1976] that, depending on the share of exports in world trade and of exports in national income, there is a presumption that foreign or non-traded prices

[14] Or elasticity of 'expenditure switching' (see Johnson [1961]) assuming no supply constraints.

will dominate making the country, respectively, a 'price-receiver' or a 'price-transmitter'; and their empirical study of OECD countries (op.cit.) has found such a presumption to be generally valid for export prices.

6.8.2. *Lagged responses*

Following the arguments of chapter 3 and of Rees and Layard [1971] we attribute a lag on η, the demand elasticity, to a convolution of order-delivery, information, adjustment and expectations lags. For convenience, we write this lag, λ_1, as geometrically declining so that:

$$t_d = \frac{\eta X \lambda_1 (S + P_t^* - P_t)}{1 - B(1 - \lambda_1)}$$

where B as usual is the backward operator.

We now write the supply elasticity with a lag, λ_2, which we take to reflect a similar convolution of lags and write similarly. Let $\lambda_2 = \lambda_1 = \lambda$, so that (6.14) and (6.15) may also stand as market-clearing equations for P_t and P_t^* in the short run and are assumed to be satisfied. Again dropping fixed P_h and P_h^*, we have from (6.14) and (6.15):

$$P_t = \frac{(\eta' - \eta'\eta^*)}{(1 - \eta'\eta^*)} S \text{ and } P_t^* = \frac{(\eta'\eta^* - \eta^*)}{(1 - \eta'\eta^*)} S \text{ where } \eta' = \frac{\eta}{\eta + \varepsilon}$$

$$\text{and } \eta^* = \frac{\eta s}{\eta s + \varepsilon(1 - s)}$$

$$\text{Hence } t = t_s = \frac{\varepsilon X \lambda}{1 - B(1 - \lambda)} (P_t) = \frac{\varepsilon X \lambda}{1 - B(1 - \lambda)} \frac{(\eta' - \eta'\eta^*)}{(1 - \eta'\eta^*)} S$$

to which we must add the terms of trade effect, $\pi = X(P_t - S - P_t^*)$ to get it into balance of payments value in home prices ($C = P_t t + \pi$).

This becomes

$$C = \left[\frac{\varepsilon X \lambda}{1 - B(1 - \lambda)} \left(\frac{\eta' - \eta'\eta^*}{1 - \eta'\eta^*} \right) + \frac{X(\eta' + \eta^* - 2\eta'\eta^* - 1)}{(1 - \eta'\eta^*)} \right] S$$

hereafter qS.

The balance of payments equation therefore becomes:

$$(q + h\Delta - h\Delta F)S = 0$$

6.8.3. *Multiple forward markets*

For convenience, we assume that there exist *forward* rates at n maturities.[15] We assume perfect interest arbitrage between maturities including spot, such that

$$S = \frac{S^{F+1}}{(1 + r - r^*)} = \frac{S^{F+2}}{(1 + r - r^*)^2} = \; . \; . \; . \; . = \frac{S^{F+N}}{(1 + r - r^*)^N}$$

where S^{F+i} are the forward rates of maturity 1 to N and $r - r^*$ is the interest differential (set at zero by assumption).

For each ith maturity, the speculative position taken is

$$hw_i(S^{F+i} - S^{E+i}) \text{ where } \sum_{i=1}^{N} w_i = 1.$$[16]

Equation (6.7) now becomes:

$$\Delta K = \sum_{i=1}^{N} hw_i(\Delta S^{F+i} - \Delta S^{E+i})$$

Since $S^{F+i} = S$, this becomes

$$\Delta K = h\Delta S - h \sum_{i=1}^{N} w_i \, \Delta S^{E+i} \qquad (6.7.2)$$

15 However, we do not need actual operating forward markets, since there is an *implicit* forward rate at every maturity given by the interest differential and the spot rate.

16 The assumption that the w_i are unaffected by the $(S^F - S^E) + i$ is only sustainable if the $(S^F - S^E) + i$ give approximately a constant relative compound rate of return per annum at all i maturities; if, for example, the relative return increased significantly at a maturity of 3 months ($i = 1$), then w_1 would rise relative to the other w_i. We therefore assume that the *term structure* of interest differentials (which governs the S^{F+i}) is such as to keep the relative incentive to speculate at the two maturities approximately constant. We would accordingly expect the *shape* of the expected path to convergence of the exchange rate to show up in the term structure of interest differentials. Strong cyclicality would therefore produce 'bumps' in the structure. By the same reasoning, one could also infer from a flat or 'smooth' term structure that expected convergence was broadly monotonic.

Instead of (6.8) we now have (6.8.1) $S^{E+i} = F^i S$ (where F is the forward operator) so that (6.7.1) can very simply be rewritten as:

$$\Delta K = h\Delta S - h \sum_{i=1}^{N} w_i F^i \Delta S \tag{6.7.3}$$

We now set $N = 2$, more or less arbitrarily on the grounds that the bulk of forward transactions would appear to be for 6 months or less. So the balance of payments equation of the last section changes to

$$(q + h\Delta - w_1 h\Delta F - w_2 h\Delta F^2)S = 0$$

which decomposes into the fourth order difference equation

$$\left\{(-w_2) + (w_2 + w_2(1-\lambda) - w_1)B + \left[\frac{\varepsilon X\lambda q_1 + Xq_2}{h} + 1 + w_1 + w_1(1-\lambda) - w_2(1-\lambda)\right]B^2 - \left[\frac{Xq_2(1-\lambda)}{h} + 1 + (1-\lambda) + w_1(1-\lambda)\right]B^3 + (1-\lambda)B^4\right\}S = 0$$

where $q_1 = \dfrac{(\eta' - \eta'\eta^*)}{(1 - \eta'\eta^*)}$

and $q_2 = \dfrac{(\eta' + \eta^* - 2\eta'\eta^* - 1)}{1 - \eta'\eta^*}$.

6.8.4. *The empirical evidence for the UK*

This fourth order difference equation can most easily be appraised numerically, so we substitute estimates for the UK derived from the work cited above (see Appendix 6.A for derivation) namely $\eta' + 0.25, \lambda = 0.14, \varepsilon = 7.5, w_1 = 0.6$, $w_2 = 0.4$, $h = 1000$, $X = 110$. We also set $\eta^* = 0$ as being small enough to neglect. This gives

$$\{1 - 0.35B - 4.3B^2 + 5.75B^3 - 2.15B^4\}S = 0$$

the roots of which are:

$$\ell = -2.472,\ 1.17,\ 0.826 + 0.25i$$

Only the last of these roots, the complex pair, is stable. It is oscillatory, with a cycle length of about five years (the model period is one quarter), and it takes about 4 years to 'eliminate' (to within 10% of its original value) an initial exchange rate deviation from equilibrium.

In Appendix 6.A, we carry out some sensitivity tests on these dynamic properties. We find there that cyclicality is almost invariably present for reasonable variations in the parameters, and the cycle generally lies in the region of 5–6 years. The length of time to convergence (to within 10%) never falls below $2\frac{1}{2}$ years or rises above 8 and for variations in one parameter only, it never rises above 6 years; the convergence period is primarily affected by variation in the size of the trade elasticity (ε, η') and the length of its lag (λ) and barely affected by variation in the speculative parameters, h, w_1 and w_2. This suggests that our 'central' result is reasonably robust, and that qualitatively we should expect convergence that is both cyclical and relatively slow, exactly how slow depending on the precise size and length of the trade response. In particular we find that even if $w_1 = 1$, that is all speculation is carried out in one, short-term, forward market alone, the stability properties are negligibly affected. This enables us to continue with the useful simplification of only one forward market in the rest of this book.

6.9. Conclusions

This chapter has considered the argument that, even with rational expectations and monetary stability, the floating exchange rate within a structural payments model may be unstable, an argument that may be extended to the floating rate within a monetary payments model including bonds and non-traded goods. It has, however, been shown that both models imply floor/ceiling constraints (boundary conditions) and that these are sufficient to rule out the possibility of even local instability; therefore, the general conclusion holds, that monetary stability is both sufficient and necessary for exchange rate stability. This is an important conclusion, since much of the debate about floating exchange rates – whether popular, policy-oriented or academic –

has centred on stability and in particular questioned whether monetary stability was an adequate condition for exchange rate stability.

With this conclusion behind us, we also considered the nature of the dynamic path of the exchange rate within these models. Since both models converge, without in general being in continuous equilibrium, and also have the same long run equilibrium exchange rate, their similarities are sufficient to justify a generalised model incorporating the less restrictive features of each, as well as some additional ones, including lags in trade adjustment and more than one time period. The solution of this (asymptotic) model is derived for the exchange rate and its convergence properties estimated with the use of available parameters for the UK; the resulting estimate, a five year cycle converging over a similar period, appears to be reasonably robust, though as one might expect the precise speed of convergence is affected by the size and length of the trade response. If approximately correct, this again would seem to be an important finding. Controversy about floating rates has tended to polarise between 'optimists' (such as Sohmen [1969], Friedman [1953]) on the one hand, arguing that speculators would stabilise the rate towards the equilibrium level, corrected for the interest differential, regardless of shocks; and 'sceptics' (the majority until recently) on the other who have doubted that the equilibrium level affected the current rate at all. Our conclusion, based on the assumption that speculators are risk-averse and therefore do not completely iron out shocks to the rate, is that while shocks shift the rate away from equilibrium, as a result of speculation the rate is thereafter pushed back towards equilibrium over a period of several years while it may in the process overshoot. This (broadly optimistic) conclusion is provisional, reached by giving the coefficient of speculative response (the parameter h) the value estimated for the fixed rate period. In subsequent chapters we proceed to question and modify this assumption. Nevertheless, it is of interest because alteration of this parameter is likely to occur slowly, as speculators learn about the new system.

Appendix 6.A: Derivation of parameter estimates for UK model and Sensitivity Tests

1. Current account parameters. These parameters, η', ε, λ and X, relate to the behaviour of the current account balance in response to an exchange rate change, the 'J-curve'. The estimated relation for the UK is given as eq. (5.1), p. 131 of chapter 5, and is based on the work cited there. That relation is however the reduced form of a large number of equations, while the parameters we have chosen to represent it, admittedly crudely, are structural if at a rather aggregated level. We now attempt to find values for them which roughly satisfy both what we know about the structure and the relation, the b_i, of eq. (5.1).

We begin with some plausible guesses based on structure, and then check them against the b_i.ε, the 'supply' elasticity, is the sum of the two elasticities for exports and imports. We have that for manufactured exports from chapter 3 as 3.9. In the absence of evidence for the supply elasticities of other exports or of imports, we might guess that they were similar and that ε might accordingly be around 7–8. η' is the ratio of η, the 'demand' elasticity (again the sum of two elasticities), to $\eta + \varepsilon$. We have the demand elasticity for exports of manufactures from chapter 3 as 1.5, and that for imports of goods as 0.5 from Rees and Layard. We may reasonably think of η therefore as being in the range of 2–3. This would imply η' as 0.2–0.3.

X is simply set at the value in £ million p.a. of UK exports of goods and services in 1968 (a year representative of our period) or about £11 000m., divided by 100 because our units for S, the exchange rate, are percentage deviations from some base level. Thus $X = 110$.

λ, the lag parameter, poses more difficulty because it is exponential whereas most of the structural lags were polynomial of second or higher degree. We may however make some inference from the average and total lag lengths in the reduced form relation, which are respectively 9 quarters (calculated for the positive coefficients only) and 23. A λ of 0.2 gives approximately the right total lag length if the very small tail values of the exponential are neglected. The average lag implied, of only 4, is too small. However, there is a trade-off between average lag and total lag, since a λ of 0.1 gives an average lag of 9, but an excessively long total lag of over eight years. Choice within this range is therefore a matter of taste, depending on the purpose in hand.

After some experimentation with values in these vicinities, we selected $\eta' = 0.25$, $\varepsilon = 7.5$, $\lambda = 0.14$; with these values the cumulative lag coefficients for the b_i and our representative structure compared as shown in Table 6.A.1.

Table 6.A.1
Cumulative effect of 1% exchange rate depreciation on current account, for: (1) reduced form relation (b_i) and (2) relation imposed through selected parameters (£m. per quarter).

Period	(1) Reduced Form	(2) Imposed Structures ($\eta' = 0.25$, $\varepsilon = 7.5$, $\lambda = 0.14$, $X = 110 \div 4 = 27.5$)
0	−8.34	−13.40
1	−8.41	−7.19
2	−9.38	−1.86
3	−6.93	2.73
4	−1.70	6.67
5	3.01	10.07
6	6.85	12.99
7	8.67	15.50
8	11.16	17.66
9	13.68	19.62
10	16.11	21.22
11	18.49	22.59
12	20.69	23.77
13	21.96	24.78
14	23.55	25.65
15	24.75	26.40
16	26.08	27.05
17	27.12	27.61
18	28.08	28.09
19	29.04	28.50
20	29.51	28.85
21	30.01	29.15
22	30.13	29.41
23	30.39	29.63

It can be seen that the approximation is not really bad, given the large margin of error on such relationships. Thus the maximum cumulative divergence in a single quarter is in period 3 when it is nearly 10 (or £40m. p.a.), as against a standard error of forecast possibly ten times this. The impact and long run effects are very similar, as is the effect after about three years. The main defect of the imposed structure is some shortening of the average lag, to about 6 quarters.

2. Capital account parameters. To obtain a value for h, we simply take the average of h_o, Σh_i, j_o, Σj_i $(i \geq 1)$ in eq. (5.2). Implicitly we assume that had we estimated the relationship as a first difference instead of with a lag structure:

1) the h_i and j_i $(i \geqslant 1)$ would have cumulated on h_i and j_i respectively, and
2) that h would have been constrained to take an average of the 4 values, h_o, j_o, h_i, j_i.

1) is likely because of collinearity between the lagged values, and
2) is simply the result of least squares, though the averaging may not be simple as assumed here. This results in $h = 1038$ (£million at an annual rate), or in round numbers, 1000.

Finally, the weights w_1 and w_2 are derived by calculating from the model as set out in chapter 4 the effect on ΔK of respectively S^{E+1} and S^{E+2}. We find that in equation (4.10) FL (our proxy for S^{E+4}, the 1-year rate expected) has an effect of about 60 on a first difference basis as just discussed; in equation (4.12) $e/(e + d) = 0.51$, multiplied by 365, is the coefficient on S^{E+1}, which gives 186. Thus given only 3-month and 1-year forward markets the weights are respectively 0.74 and 0.26. We now interpolate weights on the 6- and 9-month markets as 0.58 and 0.42 respectively; if we then assume that we have only the 3- and 6-month markets, we can recalculate the weights as, for the 3-month, $0.74/(0.74 + 0.58)$ or 0.6 approx. and for the 6-month, 0.4.

3. Sensitivity tests. These parameter estimates are derived from what econometric evidence we have for the UK, but the derivation is approximate, the evidence is incomplete and what evidence we have is subject to error. In these circumstances, we cannot establish 'confidence limits' for the parameters, and we are compelled instead to perform sensitivity tests, varying the relevant parameter by an amount which reflects our subjective assessment of the 'confidence limit' (in a Bayesian manner). We show below in Table 6.A.2 the stability properties of the exchange rate when the parameters are varied in this way.

It can be seen that the speed of convergence varies considerably from $2\frac{1}{2}$ years to about 8 years. Provided only one of the parameters is varied, it narrows somewhat to the range of $2\frac{1}{2}$ to 6 years, with eight cases out of twelve being clustered around 4 years. This suggests that for minor parameter variation we would expect convergence to take roughly the length of the J-curve lag. It is clear that variation in the 'speculative' parameters (h, w_1, w_2) makes little difference. In particular, it turns out that having more than one forward market makes a negligible difference to the stability properties: compare (a) and (c3). In what follows we will therefore return to the useful simplifica-

Table 6.A.2
Stability properties of UK exchange rate as parameter estimates are varied by subjective confidence limit.[a]

Parameter Values	η'	ε	λ	w_1	w_2	h	X	Roots (unstable roots bracketed)	Cycle length if any (Quarters)	Approx. time to eliminate an exchange rate disturbance*, Quarters
(a) Central estimates	0.25	7.5	0.14	0.6	0.4	1000	110	(−2.473, 1.163) 0.830 ± 0.244i	21.9	16 (0.865)
(b1) Longer lags (lower λ)	0.25	7.5	0.1	0.6	0.4	1000	110	(−2.465, 1.126) 0.870 ± 0.233i	24.0	23 (0.893)
(b2) Shorter lags (higher λ)	0.25	7.5	0.2	0.6	0.4	1000	110	(−2.474, 1.188) 0.793 ± 0.228i	22.4	12 (0.825)
(c1) More speculation short term (higher w_1)	0.25	7.5	0.14	0.7	0.3	1000	110	(−3.295, 1.173) 0.827 ± 0.239i	22.4	16 (0.861)
(c2) Less speculation short term (lower w_1)	0.25	7.5	0.14	0.5	0.5	1000	110	(−1.972, 1.152) 0.840 ± 0.227i	23.8	17 (0.870)
(c3) All speculation is short term ($w_1 = 1$)	0.25	7.5	0.14	1	0	1000	110	(1.173) 0.814 ± 0.258	20.5	15 (0.855)
(d1) Smaller speculative response (lower h)	0.25	7.5	0.14	0.6	0.4	800	110	(−2.464, 1.172) 0.821 ± 0.265i	20.1	16 (0.862)
(d2) Higher speculat-								(−2.476, 1.137)		

elasticity (lower ε)	0.25	6.0	0.14	0.6	0.4	1000	110	0.846 ± 0.237i	23.0	18 (0.879)
(e2) Higher trade elasticity (higher ε)	0.25	9.0	0.14	0.6	0.4	1000	110	(−2.480 0.778), (1.026 ± 0.250i)	No cyc. (monotonic)	10 (0.778)
(f1) Less 'openness' (lower η′)	0.2	7.5	0.14	0.6	0.4	1000	110	(−2.466, 1.100) 0.858 ± 0.238i	23.2	20 (0.890)
(f2) More 'openness' (higher η′)	0.3	7.5	0.14	0.6	0.4	1000	110	(−2.476, 1.186) 0.820 ± 0.245i	21.7	15 (0.856)
(g1) All changes made in (b1)(c1)(d1)(e1) (f1) those 'unfavourable' to stability	0.2	6.0	0.1	0.7	0.3	800	110	(−3.275, 1.053) 0.894 ± 0.264i	21.9	33 (0.932)
(g2) All changes made in (b2)(c2)(d2) (e2)(f2) ie. favourable to stability	0.3	9.0	0.2	0.5	0.5	1200	110	(−1.987, 1.240) 0.773 ± 0.226	22.1	11 (0.805)
(h1) [a]	0.2	6.0	0.1	0.5	0.5	1200	110	(−1.971, 1.050) 0.910 ± 0.203	28.6	33 (0.932)
(h2) [a]	0.3	9.0	0.2	0.7	0.3	800	110	(−3.312, 1.300) 0.739 ± 0.270i	17.9	10 (0.787)

[a] *Notes:* * to within 10% of the original disturbance. The damping factor is bracketed after the number of quarters.
(h1) Mixture of changes in (c2), (d2) and (b1), (e1), (f1) ie. speculative favourable, elasticity unfavourable.
(h2) Mixture of changes in (c1), (d1) and (b2), (e2), (f2) ie. reverse of (h1).

tion that there is only one active forward market, namely that at three months and therefore that $w_1 = 1$, $w_2 = 0$.

However, variation in the 'elasticity' parameters (λ, η', ε) is important. Thus longer lags (case b1) pushes convergence to 6 years, while longer lags and lower η', ε together push it to 8 years (g1); vice versa, shorter lags push it to 3 years, and together with higher η', ε to $2\frac{1}{2}$ years (g2).

The cyclicality is almost invariably present, with cycle lengths of 5–6 years when a single parameter is varied, and $4\frac{1}{2}$–7 years in the mixed cases (h1) and (h2). The one case (e2) where convergence is monotonic looks like a curiosum. These results suggest that we should expect a cycle length of about or somewhat greater than the length of the J-curve lag.

Chapter 7

RATIONAL EXCHANGE RATE SPECULATION UNDER FIXED AND FLOATING EXCHANGE RATES[1]

7.1. Introduction

In the earlier chapters of this book we reported relationships for the UK trading and capital accounts estimated over data for the fixed exchange rate period ending in 1971. In chapters 5 and 6 we used these same relationships to solve for the market-clearing floating exchange rate, rather than for reserves changes as in the fixed rate regime. However, it is clear enough and has been frequently noted, that the change of regime is likely to affect market behaviour, especially in the capital account, where expectations previously geared to the risks of a once-for-all parity adjustment must now take account of the probably-continuous pace of exchange rate change.

This and the next chapter is devoted to the important problem of how capital account behaviour is affected, and, more precisely, to deriving numerical estimates of the changes in the relevant coefficients. This might be objected to on the grounds that such an undertaking is absurdly ambitious, in the absence of data from the floating rate period. The answer must be that anyone who wishes to use econometric results for forecasting or for simulation must make allowances for the changes in the economic structure that have almost invariably occurred since his estimation period (or else late within it, so that they are not properly mirrored in the coefficient estimates).

[1] This chapter has benefited from discussions in the Manchester Inflation Workshop, and particularly from comments by Tapan Biswas, Alvin Marty and Michael Parkin.

The transition to floating is simply one such change, and not necessarily an extreme example (if one thinks of the frequent structural changes in public finance in the UK, for example). If one has to make an allowance, it is best to make it on the basis of systematic argument, however shaky.

We could, it is true, go directly to the latest data, limited as it is, and estimate an exchange rate equation from it. However, a recurring theme of this book has been the various initial stages through which the floating rate will go; so this would be little help. More importantly, it would deprive us of the information contained in the experience of the fixed rate period. This information turns out to be considerable; particularly in so far as the system of 'dirty' floating, within which the UK has been operating for most of the time since 1971, is of course a hybrid of the fixed and floating system. It is for these reasons that we now plunge into the attempt to re-examine and modify the structure of the capital flows equations.

7.2. The equation for capital flows

Consider three exchange rate regimes; (1) the rate fixed irrevocably for all time, (2) the rate fixed-but-occasionally-adjustable, and (3) a floating rate. Under (1), exchange rate speculation will be uninteresting, since there is no exchange rate risk and the expected will always be the same as the actual rate. However, under (2) and (3) there is uncertainty about the future rate, and the question arises: how does the different nature of this uncertainty affect the speculative schedule?

For expositional convenience, suppose two countries only, one (3-months) forward market only[2], perfect interest arbitrage between the spot and the single forward market and no interest rate differential so that spot and forward rates are equal. Speculative (stock) demand for the home country's currency is then under both regimes: $K = h(S - S^E) + h^*$ where S is the price of foreign currency, S^E its expected price in the next period (both measured in % deviation from equilibrium). The change of regime can therefore affect the two parameters, h and h^*, and the variable, S^E.

We assume that speculators are rational, in the sense defined by Muth and as in chapter 6. This assumption, while not likely to be strictly realistic

[2] The model for the UK, to which the analysis is specifically related, is quarterly.

at a time when there has just been a large structural change (as in the transition to floating), will be as argued earlier the asymptotic situation towards which speculative expectations should tend as the system 'settles down'. It is therefore of the maximum interest; even if it does not help much in understanding the transitional problems of the system in its early stage, it may not be too difficult to supply the missing short-run stories once we have an idea where the system is going.

It will be argued that under these conditions the change of regime will in general affect S^E and h, though not h^*, but that a priori information may be used to derive estimates of the change, so that parameters estimated under one regime may be used, suitably modified, to simulate the behaviour of the other.

7.2.1. The floating regime

As in chapter 6, let the market-clearing equation for the foreign exchange market be (in stochastic form):

$$(\eta - 1)XS + h(\Delta S - \Delta S^E) + u = 0 \tag{7.1}$$

where u is an error term representing the supposedly random behaviour of omitted variables (the included variables, other than the exchange rate, determine the equilibrium and so are not explicitly shown here, since S is in terms of deviations from equilibrium). The addition of this error term is necessary now because we are proceeding to consider the effects of errors or uncertainty within a changed economic structure.

Whereas in chapter 6 we were able to use ordinary difference-equation methods to find the solution of the equivalent deterministic equation, for our present stochastic version we need to use a rather more elaborate procedure, which is set out in Muth [1961] pp. 325–30 for his essentially similar inventory-speculation model. This procedure is a special case of the general procedure for solving a model of stochastic equations in which rational expectations are an argument (see Hilliard [1976]). It is applicable to our model because this model is reducible under our assumptions to a final equation in the exchange rate with only one error term; for our purposes this is convenient since the problems would otherwise become intractable.

In equation (7.1), the only independent determinants of S are $u_{-i}(i=0, 1,\ldots, \infty)$. S^E is not an independent determinant of S because, by the assumption of rational expectations, it is the mathematically expected value, conditional on present information, of S_{+1}. So we may write:

$$S = \sum_{i=0}^{\infty} W_i u_{-i}; \tag{7.2}$$

$$S^E = W_0 E u_{+1} = \sum_{i=1}^{\infty} W_i u_{+1-i} = \sum_{i=1}^{\infty} W_i u_{+1-i}, \tag{7.3}$$

where $Eu_{+1} = 0$ because u_{+1} is a random variable on which no current information exists. Substituting from (7.2) and (7.3) into (7.1) gives an equation in the u_{-i}:

$$\{(\eta-1)X+h\}\sum_{i=0}^{\infty} W_i u_{-i} - h\sum_{i=0}^{\infty} W_i u_{-i-1} - h\sum_{i=1}^{\infty} W_i u_{+1-i} + h\sum_{i=1}^{\infty} W_i u_{-i} = -u \tag{7.4}$$

It is convenient to rewrite this as:

$$\left\{[(\eta-1)X+h]\sum_{i=0}^{\infty} W_i - h\sum_{i=1}^{\infty} W_{i-1} - h\sum_{i=0}^{\infty} W_{i+1} + h\sum_{i=1}^{\infty} W_i\right\} u_{-i} = -u \tag{7.5}$$

For equation (7.5) to hold for all possible values of u_{-i}, the coefficients on u_{-i} must be equal for all i. This yields the following equalities:

$$(\text{for } i=0)\quad \{(\eta-1)X+h\}\, W_0 - hW_1 = -1 \tag{7.6}$$
$$(\text{for } i \geqslant 1)\quad -hW_{i+1} + \{(\eta-1)X+2h\}W_i - hW_{i-1} = 0 \tag{7.7}$$

The solution for (7.7) is $W_i = W_0\mu^i \ (i \geqslant 1)$ (7.8)
where $-1<\mu<1$ is the only stable root of the characteristic equation $\mu^2 - \left\{2 + \frac{(\eta-1)X}{h}\right\}\mu + 1 = 0$; and where W_o is given by substitution from (7.8) into (7.6) as $W_0 = \frac{-1}{(\eta-1)X + h(1-\mu)}$.

We therefore finally have:

$$S = W_o \sum_{i=0}^{\infty} \mu^i u_{-i} = W_0 u + \mu S_{-1} \tag{7.9}$$

$$S^E = W_0 \sum_{i=1}^{\infty} \mu^i u_{+1-i} = W_0 \sum_{i=0}^{\infty} \mu^{i+1} u_{-i} \tag{7.10}$$

$$S_{+1} - S^E = W_0 u_{+1} \tag{7.11}$$

7.2.2. *The adjustable peg*

In order to reach quantitative conclusions about the adjustable peg system, we need to define its essential features clearly and no doubt somewhat artificially. The 'Bretton Woods system' was in principle the system defined in the Bretton Woods [1944] agreement. Its practical operation was somewhat different but uncodified.

A useful account was given, in a Report on the role of exchange rates in adjustment, by the executive directors of the IMF[1970]. The crucial sentence states: 'A change in the parity of a member's currency may be made only on the proposal of the member; but members agree that they will not propose such a change except to correct a fundamental disequilibrium' (p. 5, para. 1). Later, the report continues: 'The term "fundamental disequilibrium" is not defined in the Articles, and the Fund has never attempted to formulate a definition. The concept is a profound and subtle one, which lies at the heart of the Bretton Woods system, and has been tested by experience with that system' (p. 47, para. 2). On p. 7 and pp. 47–49, the Report spells out this concept. In effect, a disequilibrium is considered fundamental when it is not the result of temporary or cyclical fluctuations, or of excess or inadequate domestic expenditure ('absorption'), but rather: 'The payments disequilibrium may have been caused by an excess (or a deficiency) on domestic spending, but delay in corrective action may have led to a disparity in domestic and international prices, creating a new and more enduring source of disequilibrium. In such cases, even after domestic expenditures are adjusted in real terms, domestic costs may remain out of line and external equilibrium will not be restored. In these conditions, adjustments in domestic financial policy need to be accompanied or followed by a change in relative prices... Adjustment of the exchange rate effects this change in relative prices in a non-discriminatory way' (p. 7, para. 3).

However; 'The concept of fundamental disequilibrium does not itself specify at what stage of a disequilibrium the exchange rate should be adjusted'

(p. 48, para. 4). The Report admits: 'In the past, adjustment of parities has often been considered appropriate only when evidence of fundamental disequilibrium has become overwhelming' (p. 50, para. 2). 'During the second half of the 1960s, the international monetary system was believed by some to be so fragile that there was a strong tendency on the part of the major countries to forestall the devaluation of any major currency lest it upset the stability of other currencies. This attitude contributed to a general willingness to extend balance of payments credits and to tolerate the application of trade and payments restrictions.'

These passages convey the strong bias in the system against a parity change, and also the difficulties in assessing when disequilibrium was fundamental. 'The evidence' had to be 'overwhelming', even though the concept based on relative price disparities was simple enough; the key to these difficulties lay in problems with unit value indices, the sole indicators of traded goods prices, later analysed by Kravis and Lipsey [1971], and also in disagreements about how far such disparities could be reversed within reasonable time by domestic policy alone. In practice, the 'overwhelming' evidence was cumulative loss (or gain) in reserves to a point at which the authorities could no longer maintain 'orderly' foreign exchange markets (Article 1 section (iii) of the Bretton Woods agreement) without sacrificing the objectives of 'the promotion... of high levels of employment' (Art. 1, section (ii)) or of the 'elimination of foreign exchange restrictions' (Art. 1, section (iv)).

When a parity change came to be finally agreed because of such a situation, it clearly had to be of sufficient magnitude to convince speculators that equilibrium would return after the new policies had had time to take effect. At the same time, it must not be so large that it would create a serious disequilibrium in the opposite direction. Here again, the measure of relative price disparity was, for the same reason, hard to apply in gauging the required size of exchange rate change. In the context of the relative price disparities that developed during the 1960s, it would appear that the figure of ten percent was used as a 'norm' for parity changes. Indeed, of the 5 parity changes for major industrial countries, 3 (Canada in 1962 of −12%, France in 1969 of −11%, and Germany in 1969 of +9%) were within 2 percent of this norm; the other two were the UK at −14% in 1967 where the delay had by all accounts been unusually great, and Germany at +5% in 1961, where revaluation was strongly resisted by the German authorities.

In what follows we assume that in the peg system there are 2 'rules' of exchange rate adjustment, which encapsulate in a necessarily over-simplified form the foregoing discussion:

Rule (1): The parity will be changed in the next period if and only if cumulative intervention, I, up to that period, weighted by an exponential lag, δ, numerically exceeds a (positive) parameter, $\frac{1}{\alpha}$, that is if:

$$\left| \alpha(1-\delta) \sum_{i=0}^{\infty} \delta^i I_{-i+1} \right| > 1 \qquad (7.12)$$

where the number of periods since the peg was last fixed (at the value S_0) is assumed to be large. α is assumed to be fixed in such a way that the exchange rate is expected in the long run to converge on its equilibrium value. Hence we assume in this rule that the authorities use the loss of reserves as the sole objective 'indicator' but that they react to the loss in a way designed to reflect fundamental pressures.

Rule (2): The change in the rate next period, ΔS_{+1}, is restricted to 0 or $\pm A$, where A is a single number. This number, corresponding to the 'norm' parity change, is thus assumed to be universally and inflexibly prescribed.

These two rules are sufficient to generate the comparisons we need between the pegged and floating system. We will be building on the familiar property of the pegged system, that the peg moves discontinuously whereas the variables that trigger its movement (in our analysis, reserves is the single variable involved) move continuously. The speculator, who knows the current state of the reserves, is faced with the prospect of reserves loss (gain) in the next period. If reserves are low, then under Rule (1) a small loss in the next period would be sufficient to trigger a devaluation of A; but it would require a very large rise to trigger a revaluation. The opposite is true if reserves are high. Only if reserves are roughly at their required level will the loss and gain in reserves required to trigger a devaluation and revaluation be roughly symmetrical. Figure 7.1 illustrates.

If the authorities were to move the parity continuously in response to next period's reserves change, where the movement is calibrated so as to produce the same devaluation should $\alpha(1-\delta)x = 1$ (the same revaluation should $\alpha(1-\delta)x = -1$), then the mean or expected value of the probability distribution of the implied exchange rate level in the next period, denoted as $\hat{S}_{+1}$ would be S^*_{+1} shown on the lower scale in Figure 7.1 below the peak of

Figure 7.1
The probability distribution of a change in reserves at the end of the next period.

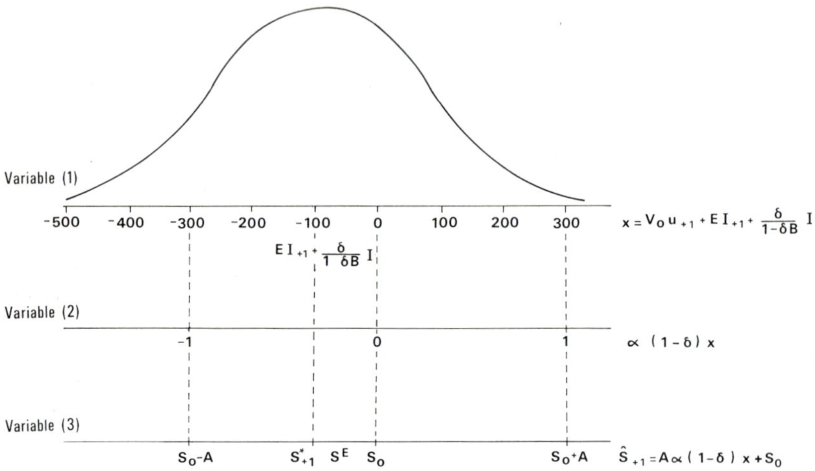

Variable (1), x, is reserves change next period *plus* past reserve changes exponentially weighted (£ million).
Variable (2), according to Rule (1), triggers parity change when $|\alpha(1-\delta)x>1$.
Variable (3), $\hat{S}_{+1}$, is the parity level next period that would be implied by $\alpha(1-\delta)x$, if parity changes were made continuously, i.e. not by Rules (1) and (2), but by the rule $\Delta\hat{S}_{+1} = A\alpha(1-\delta)x$.

the distribution. We call $\hat{S}_{+1}$ and S^*_{+1} the 'as if' actual and expected values of S_{+1} (as if the distribution over S_{+1} were continuous). However, this is not in general the expected value, S^E, of next period's parity, when the parity is moved discontinuously by $\pm A$ (as dictated by Rule (2) of the peg system); it will only be so when the exponentially weighted sum of past reserve changes *plus* the expected next period reserve change is 0, because only in this case are the probabilities of devaluation and revaluation equal. This can be seen by comparing Fig. 7.1 with Fig. 7.2 which shows the 'degenerate' probability distribution over S_{+1} when the parity is moved discontinuously. The fact that the area between $S_0 + A$ and $S_0 - A$ in the continuous distribution of Fig. 7.1 is 'piled up' on S_0, because there is no parity change, means that S^E is closer to S_0 than S^*_{+1}. Thus in this example the area of the bar over S_0 is 0.8, that over $S_0 - A$ is 0.19, that over $S_0 + A$ is 0.01. If $A = 10$, $S_0 = 0$, then $S^*_{+1} = -2.7$, $S^E = -1.8$.

Figure 7.2
Corresponding probability distribution of parity changes under the pegged system.

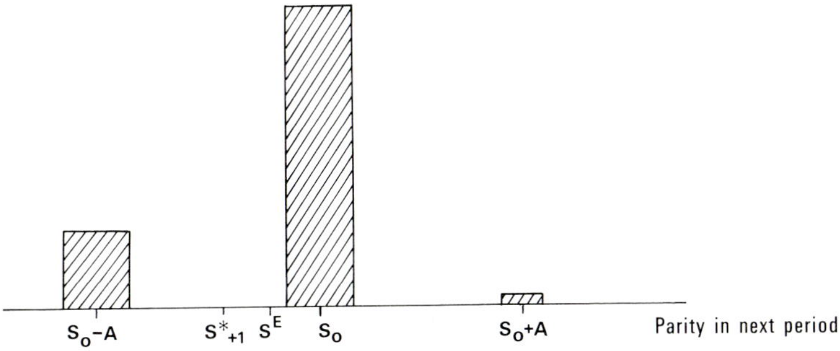

We call the gap between S^E and S^*_{+1} the 'bias factor', and approximate it by the linear funtion $S^E - S^*_{+1} = b(S_0 - S^*_{+1})$. The true function is non-linear, as given by the properties of the normal distribution. Thus b increases as S^*_{+1} diverges from S_0 (because of past or expected reserves change). However, we will be concerned in what follows with the behaviour of the peg system under 'normal' circumstances where the past reserves losses or gains have not cumulated to an extreme extent. Under other, 'crisis', circumstances it is a familiar point that speculators enjoy a one-way option in a peg system, so that not only b but also the coefficient h (the response of capital flows) increase sharply, the latter causing abnormally large pressure on the peg. In the region we are concerned with, the assumption of constancy for b, as for h, seems reasonable.

The algebraic expression for S^*_{+1} is thus derived directly from Rule (1) of the peg system as:

$$S^*_{+1} = E\hat{S}_{+1} = EA\alpha(1-\delta)x + S_0 = A\alpha(1-\delta)EI_{+1} + \frac{A\alpha(1-\delta)\delta}{1-\delta B} I + S_0 \tag{7.14}$$

where E is the expectations operator, meaning the expected value conditional on information available at time t when expectations are formed, and B is the lag operator. This expression simply restates what was illustrated in Fig. 7.1. To it we add the bias factor to obtain S^E as:

$$S^E = A\alpha(1-\delta)(1-b)EI_{+1} + \frac{A\alpha(1-\delta)\delta(1-b)}{1-\delta B} I + S_0. \tag{7.15}$$

We derive EI_{+1} and I by solving the market-clearing equation for the peg system, in which now the dependent variable is not the exchange rate but the amount of intervention, I. This equation, which under floating was (7.1), is now written as:

$$(\eta - 1)XS_0 - h\Delta S^E + u + I = 0 \tag{7.16}$$

where u is the same error term as in (7.1).

We follow Muth's general approach for solving this equation, just as in the floating case. From (7.15) we substitute into (7.16) for ΔS^E, so obtaining an expression in EI_{+1} and I. We then take deviations of I from its equilibrium value, $\bar{I}$, which is obtained from (7.16) by setting $\Delta S^E = 0 = u$ as:

$$\bar{I} = -(\eta - 1)XS_0 \tag{7.17}$$

where $i = I - \bar{I}$ and $h'' = hA\alpha(1 - \delta)(1 - b)$, this gives us:

$$-h''\{1-(1+\delta)B+\delta B^2\}Ei_{+1} + \{(1-\delta h'')+(h''\delta-\delta)B\}i = -(1-\delta B)u \tag{7.18}$$

We now write:

$$i = \sum_{i=0}^{\infty} V_i u_{-i} \tag{7.19}$$

$$E(i_{+1}) = \sum_{i=1}^{\infty} V_i u_{-i+1} = \sum_{i=0}^{\infty} V_{i+1} u_{-i} \tag{7.20}$$

Substituting (7.19) and (7.20) into (7.18) gives:

$$-h''\sum_{i=0}^{\infty} V_{i+1}u_{-i} + (1+\delta)h''\sum_{i=1}^{\infty} V_i u_{-i} - \delta h''\sum_{i=2}^{\infty} V_{i-1}u_{-i}$$

$$+(1-\delta h'')\sum_{i=0}^{\infty} V_i u_{-i} + (h''\delta - \delta)\sum_{i=1}^{\infty} V_{i-1}u_{-i} = -u + \delta u_{-1}. \tag{7.21}$$

This yields the following identities in u, u_{-1}, and u_{-i} $(i \geqslant 2)$:

$$-h'' V_1 + (1 - \delta h'')V_0 = -1, \tag{7.22}$$
$$-h'' V_2 + (1 + h'')V_1 + (h''\delta - \delta)V_0 = \delta, \tag{7.23}$$
$$-h'' V_{i+1} + (1 + h'')V_i - \delta V_{i-1} = 0 \text{ for } i \geqslant 2, \tag{7.24}$$

from which we derive V_0, V_1 and $V_i = V_1 l^{i-1}$ $(i \geqslant 2)$, being the only stable root of (7.24), provided the roots are not imaginary. This gives $V_0 = \{1 + h''(1 - \delta - l)\}/d$ and $V_1 = \delta h''(\delta - 1)/d$ where $d = h''(2\delta + l - 1) - 1 - l\delta h''^2$.

Returning now to S^E, we substitute from (7.19) and (7.20) into (7.15) and collect terms, to obtain:

$$S^E = A\alpha(1 - b)\bar{I} + S_0 + A\alpha(1 - \delta)(1 - b)\left\{\sum_{i=0}^{\infty} V_{i+1} + \right.$$
$$\left. + \sum_{i=0}^{\infty} \delta^{i+1} B^i \sum_{i=0}^{\infty} V_i \right\} u_{-i} \tag{7.25}$$

We can simplify this further by appealing to that part of Rule (1) which specifies the method for fixing α, namely at a level such that the exchange rate is expected in the long run to converge on its equilibrium value. If we define S^{E+j} as the exchange rate currently expected to prevail j periods from now, then:

$$S^{E+j} = A\alpha(1 - b)\bar{I} + S_0 + A\alpha(1 - \delta)(1 - b)$$
$$\left\{\sum_{i=0}^{\infty} V_{i+j} + \sum_{i=0}^{\infty} \delta^{i+1} B^i \sum_{i=0}^{\infty} V_{i+j-1} \right\} u_{-i} \tag{7.26}$$

Since V_i is a series declining asymptotically to zero, as $j \rightarrow \infty$ so the terms in the u_{-i} tend to disappear and $S^{E+j} \rightarrow A\alpha(1 - b)\bar{I} + S_0$, which is therefore the expected long run exchange rate. Since by Rule (1) this must be the equilibrium exchange rate (i.e. zero given our measurement of S in terms of deviations from equilibrium), we have:

$$A\alpha(1 - b)\bar{I} + S_0 = 0 \tag{7.27}$$

Because $\bar{I} = -(\eta - 1)XS_0$, this gives us the required restriction on α:

$$\alpha = \frac{1}{(\eta - 1)X(1 - b)A} \tag{7.28}$$

It also allows us to write S^E simply in terms of the current and past errors, u_{-i}:

$$S^E = A\alpha(1 - \delta)(1 - b)\left\{\sum_{i=0}^{\infty} V_{i+1} + \sum_{i=0}^{\infty} \delta^{i+1} B^i \sum_{i=0}^{\infty} V_i\right\} u_{-i} \tag{7.29}$$

Note also that, as illustrated in Figure (7.1):

$$\hat{S}_{+1} - S^*_{+1} = A\alpha(1 - \delta)V_0 u_{+1}. \tag{7.30}$$

(7.29) is an important and helpful finding, as can be seen by comparing it with (7.10), the expression for S^E in the floating rate system. In both regimes the expected exchange rate depends solely on the (same) current and past errors, with no constant term. The difference relates solely to the coefficients on those errors; the coefficients will in turn depend on the complete set of model parameters entering respectively into the pegged and floating equations. The two sets will not in general be the same; apart from the inclusion of the parameters A, α, δ, b in the peg system and which are not present in the floating case, we will next be discussing the possible difference in the capital flows parameter, h. But the strong implication nevertheless remains that the *systematic* determinants of and expression for the expected exchange rate (ie. omitting the error terms) are identical, whether the exchange rate is fixed or floating.

7.2.3. *Comparing h and h* under pegged and floating rates*

h, in standard portfolio theory, depends on the variance of S_{+1} around S^E (see for example Tobin [1958] and chapter 4), in the function $K = h(S - S^E) + h^*$. It is clear from casual illustration that, in general, the variance of S_{+1} need not be the same between regimes:

Figure 7.3
Probability distributions of pegged and floating rates.[1]

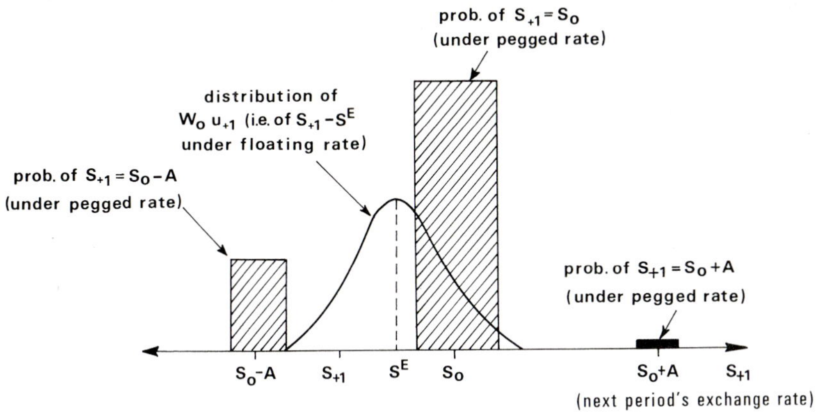

S^E, the expected exchange rate, is assumed in this illustration to be the same under both regimes.

However, standard portfolio theory is not set up ideally for dealing with non-symmetric distributions. It has been argued (see for example Markowitz [1959] chapter 9, pp. 188–201) that the semi-variance should be substituted for the variance when the distribution is non-symmetric; this may be seen as a way of allowing for skewness without resort to the (inconvenient) third moment.

The use of variance as a measure of risk has also been attacked by Rothschild and Stiglitz [1970] as being 'misleadingly general', because the relative risk of two probability distributions with the same mean will only be correlated with their relative variance under highly restrictive assumptions about the nature of either the probability distributions (eg. if both distributions are normal) or the utility function (eg. if the function is quadratic and concave). Clearly in our case no such restrictions can reasonably be applied; as is perfectly clear from Figure 7.3, even if the variances of S (pegged) and S (floating) were the same, the riskiness of the two distributions would not be because the distribution of S (pegged) is asymmetrical.

The semi-variance measure of risk is not open to the objection of asymmetry. It is also clear that, if the relative semi-variance of the two distributions increases, so too does the relative risk. Thus it would appear satisfactory for our purposes here. Of course, we also make the strong (cardinal) assumption that, if the semi-variance of the two distributions is the same, then the risk is *equal*. This, like most cardinal assumptions, cannot and in fact need not be defended as precise; all we say is that given that some such quantitative assumption must be made, no better one is available and that as an approximation it is satisfactory.[3]

We therefore measure expected risk in the floating case not by the variance, σ_F, but by the expression,

$$E(S)^2 = \sigma_F^2 \int_{S_{+1}=S}^{(\pm)\infty} \frac{1}{\sigma_F\sqrt{2\pi}} e^{-\frac{1}{2}\frac{(S_{+1}-S^E)^2}{\sigma_F}} \cdot dS_{+1}, \quad \text{where} \quad \sigma_F = \sigma_u W_0 \tag{7.31}$$

(and the bound is $\pm\infty$ depending on $S \gtrless S^E$). Similarly, in the pegged case, risk becomes

$$E(S)^2 = A^2 \int_{S_{+1}=S_0(\pm)A}^{(\pm)\infty} \frac{1}{\sigma_p\sqrt{2\pi}} e^{-\frac{1}{2}\frac{(\hat{S}_{+1}-S^*_{+1})^2}{\sigma_p}} \cdot dS_{+1},$$

$$\text{where } \sigma_p = \sigma_u A\alpha(1-\delta)V_0 \tag{7.32}$$

[3] To satisfy ourselves that it is a reasonable approximation we may perform the following arithmetical experiment to compare the expected utility of two relevant distributions with the same semi-variance. One distribution was standard normal (eg. the floating case) and thus had a semi-variance of 0.5. The other was skewed with a non-negligible probability of a large loss, a negligible probability of a large gain, and a residual probability of no change (eg. the pegged case). For this other, the large gain was set at 2 (standard deviations) with probability 0.01; the large loss was set variously at -1 with probability 0.5, -1.5 with probability 0.222, -2 with probability 0.125, and -3 with probability 0.055, all of these yielding a semi-variance of 0.5. Two extreme utility functions were tried; one highly concave (u_1) and one linear or risk-neutral (u_2). The values of u for 'income' of -2, -1, 0, $+1$, $+2$ were: (u_1) 10, 22, 29, 33, 36, and (u_2) 10, 25, 40 etc. The expected utility of the skewed distribution expressed as a percentage of that for the normal distribution were:

Large Loss (Probability)	u_1 *(Highly concave)*	u_2 *(Linear)*
−1 (0.5)	95	84
−1.5 (0.222)	98	90
−2 (0.125)	100	94
−3 (0.055)	102	96

This experiment indicates that the error in using the suggested cardinal assumption is most unlikely to exceed 16 per cent (and will probably be considerably less). That sort of error is trivial relative to the margin of error on most of our parameter estimates.

(and again the signs of $S_0 \pm A$, $\pm\infty$ are set by $S^*_{+1} \gtrless S_0$). The integrals measure the area under the standard normal curve covered respectively by the distributions of $W_0 u_{+1}$ and $V_0 A\alpha(1-\delta)u_{+1}$; and subscripts F and P denote floating and pegged regimes respectively. These expressions measure the variance of $S_{+1} - S$, $S_{+1} - S_0$, respectively, for the values of these variables which cause actual loss to the speculator; for values implying a profit, $S_{+1} - S, S_{+1} - S_0 = 0$. Now we write the expected utility on a portfolio of two currencies (with only one independent exchange rate, measured with currency 2 as numeraire) as a linear function of expected return and expected risk in the sense defined:

$$\frac{E(u)}{p} = \left[\gamma \sum_{i=1}^{2} \frac{p_i}{p} E(r_i)\right] - \left[(1-\gamma) \sum_{i=1}^{2} \left(\frac{p_i}{p}\right)^2 \int (r_i - Er_i)^2\right] + \beta \qquad (7.33)$$

where $E(r_i)$ is expected return on currency i, p_i is the proportion of the portfolio p held in currency i and the $\int$ sign stands for the appropriate integral over the normal distribution. Since currency 2 is the numeraire, $Er_2 = r_2 = 0$ so we will simply write $Er_1 = Er$ in what follows; also of course $\frac{p_2}{p} = 1 - \frac{p_1}{p}$, in our two-currency world.

For each country's residents, we assume that the domestic currency is free of exchange rate risk and gives no return.[4] For residents of country II, this implies straightforwardly that their expected utility is:

$$\frac{E(u)^{II}}{p^{II}} = \gamma\left(\frac{p_1^{II}}{p^{II}}\right) Er - (1-\gamma)\left(\frac{p_1^{II}}{p^{II}}\right)^2 E(S)^2 + \beta^{II} \qquad (7.34)$$

[4] It is not, of course, free of price-level risk and may give a price return and, fully specified, the speculative schedule would also have a coefficient on the expected price return as well as a further element in the constant term, whose values would be dependent on this risk. However, here we assume expected price level return and risk to be both zero in order to focus purely on the coefficients h and h^*. Similar points apply to differential interest rate return and risk; we assume here that the interest rate differential is zero and riskless. While strict, these assumptions concerning prices and interest rates may be partly justified on the grounds that in this quarterly model the covariances between the exchange rate and each of these are likely to be negligible; expected returns and risk on the different aspects of the portfolio are then additive. Nevertheless, the variances of the other aspects would still enter into the expression for h (in the divisor). Neglect of these variances is purely a matter of convenience and leads to some over-statement of the effect of regime-change. However, the existence of a 3-monthly debt instrument (with zero capital variance) and the predictability of prices 3 months ahead suggest that in this quarterly context it may not be too serious.

Er here represents the expected appreciation of currency 1 against currency 2 (in terms of currency 2). $E(S)^2$ represents the semi-variance of the r distribution (i.e. the risk of currency 1 depreciating). The II superscript indicates that these are country II variables.

For residents of country I, the assumption implies that expected utility is given by:

$$\frac{E(u)^I}{p^I} = \gamma\left(1 - \frac{p_1^I}{p^I}\right)(-Er) - (1-\gamma)\left(1 - \frac{p_1^I}{p^I}\right)^2 E(-S)^2 + \beta^I. \tag{7.35}$$

Here $-Er$ is the expected appreciation of currency 2 against currency 1, while $E(-S)^2$ represents the semi-variance arising from the risk of currency 2 depreciating (ie. the opposite side of the r distribution to that which worries residents of country II). So residents of country I, like those of country II, are only concerned with returns and risks on their holdings of *foreign* currency.

Maximising these with respect to $\frac{p_1^I}{p^I}$ and $\frac{p_1^{II}}{p^{II}}$ respectively gives:

$$0 = \frac{\delta E(u)^I/p^I}{\delta p_1^I/p^I} = \gamma Er - 2\frac{p_1^I}{p^I}E(-S)^2(1-\gamma) + (1-\gamma)2E(-S)^2 \tag{7.36}$$

and

$$0 = \frac{\delta E(u)^{II}/p^{II}}{\delta p_1^{II}/p^{II}} = \gamma Er - 2(1-\gamma)\frac{p_1^{II}}{p^{II}}E(S)^2 \tag{7.37}$$

Let $p^I = wp$ where p is the total world speculative portfolio; then summing the two implied demand curves p_1^I and p_1^{II} gives:

$$p_1 = p_1^I + p_1^{II} = \frac{p\gamma}{2(1-\gamma)} Er\left\{\frac{1-w}{E(S)^2} + \frac{w}{E(-S)^2}\right\} + wp \tag{7.38}$$

and, of course, $p_2 = p - p_1$.

Since $Er = S - S^E$,

$$h = \tfrac{1}{2}p\left(\frac{\gamma}{1-\gamma}\right)\left\{\frac{1-w}{E(S)^2} + \frac{w}{E(-S)^2}\right\} \text{ and } h^* = wp \tag{7.39}$$

h^* is identical in the two regimes. As for h, in both regimes there is the similarity that $h \to \infty$ as $Er \to \infty$, because $E(S)^2 \to 0, E(-S)^2 \to \sigma_F^2$ (floating) or A^2 (pegged). This is a cautionary reminder that h is not a constant. However, for our purposes we take it at its average value over the estimation period (excluding 'crisis' quarters); and as such it will in general not be the same in the two regimes. How we may estimate the difference we proceed to discuss in the next section.

7.2.4. *Estimating the effect of a change of regime on h*

It is helpful to define a new parameter of the pegged regime, k, such that $A = k\sigma_p$. This parameter indicates the relative priorities attached by the authorities to, on the one hand, the risk that the party change will be inadequate to prevent continued reserves losses (gains), and on the other hand, the risk of 'overkill', with the consequent need to reverse the parity change. The higher k, the less the relative fear of overkill, and the higher the parity change relative to the identified disequilibrium.

We may conveniently write h_p and h_F as:

$$h_p = \frac{p'}{A^2}\left\{\frac{(1-w)A^2}{E(S_p)^2} + \frac{wA^2}{E(-S_p)^2}\right\} \tag{7.40}$$

and

$$h_F = \frac{p'}{\sigma_F^2}\left\{\frac{(1-w)\sigma_F^2}{E(S_F)^2} + \frac{w\sigma_F^2}{E(-S_F)^2}\right\}, \text{ where } p' = \tfrac{1}{2}p\frac{\gamma}{1-\gamma}. \tag{7.41}$$

In these expressions, $\dfrac{A^2}{E(S_p)^2}, \dfrac{A^2}{E(-S_p)^2}$ are functions of the standard normal variable $\dfrac{S^*_{+1} - S_0}{A/k} = S_p^d$;

$\left\{\dfrac{\sigma_F^2}{E(S_F)^2}, \dfrac{\sigma_F^2}{E(-S_F)^2}\right\}$ are functions of $\dfrac{S_F^E - S}{\sigma_F} = S_F^d$. S_p^d and S_F^d, both expressed in the same units as the standard normal variable, measure the gap between the mean of the normal distribution and the current level of the pegged or floating exchange rate.

We are principally interested in the central limit h_p and h_F as (S^*_{+1}, S^E_{FI}) tend to (S_0, S); that is, as the means of the distributions tend to the current level of the exchange rate. This is the region in which the data should lie if 'crisis' experience is excluded, and will therefore be relevant to our estimate of h. We might conceivably wish to refine on this if the data lay seriously to the 'left' or 'right' of the central limiting value. But in practice such refinement is complicated and unlikely to yield a sufficient return, given the margin of error on the original parameter estimates.

We know that at this central limit

$$\frac{E(S_p)^2}{A^2} \to \frac{E(-S_p)^2}{A^2} \to f(k) \text{ and } \frac{E(S_F)^2}{\sigma_F^2} \to \frac{E(-S_F)^2}{\sigma_F^2} \to 0.5,$$

where $f(k)$ is the tail cut off by k standard deviations (eg. for $k = 2, f(k) = .025$). Hence at the limit $\frac{h_p}{h_F} = \frac{\sigma_F^2}{A^2}\left\{\frac{1/f(k)}{1/.5}\right\}$.[5] We may also evaluate the bias factor at the limit. We find that $(1 - b) = \{f(k - S_p^d) - f(k + S_p^d)\}\frac{k}{S_p^d}$[6] which evaluated for $S_p^d \to 0$ is a function of k.

It is also possible to go further and derive the full *function*, $h_p = f(Er_p)$, from the *function*, $h_F = ø(Er_F)$, and *vice versa*.[7] However, this is of little practical interest to us here, since we assume h to be constant, and is not pursued further.

[5] Chapter 8 discusses how this expression can be estimated numerically from estimates solely from data for the pegged regime.

[6] Since by definition $S_p^E = S_0 + A\{f(k - S_p^d) - f(k + S_p^d)\}$, and $S_p^E = (1 - b)S^*_{+1} + bS_0$.

[7] The procedure involves substituting for $1/f(k)$ and $1/0.5$, in the expressions for h_p and h_F, the values of

$$\left\{\frac{(1 - w)A^2}{E(S_p)^2} + \frac{wA^2}{E(-S_p)^2}\right\} \text{ and } \left\{\frac{(1 - w)\sigma_F^2}{E(S_F^2)} + \frac{w\sigma_F^2}{E(S_F^2)}\right\}$$

as $E(r_p)$ and $E(r_F)$ change. For this we also need to know w, which should be avalable from world financial statistics.

7.3. Conclusions

This chapter has derived the relevant expressions for S^E and for the parameters h and h^* under the pegged and floating regimes. We have, therefore, shown how, under the assumptions made that there are two currencies, one forward market and expectations are rational, we should proceed to adjust the speculative schedule $K = h(S - S^E) + h^*$ for a change in regime between pegged and floating rates, even though in general h and S^E are not the same. The assumptions are strict, deliberately so in order to extract a precise comparison capable of being translated into numerical form. Nevertheless, they are extremely relevant. The second currency can be regarded as an index of all foreign currencies. We may similarly regard S^E as an index of expected exchange rates at all future time periods. Expectations are, we have argued, likely to tend towards rationality and so to assume rationality will be most relevant for the new regime once it has 'settled down'; for analysis up to that point much guesswork would in any case be inevitable. In the next chapter we will explore the numerical consequences of the algebra we have developed in this one.

Chapter 8

THE FLOATING RATE MODEL WITH MODIFIED SPECULATIVE RESPONSE: STABILITY PROPERTIES REVISITED

8.1. Introduction

In chapter 7, it was shown that under certain assumptions the shift of exchange rate regime can be allowed for in the parameter estimates. The example of rational expectations in two simple models was worked through in detail. We now apply the technique exemplified there to the floating rate model for the UK. Hitherto, we have assumed that the coefficient, h, of speculative response is invariant with respect to the regime shift; on this assumption, we derived the stability properties of the UK floating rate model in chapter 5 given 'semi-rational', and in chapter 6 given 'fully-rational' expectations. In sections 8.2 and 8.3 of this chapter respectively, we go through the equivalent exercises with an appropriately modified h coefficient.

8.2. Semi-rational expectations

It will be recalled that the semi-rationality of speculators consisted essentially in their ignorance of the lag in current account response to the exchange rate (or the 'J-curve') and in their confusion of random with underlying payments factors. Thus we suggested that speculators believed in the models set out in chapter 7, solved these for their expectations, and then substituted an estimate for the resulting expression. The expected exchange rate derived in this way is then substituted into the 'true' model of chapter 5 to obtain the behaviour of the actual rate.

The derivation of h in chapter 7 was shown to involve the semi-variance of the exchange rate. It is clear that the relevant semi-variance is that perceived subjectively by the speculators themselves, since it is their assessment of the uncertainties that influences their willingness to take open positions. Since semi-rational speculators believe the models of chapter 7, it follows that they also estimate the semi-variances from these models. Thus to modify the parameter h for regime change we simply need to compare these models, and may therefore adopt the correction factor proposed there, namely

$$\frac{h_F}{h_p} = \frac{A^2 f(k)}{\sigma_F^2 (0.5)}.$$

Estimating the correction factor

A we supposed to be available from knowledge of the rules governing the fixed rate regime. We can reasonably set $A = 10\%$ for the 1960s, as argued in Chapter 7.

For k, we have from the definition given earlier:

$$k = A/\sigma_p \tag{8.1}$$

where

$$\sigma_p = \sigma_u A\alpha(1 - \delta)V_0, \tag{8.2}$$

as given in equation (7.32).

We derive σ_u on the assumption that UK government policy in the period was set with the aim of preventing the reserves changing; thus, it is assumed that their post-policy forecasts would have predicted zero change. We therefore took σ_u as the standard deviation from 0 of actual quarterly reserves changes ('currency flow') from 1963 *Q*1 to 1971 *Q*2, the period for which h_p was derived; on this basis, $\sigma_u = 1600$ (expressed as £ million per annum).

The fact that evidence of a 'fundamental' disequilibrium had to be 'overwhelming' suggests a long lag before reserve losses trigger a parity change, and consequently a high δ. We choose $\delta = 0.9$, which implies that a steady reserve loss at the rate of $1/\alpha$ would take about four years to trigger a devaluation; a reserve loss at the rate of $2/\alpha$ would take about $1\frac{1}{2}$ years. This appears to tally roughly with the UK experience in the run-up to the 1967 (November 18th) devaluation; reserve losses were not serious prior to 1964 but in the four years 1964–7 they averaged £580 million per annum, which is acceptably close to $1/\alpha$ (given $\alpha = 0.002$ as estimated below).

From p. 00, we obtained $V_0 = \dfrac{1 + h''(1 - l - \delta)}{h''(2\delta + l - 1) - 1 - lh''^2}$,
where $h'' = h_p A\alpha(1 - \delta)(1 - b)$.
This depends on the parameters A, h_p, α, δ, b, and l; of these b, l, α in turn depend on h_p and $(\eta - 1)X$.

Thus, by Rule (1) of the peg system we have $\alpha = \dfrac{1}{(\eta - 1)X(1 - b)A}$.

From p. 196 we have $b = 1 - \{f(k - S_p^d) - f(k + S_p^d)\}\dfrac{k}{S_p^d}$, which we evaluate for $S_p^d \to 0$.

Then (7.24) gives $l = \dfrac{(1 + h'') - \sqrt{(1 + h'')^2 - 4h''\delta}}{2h''}$

Finally, we have $h_p = 1000$, as (see Appendix 6.A) the approximate equivalent (at an annual rate) of the distributed lag parameters in (5.2); and (5.1) gave the total long run exchange rate effect (at an annual rate) on the current balance (Σb_i) as 122, which is the relevant estimate of $(\eta - 1)X$.

It turns out that the following (rounded) numerical values solve this nonlinear system in b, ℓ, α, and k: $b = 0.55$, $\ell = 0.75$, $\alpha = 0.002$, $k = 1.3$ ($f(k) = 0.1$). Hence also $h'' = 0.88$, $V_0 = -2.5$, $\sigma_p = 7.5$.

To complete estimation of the correction factor,
we require $\sigma_F^2 = \sigma_u^2 W_0^2$. From p. 182, $W_0 = \dfrac{1}{(\eta - 1)X + h_F(1 - \mu)}$ where the root

$$\mu = \frac{\left\{\dfrac{(\eta - 1)X}{h_F} + 2\right\} - \sqrt{\left\{\dfrac{(\eta - 1)X}{h_F} + 2\right\}^2 - 4}}{2}$$ comes from (7.7).

From the correction factor together with our estimates of A and k, we have
$\dfrac{h_p}{h_F} = \dfrac{\sigma_F^2}{100}\left\{\dfrac{0.5}{0.1}\right\} = 0.05\,\sigma_F^2.$

Substituting into this for σ_F^2, we obtain

$$\frac{h_p}{h_F} = 0.05 \frac{\sigma_u^2}{\{(\eta - 1)X + h_F(1 - \mu)\}^2}. \tag{8.3}$$

This is solved for the single remaining unknown, h_F, of which μ is also a function, to give $h_F = 4500$, $\mu = 0.86$. Thus the correction factor (h_F/h_p) is 4.5. We also have $\sigma_F = 2$, which is of some interest in itself.

It may cause some surprise that the necessary modification is so large and in an upward direction. However, the explanation is that there are two opposing forces influencing the degree of uncertainty and so h, as we move from a pegged to a floating regime. On the one hand, the probability of a rate change is increased since the authorities are no longer intervening. On the other hand, the size of the change – when it comes – is smaller with a floating rate. Thus floating carries the connotation of 'a lot of little' rate changes, a pegged rate few but large.

The precise correction factor turns out to be very sensitive to small variations in the relative strength of these two opposing forces. Thus, if we keep the other parameters, σ_u^2 and h_p, constant, we may gauge the effect of the first force by varying $f(k)$, which measures the probability of a peg change or the degree of 'fixity' in the peg, and of the second force by varying A, the size of peg change. The table below shows the correction factor for 10% variations of these parameters:

Table 8.1
The Correction Factor (h_F/h_p) for 10% variations of A, $f(k)$.

A	$f(k) =$	0.12 ($k = 1.2$)	0.1 ($k = 1.3$)	0.09 ($k = 1.4$)
11		> 50	> 50	20
10		20	4.5	3
9		5	2	1.5

Note: Correction factors corresponding to $f(k)$, A, are shown in cells.

The degree of sensitivity is such that there is little point in re-running the semi-rational floating rate model for simply the one 'central' modification. In order to gauge the stability of the resulting exchange rate equation, we assume that the expected exchange rate is given 'semi-rationally' by the expression developed in Appendix 5.A, namely:

$$S^{E+4} = \Sigma w_i\left(-\frac{C_{-i}}{b} + S_{-i}\right) \qquad \text{`modified' model} \tag{8.4}$$

and $$S^{E+4} = \Sigma w_i\left(\frac{-C_{-i}}{b}\right) \qquad \text{`unmodified' model} \tag{8.5}$$

We approximate the Σw_i as $w(B) = \dfrac{0.2B}{1-0.8B}$, which is a reasonably close fit to the lag structure in eq. (5.A.8) on p. 146. We then embed this equation for S^{E+4} in the following approximation (see Appendix 6.A) to the model of chapter 5:

$$C + \Delta K = 0 \tag{8.6}$$

$$C = \left\{\frac{\varepsilon X\lambda\eta'}{1 - B(1-\lambda)} + X(\eta' - 1)\right\} S \tag{8.7}$$

$$\Delta K = h(\Delta S - \Delta S^{E+4}) \tag{8.8}$$

So the 'modified' model consists of (8.4) and (8.6–8), while the 'unmodified' model consists of (8.5) and (8.6–8).

We found that the modified model was unstable, however high the corrected h became. Thus at $h_F = 1000$, the roots were 0.55 and a complex pair with damping factor 1.14; as $h_F \to \infty$, they tended to 0.57 and a complex pair with damping factor 1.09.

The unmodified model however was stable, provided the corrected h_F was greater than 1500. At $h_F = 1500$, the roots were 0.54 and a complex pair with damping factor of 1. At $h_F = 1000$, the first root was 0.53 and the damping factor became 1.01. However at $h_F = 2000$, these numbers became respectively 0.6 and 0.93. As $h_F \to \infty$, they tended to 0.53 and 0.98.

The actual standard error of the one-period-ahead exchange rate forecast, se_F (as opposed to the variance expected by semi-rational speculators, σ_F), is given for both modified and unmodified models by

$$se_F = \frac{\sigma_u\sqrt{1 + (1.8-\lambda)^2 + 0.64(1-\lambda)^2}}{\{\varepsilon X\lambda\eta' + X(\eta' - 1) + h_F\}};$$

note that the next period's error is the moving average process $-u_{+1} + (1.8 - \lambda)u - 0.8(1 - \lambda)u_{-1}$, where u is assumed to be serially uncorrelated. Even given $\sigma_u = 1600$; $\eta' = 0.25$, $\lambda = 0.14$, $\varepsilon = 7.5$, $X = 110$, se_F nevertheless ranges massively, according to the appropriate correction factor from 2.3 ($A = 9, f(k) = 0.09$) to a negligible 0.06 ($A = 11, f(k) = 0.12$).

These results for the semi-rational models are to be interpreted as applying to the behaviour of the floating rate in its early years. They suggest that, while the speculative response would be at least as large and probably larger than under the pegged system, there would be tendencies towards instability. These, however, might not be quantitatively too serious in that the system could be converging on full rationality before the roots had cumulated massively. For example, a damping factor of 1.14^t (the highest encountered) has cumulated to only 4.8 by the end of 3 years. This would appear to give ample time for the necessary learning by speculators about the long lag structures embedded in the system.

8.3. Fully rational expectations

The correction factor of the previous section remains the appropriate one as the floating rate model tends to full rationality, namely $h_F/h_p = \dfrac{A^2 f(k)}{\sigma_F^2 0.5}$ However, now $\sigma_2^u = \sigma_2^u Z_0$, where Z_0 is derived from the fully rational model of chapter 6, section 6.8, but assuming only one forward market and incorporating a random error term u as in chapter 7. This gives us the market-clearing equation:

$$qS + h\,\Delta(S - S^E) + u = 0 \tag{8.9}$$

where since η^* is set at zero, $q = \dfrac{\varepsilon X \lambda \eta'}{1 - B(1 - \lambda)} + (\eta' - 1)X$.

Following the procedure of chapter 7, we specify

$$S = \sum_{i=0}^{\infty} Z_i u_{-i}, \text{ so that} \tag{8.10}$$

$$S^E = \sum_{i=1}^{\infty} Z_i u_{-i+1}. \tag{8.11}$$

We substitute from (8.10) and (8.11) into (8.9), and obtain from the resulting three identities in u, u_{-1}, and u_{-i} $(i \geqslant 2)$ the relevant expressions for Z_0, Z_1 and the stable roots of the equation for the Z_i $(i \geqslant 2)$, which will be a complex pair as in chapter 6, Appendix 6.A. Their derivation is given in Appendix 8.A.

We now re-arrange terms in the correction factor and substitute $\sigma_u^2 Z_o^2$ for σ_F^2 to obtain:

$$Z_0^2 h_F = \frac{A^2 h_p f(k)}{\sigma_u^2 \, 0.5} = 0.0078, \tag{8.12}$$

from the estimates given earlier of $A = 10$, $f(k) = 0.1$, $h_p = 1000$, $\sigma_u = 1600$. Given our estimates of the other parameters, namely $\eta' = 0.25$, $\varepsilon = 7.5$, $X = 110$, $\lambda = 0.14$, we solve iteratively, picking an h_F, solving for the root, deriving Z_0, and checking against (8.12).

It turns out that the values of h_F and Z_0 consistent with these estimates are approximately $h_F = 14000$, $Z_0 = -0.00075$ and the correction factor is of course 14. The stable root is the complex pair $0.878 \pm 0.105\sqrt{-1}$; this implies a (very slow) cycle of about 13 years which also takes about 5 years to converge to within 10%; the convergence factor is 0.884. This central result (case (a) of Table 8.2) plausibly implies that once speculators have learnt 'fully', the speculative response becomes very much more elastic. The variance of the exchange rate around equilibrium becomes $\sigma_F^2 = Z_0^2 \sigma_u^2 = 1.42$ and the standard deviation 1.2%.

This result is less sensitive to variations in A and $f(k)$ (and correspondingly in σ_u and h_p) than the earlier semi-rational case. For 10% variations in each (in all permutations as in Table 8.1 above) h_F lies within the range 11,000–19,000 (Table 8.2, cases (k) – (p)). At the lower end of this range the only change from the central result is that σ_F rises to 1.4 – 1.6%. At the higher end, σ_F falls to 0.9 – 1.0%, the convergence period lengthens slightly to 6 years and the cycle length nearly doubles to 24 years. Curiously, however, the *higher* A or $f(k)$, the lower h_F becomes, unlike in the semi-rational case and unlike what one might expect (the more risky the peg system, the lower h_p could be *relative* to h_F). For example, for $A = 11$, $f(k) = 0.12$, we have $h_F = 11000$ (as against $h_F = 19000$ for $A = 9$, $f(k) = 0.09$). The reason for this lies in the sensitivity of Z_0 and so the variance of the exchange rate, σ_F^2, to h_F.

Table 8.2
Stability properties of UK exchange rate with fully rational expectations and corrected h.[1]

	A	$f(k)$	h_p	σ_u	η'	ε	λ	h_F (corrected)	Roots (unstable bracketed)	Cycle length (quarters)	Z_0	$\sigma_F(\%)$	Approx. number of quarters to converge[2] (damping factor)
(a)				)	0.25	7.5	0.14	14000	(1.1), $0.878 \pm 0.105i$	53	−0.00075	1.2	19 (0.884)
(b)				)	0.25	7.5	0.1	$\to\infty$	$>\to 1$, $<\to 1$, $\to 0.9$	—	$\to 0$	$\to 0$	—[3]
(c)				)	0.25	7.5	0.2	14000	(1.1), $0.849 \pm 0.084i$	64	−0.00075	1.2	15 (0.853)
(d)				)	0.2	7.5	0.14	$\to\infty$	$>\to 1$, $<\to 1$, $\to 0.86$	—	$\to 0$	$\to 0$	—[3]
(e)				)	0.3	7.5	0.14	14000	(1.1), $0.878 \pm 0.101i$	55	−0.00075	1.2	19 (0.884)
(f)	10	0.1	1000	1600)	0.25	6.0	0.14	$\to\infty$	$>\to 1$, $<\to 1$, $\to 0.86$	—	$\to 0$	$\to 0$	—[3]
(g)				)	0.25	9.0	0.14	14000	(1.1), $0.878 \pm 0.105i$	53	−0.00075	1.2	19 (0.884)
(h)				)	0.3	9.0	0.2	9000	(1.12), $0.839 \pm 0.100i$	53	−0.00095	1.5	14 (0.845)
(i)				)	0.2	6.0	0.1	$\to\infty$	$>\to 1$, $<\to 1$, $\to 0.9$	—	$\to 0$	$\to 0$	—[3]
(j)				)	0.2	6.0	0.2	$\to\infty$	$>\to 1$, $<\to 1$, $\to 0.80$	—	$\to 0$	$\to 0$	—[3]
(k)	11	0.12	1000	1600)								1.6	
(l)	10	0.10	1450	1600)	0.25	7.5	0.14	11000	(1.1), $0.878 \pm 0.105i$	53	−0.00102	1.6	19 (0.884)
(m)	10	0.10	1000	1330)								1.4	
(n)	9	0.09	1000	1600)								0.9	
(o)	10	0.10	730	1600)	0.25	7.5	0.14	19000	(1.05), $0.903 \pm 0.059i$	97	−0.00055	0.9	23 (0.905)
(p)	10	0.10	1000	1870)								1.0	

Notes: [1] $X = 110$ throughout. Values of h_F approximate to nearest '000.
[2] Convergence to within 10% of original shock.
[3] In these cases, the correction factor is infinitely large, the unstable root tends to unity from above, one stable root tends to $(1-\lambda)$, the other tends to unity from below, Z_i (for all i) tend to zero, and the rate is in continuous equilibrium.

Thus at $h_F = 11000$, $Z_0 = -0.0010$, $\sigma_F^2 = 2.62$, while at $h_F = 19000$, $Z_0 = -0.0005$, and $\sigma_F^2 = 0.77$. In the semi-rational case, we found that as h_F rose, so $|Z_0|$ (and the variance expected by speculators, σ_F^2) fell much less rapidly than in the fully rational case; at $h_F = 11000$, $V_0 = -0.0009$, $\sigma_F^2 = 2.07$ while at $h_F = 20000$, $V_0 = -0.0007$, $\sigma_F^2 = 1.25$. This lesser sensitivity accounts for the different direction of the response of h_F to A and $f(k)$.

We remarked earlier (chapter 6) that the stability properties of the floating rate model were sensitive in the fully rational case to variation in its 'basic' parameters η', ε, λ. We now investigate whether this sensitivity continues when we allow h_F to be determined by the correction factor.

Table 8.2, cases (b) – (j), show that h_F is very sensitive to small downward movements in any one of η', ε, λ, these being sufficient to induce an infinitely high capital flow response and correspondingly reduce Z_0, σ_F to zero. η' and ε are the trade elasticity parameters, so that as either falls the trade response to exchange rate change drops; as λ falls, so the lag, with which the response occurs, lengthens. Hence, as the immediate trade volume response to an external shock weakens (the perverse trade value response increases), so in a fully rational world capital mobility becomes infinite and stability total – the contrary of the usual assumption that the 'J-curve' will create instability and indeed quite different from our earlier results for full rationality (Table 6.A.2) when h_F was not corrected. This is an important result since these elasticity and lag assumptions are well within the margin of error.[1]

h_F is quite insensitive to upward movements in η', ε, λ, from their central values in case (a). Only in case (h) when all three are simultaneously reduced is there a significant effect on h_F, which falls to 9000, raising σ_F to 1.5%. Even here there is no change in cycle length, and the convergence period is only slightly reduced to $3\frac{1}{2}$ years.

In all cases, the speculative response is therefore substantially greater than under the pegged system. As a result, the standard error of the one-quarter-ahead forecast for the exchange rate also drops substantially.

As compared with semi-rational expectations, full rationality generates stability, where semi-rationality is likely to be unstable, especially in its 'modified' version. Speculative responses will probably be rather higher. The standard error of forecasts may not be very different for only one quarter

[1] A recent study by Batchelor and Minford [1977] in fact used elasticity assumptions of the order of these 'low' values.

ahead, but for longer-range forecasts the standard error of forecasts in a semi-rational world grows and ultimately explodes, while in a fully rational world it grows but ultimately converges for the very long range forecast on approximately $\frac{\sigma_F}{\sqrt{(1-r^2)}}$ where r is the damping factor (and $1\sqrt{(1-r^2)}$ is thus in the range 2–3).

Once this stage is over, fully rational expectations may well generate – with the corrected speculative response – similar stability properties to those found in chapter 6 before correction, namely a long period of convergence with a very slow cycle. But the correction turns out to raise the speculative response parameter dramatically and in so doing reduces the standard error of forecasts substantially, the one-period-ahead forecast error falling to around 1%. With lower elasticities or longer lags in trade, the speculative response goes to infinity, and the forecast error to zero, implying total stability. Our overall conclusion about the behaviour of the floating rate, once it has fully settled down, is therefore that it strongly damps and may eliminate the initial impact of any shock, because of the powerful speculative response, and that thereafter any residual impact is eliminated very slowly – with a mild trace of cyclicality.

This behaviour is, to a reasonable approximation, that asserted by the efficient market hypothesis (see Fama [1970]), which here implies insignificant divergence of the current from the expected exchange rate (adjusted for the interest differential).[2] This result has powerful implications for a full macroeconomic model of the UK; but these are left to be pursued in further work. Meanwhile, the final conclusion of this book is that, after a transitional learning period, speculators will stabilise the floating rate very close to its equilibrium, as determined by the prevailing monetary policies at home and abroad.

Appendix 8.A: Derivation of Z_i for equations (8.9) – (8.11)

Substituting from (8.10) and (8.11) into (8.9), we obtain the following expression in u_{-i}:

[2] With a non-zero differential, k', we would obtain $S^{E+j} \to 0$ as $j \to \infty$, and S, S^{E+j} would be related to it by $S - S^{E+1} = k'$ and $S^{E+j-1} - S^{E+j} = k'$ (for all j).

$$\Big\{(p+h)\sum_{i=0}^{\infty} Z_i - \{s+h(2-\lambda)\}\sum_{i=1}^{\infty} Z_{i-1} + h(1-\lambda)\sum_{i=2}^{\infty} Z_{i-2} \quad (8.A.1)$$

$$-h\sum_{i=0}^{\infty} Z_{i+1} + h(2-\lambda)\sum_{i=1}^{\infty} Z_i - h(1-\lambda)\sum_{i=2}^{\infty} Z_{i-1}\Big\} u_{-i} = -u + (1-\ )u_{-1}$$

where $p = \varepsilon X\lambda\eta' + (\eta'-1)X$ and $s = (\eta'-1)X(1-\lambda)$.
This gives rise to three identities in the u_{-i}:

$$(u)\ (p+h)Z_0 - hZ_1 = -1 \qquad (8.A.2)$$

$$(u_{-1})\ -\{s+h(2-\lambda)\}\,Z_0 + \{p+h(3-\lambda)\}\,Z_1 - hZ_2 = 1-\lambda \qquad (8.A.3)$$

$(u_{-i}, i \geqslant 2)$

$$-hZ_{i+1} + \{p+h(3-\lambda)\}\,Z_i - \{s+3h-2\lambda h\}\,Z_{i-1} + h(1-\lambda)Z_{i-2} = 0 \qquad (8.A.4)$$

The roots of (8.A.4) are those of the polynomial:

$$\rho^3 - \Big\{\frac{p}{h} + (3-\lambda)\Big\}\rho^2 + \Big\{\frac{s}{h} + 3 - 2\lambda\Big\}\rho - (1-\lambda) = 0 \qquad (8.A.5)$$

We write the solution as:

$$(\rho^3 - c)(\rho^2 + a\rho + b) \qquad (8.A.6)$$

It turns out in most of the cases in Table 8.2 that $|c| > 1$, and that the roots of the quadratic are a complex pair, with the damping factor r, less than unity in absolute terms. Thus we ignore c, and write:

$$Z_i = r^i\{A_1 \cos\theta\, i + A_2 \sin\theta\, i\}\ (i \geqslant 2) \qquad (8.A.7)$$
$$= -aZ_{i-1} - bZ_{i-2}$$

We may find the values of A_1 and A_2 from the initial values Z_0 and Z_1, or more simply we may note that:

$$Z_2 = -aZ_1 - bZ_0 \qquad (8.A.8)$$

Substituting this into (8.A.3), we may solve (8.A.2) and (8.A.3) for Z_0 and Z_1 as:

$$Z_0 = \{-c + 1 - \lambda\}/hd \tag{8.A.9}$$

and $$Z_1 = \{(1 - \lambda)\{\frac{p}{h} + 1\} + b - \frac{s}{h} - (2 - \lambda)\}/hd \tag{8.A.10}$$

where c (the first root) $= \{\frac{p}{h} + 3 - \lambda + a\}$ and

$$d = c\{\frac{p}{h} + 1\} + b - \frac{s}{h} - (2 - \lambda).$$

In cases b, d, f, i, j, of Table 8.2, the argument is unchanged except that the two stable roots, ρ_1 and ρ_2, are now both real and positive so that (8.A.7) becomes $Z_i = A_i\, \rho_1^{\,i} + A_2\, \rho_2^{\,i} (i \geqslant 2)$

$$= -a\, Z_{i-1} - bZ_{i-2}$$

REFERENCES

Adams, F.G., E. Eguchi, F. Meyer-zu-Schlochtern [1969] *An Econometric Analysis of International Trade*, OECD.

Alexander, S.S. [1952] 'Effects of a Devaluation on a Trade Balance', *IMF Staff Papers*, April.

Allen, W.A. and M.H. Miller [1974] 'The Stability of the Floating Exchange Rate', mimeo, Bank of England, September.

Almon, S. [1965] 'The Distributed Lag Between Capital Appropriations and Expenditures', *Econometrica*.

Ando, A. [1974] 'Some Aspects of Stabilization Policies, the Monetarist Controversy and the MPS Model', *International Economic Review*, October.

Armington, P.S. [1969] 'A Theory of Demand for Products Distinguished by Place of Production', *IMF Staff Papers*, Vol. XVI, pp 159–78.

Arrow, K.J., H.B. Chenery, B.S. Minhas and R.M. Solow [1961] 'Capital-Labor Substitution and Economic Efficiency', *Review of Economic Studies*, April.

Artus, J.R. [1970] 'The Short-Term Effects of Domestic Demand Pressure on British Export Performance', *IMF Staff Papers*.

Ball, R.J. [1967] 'Credit Restriction and the Supply of Exports', *Manchester School*, May.

Ball, R.J., J.R. Eaton and M.D. Steuer [1966] 'The Relationship Between United Kingdom Export Performance in Manufactures and the Internal Pressure of Demand', *Economic Journal*, September.

Batchelor, R.A. and A.P.L. Minford [1977] 'The Costs of Import Controls and Devaluation as Medium-Term Policies', Ch. 4 in R.A. Batchelor et al, *On How to Cope with Britain's Trade Position*, Thames Essay No. 8, London, Trade Policy Research Centre, January.

Beenstock, M.C. [1976] 'General macro-economic equilibrium and the balance of payments', ch. 2 of *Forward Exchange markets, international capital movements and the Balance of payments*, Ph.D. thesis, London University; also forthcoming, MacMillan.

Beenstock, M.C. and A.P.L. Minford [1976] 'A Quarterly Econometric Model of World Trade and Prices 1955–1972', in J.M. Parkin and G. Zis, (eds.) *Inflation in Open Economies*, University of Manchester, 1976.

Bispham, J.A. [1970] 'The Use of Engineering Orders for Forecasting', *National Institute Economic Review*, August.

Black, S.A. [1973] *International Money Markets and Flexible Exchange Rates*, Princeton Studies in International Finance No. 32, International Finance Section, Princeton.

Blackorby, C., G. Lady, B. Nissen and R.R. Russell [1970] 'Homothetic Separability and Consumer Budgeting', *Econometrica*, Vol. 38, No. 3, May.

Box, G.E.P. and G.H. Jenkins [1970] *Time Series Analysis: Forecasting and Control*, New York, Holden Day.

Branson, W.H. [1968] *Financial Flows in the US Balance of Payments*, Amsterdam, North-Holland.

Branson, W.H. [1972] 'The Trade Effects of the 1971 Currency Realignments', *Brookings Papers on Economic Activity*.

Branson, W.H. and R.D. Hill, Jr. [*1971*] *Capital Movements in the OECD Area,* OECD Occasional Studies, December.

Brechling, F.P.R. and J.N. Wolfe [1965] 'The End of Stop-Go', *Lloyds Bank Review*, January.

Bretton-Woods [1944] 'Articles of Agreement of the International Monetary Fund (July 22, 1944)', reprinted in *The International Monetary Fund 1945–1965, Twenty Years of International Monetary Co-operation*, Vol. III, Documents, International Monetary Fund, Washington D.C., 1969.

Britton, A.J.C. [1970] 'The Dynamic Stability of the Foreign Exchange Market', *Economic Journal*.

Chamberlin, E.H. [1932] *The Theory of Monopolistic Competition*, Harvard University Press, Cambridge, Massachusetts.

Christ, C.F. [1966] *Econometric Models and Methods*, John Wiley.

Cooper, R.A., K. Hartley and C.R.M. Harvey [1970] *Export Performance and the Pressure of Demand*: *A Study of Firms*, University of York, Studies of Economics, Allen & Unwin.

Dornbusch, R. [1973] 'Money, Devaluation and Non-Traded Goods', *American Economic Review*, December 1973.

Dornbusch, R. [1975] 'Alternative Price Stabilisation Rules and the Effects of Exchange Rate Changes', *Manchester School*, September.

Dornbusch, R. [1976] 'Expectations and Exchange Rate Dynamics', *Journal of Political Economy*, December 1976.

Eckstein, O., E.W. Green and A. Simon [1974] 'The Data Resources Model: Uses, Structure and Analysis of the US Economy', *International Economic Review*, October.

Fair, R.C. and D.M. Jaffee [1972] 'Methods of Estimation for Markets in Disequilibrium', *Econometrica*. Vol. 40.

Fair, R.C. and H.H. Kelejian [1974] 'Methods of Estimation for Markets in Disequilibrium: a further study', *Econometrica*, Vol. 42.

Fama, E. [1970] 'Efficient Capital Markets – A Review of Theory and Empirical Work', *Journal of Finance*, Vol. 25.

Friedman, M. [1953] 'Flexible Exchange Rates', in his *Essays in Positive Economics*, Chicago, University of Chicago Press, 1953.

Godley, W.A.H., et al., Cambridge Economic Policy Group [1975,6,7] *Economic Policy Review*, Nos. 1–3, Feb. 1975, March 1976, March 1977, Department of Applied Economics, Cambridge.

Griliches, Z. [1957] 'Hybrid Corn: An Exploration in the Economics of Technological Change', *Econometrica*, Vol. 25, No. 4, October.

Grubel, H.G. [1967] 'Intra-Industry Specialization and the Pattern of Trade', *Canadian Journal of Economics and Political Science*, August.

Grubel, H.G. and P.J. Lloyd [1975] *Intra-Industry Trade – The Theory and Measurement of International Trade in Differentiated Products*, Macmillan.

Hartigan, J.A. [1975] *Clustering Algorithms*, John Wiley.

Helliwell, J.F., H.T. Shapiro, G.R. Sparks, I.A. Stewart, F.W. Gorbet, D.R. Stephenson [1971] *The Structure of RDX2*, Bank of Canada Staff Research Studies No. 7.

Helliwell, J.F. and T. Maxwell [1972] 'Short-Term Capital Flows and the Foreign Exchange Market', *Canadian Journal of Economics*, May.

Henry, G.B. [1970] 'Domestic Demand Pressure and Short-Run Export Fluctuations', *Yale Economic Essays*.

Hilliard, B. [1976] 'Rational expectations – a survey', mimeo, Manchester University.

Hicks, J.R. [1950] *A contribution to the Theory of the Trade Cycle*, London, Oxford University Press.

H.M. Treasury [1974] *The Treasury Model of the UK Economy*, London, H.M. Treasury.

H.M. Treasury [1975] *Macroeconomic Model Technical Manual*, London, H.M. Treasury.

Hodjera, Z. [1973] 'International Short-Term Capital Movements: A Survey of Theory and Empirical Analysis', *IMF Staff Papers*, November.

Holt, H., F. Modigliani, J.F. Muth and H.A. Simon [1960] *Planning Production, Inventories and Work Force*, Prentice-Hall.

Houthakker, H.S. and S.P. Magee [1969] 'Income and Price Elasticities in World Trade', *Review of Economics and Statistics*, May.

Hume, David [1752] Of the Balance of Trade, reprinted in *D. Hume's Writings on Economics*, (Rotwein, ed.), Nelson, 1955.

Hutton, J.P. [1977] 'A Model of Short-Term Capital Movements, the Foreign Exchange Market and Official Intervention in the UK, 1963–1970', *Review of Economic Studies*, February.

Hutton, J.P. and A.P.L. Minford [1975] *A Model of UK Manufactured Exports and Export Prices*, Government Economic Service Occasional Paper No. 11, London, HMSO.

IMF [1970] *The Role of Exchange Rates in the Adjustment of International Payments; a Report by the Executive Directors*, International Monetary Fund, Washington D.C.

Johnson, H.G. [1961] 'Towards a General Theory of the Balance of Payments', in his *International Trade and Economic Growth: Studies in Pure Theory* (Cambridge, Harvard University Press).

Johnson, H.G. [1973] 'The Monetary Approach to the Balance of Payments' in his *Further Essays in Monetary Economics*, Allen and Unwin.

Johnson, H.G. [1973a] *The Problem of International Monetary Reform*. Stamp Memorial Lecture, University of London, Athlone Press.

Johnston, J. [1972] *Econometric Methods*, 2nd Edition, McGraw-Hill.

Jonson, P.D. [1976] 'The Monetary Approach to the Balance of Payments: The UK 1880–1970', *Journal of Political Economy*.

Junz, H.B. and R.R. Rhomberg [1965] 'Prices and Export Performance of Industrial Countries 1953–63', *IMF Staff Papers*, July.

Junz, H.B. and R.R. Rhomberg [1973] 'Price Competitiveness in Export Trade among Industrial Countries', *American Economic Review*, 63, May.

Kenen, P.B. [1965] 'Trade, Speculation and the Forward Exchange Rate', in R.E. Caves et al., (eds.), *Trade, Growth and the Balance of Payments: Essays in honour of Gottfried Habarler*, Chicago, Rand-McNally; Amsterdam, North-Holland.

Keynes, J.M. [1936] *The General Theory of Employment, Interest and Money*, MacMillan

Koyck, L.M. [1954] *Distributed Lags and Investment Analysis*, Contributions to Economic Analysis No. 4, Amsterdam, North-Holland.

Kouri, P. [1976] 'The Exchange rate and the balance of payments in the short run and in the long run', *Scandinavian Journal of Economics*, 2.

Kravis, I.B. and R.E. Lipsey [1971] *Price Competitiveness in World Trade*, National Bureau of Economic Research, New York.

Linder, S.B. [1961] *An Essay on Trade and Transformation*, John Wiley.
MacDougall, G.D.A. [1951] 'British and American Exports: A Study Suggested by the Theory of Comparative Costs', *Economic Journal*, December.
MacDougall, G.D.A. [1957] *'The World Dollar Problem'*, Macmillan.
McGee, V.E. and W.T. Carleton [1970] 'Piecewise Regression', *Journal of the American Statistical Association*.
Maddala, G.S. and F.D. Nelson [1974] 'Maximum Likelihood Methods for Models of Markets in Disequilibrium', *Econometrica*, November.
Markham, J.W. [1952] *Competition in the Rayon Industry*, Harvard University Press.
Markowitz, H.M. [1959] *Portfolio Selection: Efficient Diversification of Investment*, John Wiley.
Meade, J.E. [1951] *The Theory of International Economic Policy*, Vol. 1, The Balance of Payments, London, Oxford University Press.
Minford, A.P.L. [1975] 'Textile fibre substitution and relative prices', *Australian Journal of Agricultural Economics*, December.
Mundell, R.A. [1962] 'The Appropriate Use of Monetary and Fiscal Policy for Internal and External Stability', *IMF Staff Papers*, March.
Muth, J.F. [1961] 'Rational Expectations and the Theory of Price Movements', *Econometrica*, Vol. 29, No. 3, July.
Nerlove, M. [1958] *Distributed Lags and Demand Analysis*, Agricultural Handbook No. 141, Washington, US Govt. Printing Office.
Officer, L.H. and T.D. Willett [1970] 'The Covered-Arbitrage Schedule: A Critical Survey of Recent Developments', *Journal of Money, Credit and Banking*.
Parkin, J.M. [1974] 'Inflation, the Balance of Payments, Domestic Credit Expansion and Exchange Rate Adjustments' in R.Z. Aliber (ed.) *National Monetary Policies and the International Financial System*, University of Chicago Press.
Parkin, J.M. [1977] 'World Inflation, International Relative Prices and Monetary Equilibrium under Fixed Exchange Rates', in R.Z. Aliber (ed.), *The Political Economy of Monetary Reform*, Macmillan.
Polak, J.J. [1957] 'Monetary Analysis of Income Formation and Payments Problems', *IMF Staff Papers*, Vol. VI, 1957/58, pp 1–50.
Polasek, M. and A. Powell [1964(1)] 'Wool and Synthetics: A Statistical Analysis of Fibre Substitution in the US', *Australian Journal of Agricultural Economics*, Vol. 8 No. 1.
Polasek, M. and A. Powell [1964(2)] 'Wool versus Synthetics: An International Review of Innovation in the Fibre Market', *Australian Economic Papers*, Vol. 3 June–December.
Polasek, M. [1965] 'Synthetic Fibres and Australia's Economic Future', *Economic Record*, Vol. 41, No. 39, March.
Powell, A., M. Polasek and H.T. Burley [1963] 'Synthetic Fibres in the Wool Textile Industry: A Study of the Role of Price in Technological Adjustment', *Australian Journal of Agricultural Economics*, Vol. 7. No. 2, December.
Quandt, R.E. [1958] 'The Estimation of the Parameters of a Linear Regression System Obeying Two Separate Regimes', *Journal of the American Statistical Association*, December.
Quandt, R.E. [1972] 'A New Approach to Estimating Switching Regressions', *Journal of the American Statistical Association*, June.
Rees, R.D. and P.R.G. Layard [1971] *'The Determinants of UK Imports'*, Government Economic Service Paper No. 3, HMSO.
Renton, G.A. and M.H. Duffy [1970] 'A Model of UK Exports of Manufactures to Industrial Countries', *Applied Economics*.
Renton, G.A. [1970] 'British Exports of Manufactures to Industrial Countries', *National Institute Economic Review*, November.

Robinson, J. [1933] *Imperfect Competition*, Macmillan, London.

Robinson, P.W., T.R. Webb and M.A. Townsend [1976] *Effective Exchange Rates and Competitiveness*, mimeo, European Economic Commission, August.

Rothschild, M. and J.E. Stiglitz [1970] 'Increasing Risk: I) A Definition and II) Its Economic Consequences', *Journal of Economic Theory*, Vol. 2, No. 3, September; reprinted as Cowles Foundation Paper No. 341, 1971.

Sargent, T.J. [1973] 'Rational expectations, the real rate of interest and the natural rate of unemployment, *Brookings Papers on Economic Activity*.

Sato, K. [1967] 'A Two-Level Constant-Elasticity-of-Substitution Production Function', *Review of Economic Studies*, April.

Scherer, F.M. [1970] *Industrial Market Structure and Economic Performance*, Rand-McNally.

Shepherd, J.R., H.P. Evans and C.J. Riley [1973] *The Treasury Short-Term Forecasting Model*, Government Economic Service Occasional Paper No. 8, HMSO, London.

Shiller, R.J. [1976] 'Rational expectations and the dynamic structure of macroeconomic models; a critical review', Discussion Paper No. 366, University of Pennsylvania, December; forthcoming *Journal of Monetary Economics*.

Smyth, D.J. [1968] 'Stop-Go and United Kingdom Exports of Manufactures', *Bulletin of Oxford University Institute of Statistics*, Vol. 30.

Sohmen, E. [1969] *Flexible Exchange Rates*, (revised edition), Chicago, University of Chicago Press.

Solnik, B.H. [1973] *European Capital Markets*, Lexington, D.C. Heath.

Stern, R.M., J. Francis and B. Schumacher [1976] *Price Elasticities in International Trade – an annotated bibliography*, Macmillan, for Trade Policy Research Centre.

Stigler, G.J. [1969] 'Economics of Information', *Journal of Political Economy*.

Stoll, H.R. [1968] 'An Empirical Study of the Forward Exchange Market Under Fixed and Flexible Exchange Rate Systems', *Canadian Journal of Economics*, February.

Strotz, R.H. [1957] 'The Empirical Implications of a Utility Tree', *Econometrica*.

Theil, H. [1971] *Principles of Econometrics*, Amsterdam, North-Holland.

Tobin, J. [1958] 'Liquidity Preference as Behaviour Towards Risk', *Review of Economic Studies*, February.

Tobin, J. [1965] 'The Theory of Portfolio Selection', in F.H. Hahn and F.P.R. Brechling (eds.) *The Theory of Interest Rates*, Macmillan.

Trivedi, P.K. [1970] 'The Relation Between the Order-Delivery Lag and the Rate of Capacity Utilisation in the Engineering Industry in the UK, 1958–67', *Economica*.

Walters, A.A. [1963] 'Production and Cost Functions: an Econometric Survey', *Econometrica*, January.

Walters, A.A. [1971] 'Consistent Expectations, Distributed Lags and the Quantity Theory', *Economic Journal*, June.

Wilson, H. [1973] Presidential Address to the Royal Statistical Society, *Journal of the Royal Statistical Society*, Vol. 136, Part I.

Zarnowitz, V. [1962] 'Unfilled Orders, Price Changes and Business Fluctuations', *Review of Economics and Statistics*, November.

INDEX